Double Agents

The Middle Ages Series

Ruth Mazo Karras, Series Editor
Edward Peters, Founding Editor

A complete list of books in the series
is available from the publisher.

Double Agents

Women and Clerical Culture in Anglo-Saxon England

Clare A. Lees and Gillian R. Overing

PENN

UNIVERSITY OF PENNSYLVANIA PRESS

Philadelphia

PR
275
.R4
L44
2001

Copyright © 2001 University of Pennsylvania Press
All rights reserved
Printed in the United States of America on acid-free paper

10 9 8 7 6 5 4 3 2 1

Published by
University of Pennsylvania Press
Philadelphia, Pennsylvania 19104-4011

Library of Congress Cataloging-in-Publication Data

Lees, Clare A.
    Double agents : women and clerical culture in Anglo-Saxon England / Clare A. Lees and Gillian R. Overing.
        p.   cm.—The Middle Ages Series
    ISBN 0-8122-3628-9 (cloth : alk. paper)
    Includes bibliographical references and index.
    1. Christian literature, English (Old)—History and criticism. 2. Christian literature, Latin (Medieval and modern)—England—History and criticism. 3. Women—Religious life—England—History—To 1500. 4. Feminism and literature—England—History—To 1500. 5. Women and literature—England—History—To 1500. 6. Women—England—History—Middle Ages, 500–1500. 7. Clergy—England—History—To 1500. 7. Social history—Medieval, 500–1500. 8. Rhetoric, Medieval. 9. Great Britain—History—Anglo-Saxon period, 449–1066. 10. England—Social conditions—1066–1485. I. Overing, Gillian R., 1952–. II. Title. III. Series
PR275.R4 L44   2001
829.09′3823—dc21   2001027906

For our mothers
Winifred Pauline Lees
and Rose Overing

Contents

         Body Politics in Aldhelm's *De virginitate*   111
         Female Saints, Female Subjects?   125
         Seeing Women: Mary of Egypt   132

5   *Pressing Hard on the "Breasts" of Scripture:*
         Metaphor and the Symbolic   152

         When Is a Woman Not a Woman?   154
         Cognition and Containment   163
         Relics: Dead Bodies, Living Metaphors   167
         Over Her Dead Body   171

         Abbreviations   173

         Notes   175

         Bibliography   219

         Index   235

Acknowledgments

We have been thinking about this book for a long time. It's hard to know just when thinking about and talking through the issues of women and culture in Anglo-Saxon England became writing about them. We have been working together on a variety of projects for nearly ten years, and our recurrent concerns as Anglo-Saxonists and feminist medievalists have been issues of women, gender, power, class, and methodological clarity. Our way of working together, about which we are often asked, is still something of a mystery to us. Sometimes we write together, sometimes separately, sometimes we do both, and always we revise each other's work. Often we will read a piece and not know who wrote what. We don't question our collaborative methods too closely, we just know that they work. Our collaboration is a source of considerable intellectual enrichment, and it's fun. We try not to take ourselves too seriously, though sometimes we do; we try not to be too glib, though sometimes we relish the ironies of looking at women (especially at smart old rich ones) through the lens of patristic culture. Our collaboration is also, however, at all times a matter of feminist principle and politics.

We are also grateful to the anonymous reader who pointed out to us the analogy between our own collaboration and the collaboration "of cultural documents, histories, and literary texts" in this book. Our style too is a mixed bag: we deliberately move between dense theoretical formulation and its colloquial demystification. We do this as much for our benefit as for that of our readers.

We think the deciding factor which gave shape to this book was the publication of "Birthing Bishops, Fathering Poets: Bede, Hild, and the Relations of Cultural Production" (*Exemplaria*, 1994), which we reprint here in a slightly revised version as Chapter One. This article has received considerable attention in our field, but we always thought that it was designed to initiate questions rather than offer a program for solutions. By the time we published "Before History, Before Difference: Bodies, Metaphor, and the Church in Anglo-Saxon England" (*Yale Journal of Criticism*, 1998), this book had already come together in our thoughts and in our research. The essay is a distillation of several important themes of the book, and revised sections of it underpin our arguments in the Introduction and Chapter Four.

Collaboration is still viewed with suspicion in some quarters of the academy (we have often had to answer the question of who wrote what), but it certainly is not possible without institutional support. In this regard, we have both been fortunate in our respective institutions: Gillian wishes to thank Wake Forest University for a leave in 1998–99, without which this book could not have been written, and the Research and Publication fund of the Graduate School for its invaluable and consistent support of all her collaborative projects; Clare wishes to thank the Center for the Study of Women in Society at the University of Oregon for a one-quarter research fellowship in 1997, and the Chandler Beall endowment to the Program of Comparative Literature for additional funding for travel. We both thank Karma Lochrie for her valuable comments on the manuscript, and the editorial staff at the University of Pennsylvania Press and Wake Forest graduate research assistant Kristine Funch Lodge for the help given and care taken with its preparation. Last but certainly not least Clare thanks Tammy Stenshoel and Deborah Vukson—two remarkable women—for their support.

Introduction

This is a book about women and about Anglo-Saxon England. But first we need to conceptualize the categories of women and of Anglo-Saxon England; both require a fundamental examination of the methodologies by which women and historical periods are understood. For this reason, this is not a book about women *in*: women in *Beowulf*, women in other canonical texts of Anglo-Saxon studies (literary or historical). It is not a book about women *as* exceptional individuals, whether these be saints, queens, abbesses, or women who have otherwise sufficiently distinguished themselves to make it into the cultural record. Nor do we claim to offer a comprehensive study of women in our period. Rather, we are concerned with the formation of the cultural record itself and what this may tell us about these and many other, undistinguished (that is, unrecorded or partially recorded) women. This is a book about women's agency, but it is also a book about women's absence and presence as these may be traced in the partial record of Anglo-Saxon culture: we argue that agency, absence, and presence are profoundly interrelated in our clerical sources.

This interrelation provided us with a real theoretical conundrum. Bluntly speaking, we know women were present, but we are everywhere faced with their absence from the cultural record, or with a source that allows us only a partial glimpse of any level of women's "real" lives. We even thought of calling the book, "Getting a Life: Women and Anglo-Saxon Culture," but we still had to face the problem of making something out of nothing. What to do with absence? And what to do with the slender, but no less important, evidence that we do have for women's agency? As scholars, we needed a methodology that would respect and not diminish these problems of evidence, and that would enable us to acknowledge agency. In short, we needed a metaphor.

While our concept of double agency cannot fully encapsulate the multiplicity of female identities and agencies present, it allows us to avoid a default methodology—one that would take the patristic record as central and women's relation to it as peripheral, penumbral, or secondary. Women, in our view, did not inhabit an alternate universe, the kind of nether world constructed by our clerical sources—they were obviously an integral part of the social fabric of Anglo-Saxon England, but this does not make them proto-feminists. The female agent is a double agent: she moves in this "real" world of Anglo-Saxon society, but we can only perceive her in that penumbral, nether world to which she is relegated by clerical culture. It is our critical responsibility to be open to the multivalency of all cultural documents as we trace the activities of the female agent. If this means that we occasionally hallucinate, or that as a true double agent she must necessarily betray and confuse, so be it. We address women's entry into the patristic symbolic, by which we mean not only the cultural record itself but the symbolic order that authorizes the record. We look at women's relation to culture, to its formation, and to its processes of production and reception.

The category of "women" engages issues of gender, class, representation, history, belief, and difference. These larger methodological issues, which we outline here, structure our entire study and offer points of liaison with the study of women in other, later cultures in the Western tradition. Contemporary and medieval feminist theory has rightly problematized the category of "women," and we take care to do so as well. We engage with the work of Judith Butler, Judith Bennett, Toril Moi, and Stephanie Hollis among others, and we work firmly within the perspective of cultural materialism of critics such as Raymond Williams. Butler's theory of performativity, for example, allows us to look at women's identity as a function of repeated rhetorical patterns within Anglo-Saxon clerical culture. Moi's critique of Butler's problematic conceptualization of agency and her insistence on the importance of the historical material body accords with our own view of female agency and the physical body. Bennett encourages a rigorous historicization (as does Hollis) and a reassessment of developmental models of women's history. And we are indebted to Raymond Williams's particular contribution to cultural materialism for his understanding of the crucial relation between history, culture, and society. We cross theoretical and disciplinary boundaries in an attempt to establish a conversation about issues that so many feminists share. As Anglo-Saxonists, however, we argue that the concept of difference provides a point of connection and disjuncture with other historical cultures (including the later medieval) and their scholarly interpretation. We therefore begin with this particular problem of studying a remote historical culture.

Difference Historicized

What possibilities are there for the study of remote historical periods in the age of the postmodern? Given that the meaning of periodization itself is strongly contested, and that cultural studies largely means the study of contemporary culture, what difference can history make?

Few cultural historians, and even fewer cultural theorists, would place the study of Anglo-Saxon England at the heart of this debate. Indeed, Anglo-Saxon England has been characterized as different from other periods of English history in that it is most frequently located "before history." Narratives of Western history often omit the early medieval period; its history, compressed beyond recognition or simply omitted, is downplayed in favor of those of the Greek and Roman worlds and of the more modern West, beginning with the twelfth and thirteenth centuries. In the twelfth and thirteenth centuries, historians recognize the emergence of the individual (and the heretic), as well as familiar clerical and secular institutions (Gregorian reforms, Lateran councils, clerical celibacy, marriage, the universities, towns, a money economy). The medieval world starts to resemble, however precariously, the modern. Although recent work has loosened the hold of this master paradigm on the analysis and writing of medieval history after the Anglo-Saxon period,[1] the period itself remains emphatically pre-historical—at the origin, though not at the beginning.[2] Whether from simple ignorance of this earlier period or for reasons largely unconscious or disciplinary, debates in medieval studies on the nature of subjectivity and identity, gender, the body, sexuality, representation, and power continue to operate from, or are conditioned by, the premisses of this master paradigm.[3] Cultural history before the twelfth century is thus alienated, offering a history different from that of later periods, yet one whose difference goes unrecognized and uncontested. The continuing processes of differentiation that construct the Anglo-Saxon period can be seen in a variety of contexts, whether in terms of origins (and their connections to European and North American nationalism), periodization (that is, not post-Conquest England), social formations (tribal to civil state), language (not Latin, not Middle English), religion (pagans and/or Christians), gender (the so-called "golden age" of Anglo-Saxon women), or sexuality (no sex please, we're Anglo-Saxon).[4] Interestingly enough, however, in these processes of differentiation, women are not differentiated enough. The aristocratic nature of the cultural record cannot be stressed too often.

From the more conventional standpoint of a developmental model of history, Anglo-Saxon England is originary—inescapably different from and often irrelevant to subsequent medieval periods. Commonly held distinctions for periodization (to which we do not necessarily subscribe) are that the Anglo-Saxon period traditionally ends around 1066. Excluding the problem of when to locate the "early medieval," the medieval period itself usually extends either to 1400 or 1500, depending on one's views on when "high medieval" begins and ends, and on where and when one locates the Renaissance; the newer term "early modern" can encompass late medieval through to the late seventeenth century and beyond. The Anglo-Saxonist working within the field might find these continually asserted and often commutable distinctions as puzzling and arbitrary as might the Modernist. What such periodic gradations do elucidate, however, is an ongoing process of *dependent* differentiation, where one period defines itself against another, and where each preceding period is necessarily constructed as "pre-historical."

Definition by means of difference, therefore, is not limited to the Anglo-Saxon period. The long view, moreover, reveals a further analogy: that of the larger processes by which history constructs difference and difference is constructed historically to those discursive operations that create the difference of gender in and through time. For the student of Anglo-Saxon England as for the student of other periods, the problem is how to engage with conversations about culture, subjectivity, and identity while recognizing the importance of their historical difference in relation to other formations of difference within and without specific periods. One such formation is that of gender.

Where Are Those Women?

Anglo-Saxon studies as a discipline has always actively engaged with questions of origins, whether those origins concern the history of the English language, the ethnicity of the tribes who came to be the Anglo-Saxons, or the nature of their culture and its relation to our own. Recently, Allen J. Frantzen and other Anglo-Saxonists have refocused such questions so as to include the history of our discipline and the ways our own scholarship influences, in part, the material that we study. These newer projects help highlight one particularly problematic aspect of our scholarly work of reconstruction that has yet to be considered in detail: the relation of Anglo-Saxon women to their culture and the methods by which we recover this relation.[5] Our investigation of women and culture proceeds along a dual axis that combines an examination of the cultural record (working primarily from written texts) with consideration of the methodological and theoretical questions that such evidence prompts.

When students ask teachers, or scholars ask themselves, where are the women in Anglo-Saxon England, or, more specifically, where were the women in the early Germanic invasions, whom did they marry, how were they educated, and what role did they play in the education of others—when these questions arise (and there are many more similar ones), how might we begin to formulate answers to them? A specific history of women in the methodological terms we outline is a missing piece of the Anglo-Saxon cultural record, a vacuum, or as we have already pointed out, an absence. This is not to say that there is no evidence whatsoever for a history of women in the period, or that there are no valuable individual studies of particular aspects of that history. To the contrary, certain aspects of Anglo-Saxon life—the importance of female monasticism, queens, and literary representation, for example— have been studied in some detail.[6] Indeed, one dimension of this scholarship has been an unqualified celebration of women's roles and status in Anglo-Saxon England, resulting in the so-called "golden age" hypothesis, where post-Conquest women suffer by comparison with their Anglo-Saxon forebears. This has provided us with an important starting point to ask questions about historical development, change, and the function of class in Anglo-Saxon England and in women's history more generally. We build on this substantial body of research here, and in fact our project would not be possible without groundbreaking studies like those of Stephanie Hollis.[7]

Our study differs in kind from previous examinations of women in this period because wherever possible we integrate questions about the details of women's lives and their role in cultural production into our overall critical methodology, at every level of our investigation, whether we are looking at the patristic construction of maternity, women's relation to orality and literacy, hagiography, or the intricacies of patristic metaphor. (These are just some of the key issues we have selected for analysis and all are traditional issues for Anglo-Saxonists.) What bears emphasis here is that the work of archival and material reconstruction has proceeded in a fragmentary fashion and, more important, often without much consideration of the implications of this evidence for the theories of gender developed and used in other fields in the humanities.[8] In consequence, neither the existing evidence nor its potential is widely known by gender specialists outside our field. Theories and histories of gender, culture, and sexuality in the West continue to be produced that ignore or quickly pass over the five hundred or so years of the Anglo-Saxon period.

And, as we have pointed out, cultural history before the twelfth century is alienated by the premises of a master paradigm.

As scholars and teachers of this period, we have come up against the problem of the absence of material about Anglo-Saxon women on several levels. Most anthologies of women's writing and accounts of women's history, for example, tend to exclude the Anglo-Saxon period. The reasons are not hard to discover. Such evidence as exists for women's lives in Anglo-Saxon England does not conform readily with the parameters of these more general studies (the only evidence we have for Anglo-Saxon women writers, for example, is in Latin). This exclusion, however, does tend to reinforce a general (and erroneous) perception that Anglo-Saxon culture has nothing of value to contribute to the history of women and gender in the West or, worse, that there were somehow no women in the Anglo-Saxon period. When we turn to the field of the medieval period—an area in which gender studies are now thriving—the situation is only slightly improved. Specific histories of medieval women pay scant attention to the problematic evidence of the early period, and those of Anglo-Saxon society itself rarely consider the subject of Anglo-Saxon women in any detail.[9]

The problem, as we see it, is not just a problem of the paucity of evidence about women's lives in this period, but also one of the kind of questions about that evidence that we raise as scholars. Scholars of the Anglo-Saxon period have always faced the problem of limited and fragmentary cultural sources and have mined the existing record assiduously from a variety of disciplinary and ideological viewpoints, explicit or otherwise. The "sources" we have comprise by and large a patriarchal record and a record of patriarchy, but we believe that "patriarchy" may be persuaded to divulge many a secret if we teach ourselves to interrogate it differently, and if we bring different assumptions to the process of that interrogation. The specific nature and conditions of women's "absence" from the record can point, in other words, to elements of their "presence," which we highlight using the concept of the female double agent.

Believing Women: Self, Psyche, Body

Gender is one major formation of Anglo-Saxon difference. Another is that of belief. While one well-known study of Anglo-Saxon women by Christine E. Fell, for example, excludes religious evidence on the grounds that it is biased, the presence of such bias, cultural and religious, is crucial to our study. Concepts of belief are central to questions of subjectivity, agency, and identity in western culture, yet they are repeatedly downplayed by students of cultural studies, whose models of culture are tacitly if not willfully secular.[10] To study culture, and to study the differences by which the gendered subjects of history are made, without recourse to paradigms of belief is to empty both past and present cultural formations of a significant element of their meaning. Secularity, however bound to modernity, is shadowed by its other—belief.

To the debate about the history of subjectivity now largely conducted between High Medievalists and Early Modernists, Anglo-Saxonists bring another subject: the highly conventionalized and often ignored *cultural* notion of Anglo-Saxon Christian identity.[11] Any conversation about the historical difference of Anglo-Saxon England must begin by historicizing Christianity in terms more specific than is usual. "Anglo-Saxon England" is a broad category as much constructed from within by means of (largely unexamined) developmental models as the period itself is constructed from without. Thus, the history of the period is defined as *progressing* from pagan *to* Christian, "primitive" *to* "civilized," oral *to* literate. The problem of elucidating these definitions, and the particular syncretism of Anglo-Saxon culture that is their result, is compounded by the ideological traditions of a belief system—Christianity— that represents itself as a seamless continuity with the past and disregards specific sociocultural formations. As an ideology, orthodox Christianity emphasizes sameness while expelling difference. Institutional and disciplinary forces within medieval studies complicate the issue so that specific formations like Anglo-Saxon Christianity are neglected in favor of a broader, more general model of medieval belief and practices.[12] The need to historicize is paramount; Christianity is, after all, intimately connected to social practice throughout the medieval period and is crucial to any historical understanding of such variable categories as self, psyche, and body.[13] A religious critical paradigm that leaves Christianity unhistoricized, like a modernist secular orientation that ignores belief, overlooks the importance of the self as a product of both belief and history.

Anglo-Saxon didactic literature, with its profound emphasis on sanctity as well as on traditions of Christian exegesis and moral exhortation, may appear to be unpromising material for any investigation into the historical nature of the subject, or for an examination of agency, masculine or feminine. To ignore this evidence, however, is to assume that questions of subjectivity can be framed only by modern debates about the formation of identity, gender, and sexuality. Foucault's insistence in *The History of Sexuality* on the power of private penance to construct an interiority held partly responsible for the formation of the modern subject, for example, runs the risk of ignoring a more complex notion of what a subject might be within Christian didactic literature in general.[14] By recognizing the performative power of Christian rhetoric to create a moral agent and a psyche that cannot be dismissed by such modern assumptions about psychological interiority, we admit this Christian subject into conversations about the history of the subject and/or self in later periods. It is precisely the dissonance of the various theories of discourse and performativity, as opposed to Moi's analyses of agency, subjectivity, or historical materialism more generally, that offer us a rich terrain for critical inquiry by acknowledging the power both of representation and of the individual subject.[15] In short, belief and its sociohistorical formations are of prime relevance to historical questions of identity and gender, subjectivity and agency.

Concepts of Christian subjectivity are related historically and dialectically to concepts of gender because components of self, pysche, and body are constructed by Christian didactic literature. For many, this is a nonsubject because of the high degree of conventionality of this discourse and of the subject it creates: Anglo-Saxon Christian subjects are hardly distinguished by the marks of "individuality" that we have come to expect from modern, liberal notions of the subject. Nevertheless, didacticism is predicated on a notion of a desiring and volitional self who is educable through such disciplinary processes as exegesis (spiritual interpretation of Scripture, sermons, saints' lives) and ritualized behavior (monastic rules, attendance at mass, public penance, almsgiving, tithing, etc.). Anglo-Saxon England produced the largest and earliest body of such literature in the early medieval period. Acknowledging that didactic discourses enact a Christian subject necessitates a close examination of their rhetoric and of the power of their metaphors, both of which are heavily influenced by patristic conventions. To what extent this subject is gendered within the Anglo-Saxon period thus negotiates such larger issues as periodization and historical change, belief, and its gendered subjects.

The Christian subject is ineluctably produced by disciplines of the body as well as of the will; male bodies are crucially differentiated from female ones in the cultural record, although we concentrate here especially on female bodies. The many contradictory representations of the body in this period are evidence for a distinctively Anglo-Saxon cultural syncretism and the ideologies it negotiates. In Bede's *Ecclesiastical History*, for example, male wet dreams and female menstruation or pregnancy attest to the referentiality of bodily functions because they pose doctrinal problems for the newly converted English and their priesthood.[16] Elsewhere in the same text, however, the female body is emptied of all sex and matter, washed and sterilized for clerical metaphorical use, as in the cases of Hild and Æthelthryth.[17] Such tensions between representation and reference, bodies and metaphors, offer a way of rethinking the history of bodies and selves throughout the period. In order to engage with theoretical debate about questions of gender and history, one aspect of our study traces how the body enters the Anglo-Saxon symbolic order.

Representation and Referentiality

Our approach takes language very seriously, acknowledging its power to create the social symbolic in close tandem with the religious. We are therefore interested in tracing the complex and often convoluted relations between representation (how bodies and women are represented or metaphorized in discourse), and referentiality (how such discourse points to "real" bodies and "real" women outside the text). This is not to say that, when we read about tortured martyred female bodies in Aldhelm's *De virginitate*, composed for a community of nuns in the late seventh century, women were dying in the streets, or even being horribly maimed. Bede tells us, possibly with a tone of mild surprise as well as an element of satisfaction, that in Edwin's peaceful reign (mid-seventh century) "the proverb still runs that a woman could carry her new-born babe across the island from sea to sea without any fear of harm" (*EH* 2, 16). And whether they were proverbially or otherwise safe in the seventh century, women did not until the ninth start literally cutting off their noses to spite their faces, as a means of avoiding rape at the hands of the Vikings.[18] Rhetoric is important, but its operations are far from straightforward, and, of course, there is no necessarily direct correlation between representation and the real without the mediation of ideology. The female body's continual, repeated entry into the Anglo-Saxon Christian symbolic does not necessarily signify its increased absence or presence, or its "actual" freedom or restraint. The female body is translated, contained, or recontained by various social formations and their discourses: for example, clerical history which elides women (Bede's silence about women can be more informative than his eloquence); hagiography which reads and writes up the female saint and her body; the ecclesiastical institution which translates that dead body as or into a relic, or metaphorizes it as an icon of chastity; written discourse that records the oral trace of women within the literate document. Such representations of women may tell us less about "actual women" than they do about a change in the relation between referential and representational practices. We scrutinize the liaison between specific ideological discourses and the historicized instance to identify tensions between representation and reference, bodies and metaphors. In these sites of tension and often paradox we gain an enhanced understanding of the historical body's multivalence, of the possibilities for agency, and also of our own rhetorical categories of definition.

In considering the liaison between ideological discourses and the historicized instance, our argument claims the space between the literary and the historical, with all its attendant critical problems. We do not expect to be historical enough for historians or literary enough for the literary scholars. We accept the drawbacks of hybridization, believing that the peculiar syncretism of the Anglo-Saxon period necessitates a flexible and varied critical stance. As Anglo-Saxonists interested in critical theory, we share the double bind of all similarly minded students of the past; we negotiate dialectically the difference of the past with the available critical apparatus of the present, but we do so maintaining a respect for historical difference and its own sites of critical resistance.

A Feminist Patristics?

Our interdisciplinary examination of aspects of the extant cultural record reconfigures scholarly paradigms by placing gender at the most basic structural level of critical discourse. To place gender at the heart of the critical discourse of Anglo-Saxon studies is to challenge the paradigmatic methodology of patristic analysis, but it is also to open up patristic discourse to feminist methodology. We use the term patristic analysis in a double sense, as is common among Anglo-Saxonists: patristics refers not only to the Christian exegetical traditions of textual interpretation dominant in the medieval period, but also to modern methods of analysis of those traditions. We revisit many familiar issues within the Anglo-Saxon scholarly tradition—orality and literacy, documentation and authenticity, sources and analogues—and look at some of the core patristic authors of our period—Bede, Aldhelm, Ælfric, who continue the intellectual traditions of the early Church fathers into the Anglo-Saxon period. But we bring to our patristic analysis contemporary feminist theories of performativity, subjectivity, the body, sexuality, the dynamics of the gaze, and history. In this regard, our use of the term feminist patristics to describe our methodology also gestures toward the practices of modern feminist scholarship engaged with the study of the Bible and early Christian texts, whether written by men or women.[19] We see ourselves as engaging in a feminist patristics and we are fully aware of our own roles as double agents in this territory. While we take on traditions in Anglo-Saxon scholarship in nontraditional ways, we also take on traditions in contemporary feminist scholarship.

As we have said, this is a book about women: our study attempts to hear women's voices, to detect their possibilities for agency, to pay attention to the experience of women's bodies, to square the problem of women's recorded absence with the inescapable fact of their physical presence and material contribution. We use this book to initiate a conversation about women and culture with our colleagues in the humanities, while demonstrating to Anglo-Saxonists some of the ways in which a feminist patristics illuminates the difference of Anglo-Saxon culture.

Chapter 1, "Patristic Maternity: Bede, Hild, and Cultural Procreation," tackles one of the best-known historical anecdotes of Anglo-Saxon culture. Repeatedly anthologized and fondly rehearsed by generation after generation of Anglo-Saxonists, the elevation of the illiterate laborer Cædmon to divinely inspired poet (and almost saint) has acquired the quasimythological status of an originary narrative. It is also a story about paternity and birth on many levels. Cædmon is the so-called "father" of English poetry, who apparently generates (with Bede's help) an entire tradition of Christian vernacular poetry; with the aid of Bede's literate midwifery, Cædmon's orally inspired poetry is coopted for fathers of the Church. The overwhelmingly present language of generation with which scholars describe this event started us thinking about maternity. Where was the mother in this story? This chapter answers this question by analyzing Hild's role in the narrative and in the scholarship about it in an attempt to historicize and demystify the power of this originary narrative. Hild's striking absence from Bede's account of Cædmon, in spite of her well-attested presence elsewhere in the cultural record, prompts recurrent questions in our book: how to square absence and presence; the liaison between representation and referentiality in this particular historical instance; how patristic rhetoric appropriates female agency; the relation between orality, literacy, and femininity.

Chapters 2 and 3 are interdependent in that Chapter 2 lays the theoretical groundwork for both chapters as well as offering its own reading of the earlier material, which Chapter 3 subsequently develops. Equally, Chapter 3—in its practice of the theory—makes more accessible Chapter 2 with its necessarily denser formulations. Chapter 2 examines the recent critical focus on orality and literacy within the medieval period overall, and considers how this methodology sheds light on women within the Anglo-Saxon period. Not only do the Anglo-Saxon riddles as a genre offer rich examples of the interplay between the oral and the literate, but many of them deal with metaphors of birth—thus making concrete our association of the female and the oral/literate. We ask to what degree might the suppression and patriarchal rewriting of the feminine process (as in the masculine appropriation of metaphors of birth to signify literary creation that suppress "actual" processes of birth that we discuss in Chapter 1, for example) parallel the "disappearance" of the oral trace (the fact that evidence for orality, like evidence for birth, is represented only metaphorically within textual culture)? By contrast, the evidence from some charters, for example, suggests a different dynamic of orality and literacy, whereby class to a large extent determines which women witness charters and are thus made visible in the legal culture of the period. This much neglected evidence casts new light on women's sphere of influence in and exclusion from sociopolitical domains.

We continue this emphasis in Chapter 3 by looking at literacy and gender in the later Anglo-Saxon period. The increased evidence for literacy, both Latin and English, in the tenth and eleventh centuries prompts a reexamination of women's use of and representation in such documents as wills (a quasioral genre throughout this period) and charters, with specific reference to an early eleventh-century Hereford lawsuit. Who gets named and who does not in this evidence? Who gets represented as speaking, and how do we hear their voices? These riddles of literacy and femininity are homologous with other forms of historical evidence—the Anglo-Saxon riddles themselves mystify processes of creation, the religious material stresses the divine mysteries of Christian knowledge. We chart contrasting representations of literacy itself as well as of the literate woman in both literary and historical domains. We examine the interplay between personal names and social categories (labels such as wife, mother, widow) insofar as this evidence offers us a way of detecting the female double agent. We also consider the practice of naming from the perspective of sacred signification and the Eucharist as guarantor of the symbolic. In continuing to work with many of the same themes, preoccupations, and categories of evidence as Chapter 2, Chapter 3 prompts reexamination of the developmental model of women's history from the perspective of orality and literacy. While on the one hand, this period witnesses the increased engagement of women, especially royal women, with literate modes of communication, on the other hand, women are consistently equated with voice and not writing in the documents themselves.

If there's a voice, is there a body? Chapter 4, begins by looking at figurations of the body in Aldhelm's *De virginitate*. We offer a detailed study of the sociohistorical context of Aldhelm's elaborately literary text, its origination and reception in seventh-century monasticism, and the metaphorical construction of the female virginal body in relation to its "real" counterpart, the women in the cloister of Barking Abbey. The second part of this chapter offers a parallel study of the late tenth- and early eleventh-century vernacular contexts for female sanctity and its relation to the social imaginary of late Anglo-Saxon England.

The twists and turns of patristic metaphors for the saintly female body and the flights of masculine Christian imagination they indicate are connected to forms of the quotidian, to politics, ideology, and to sociocultural practices of restraint. Aldhelm's *De virginitate* of the seventh century and Ælfric's *Lives of Saints* of the tenth are prime texts for such an analysis.[20] Both are explicitly Christian works seldom included in analyses of gender and subjectivity—let alone agency—in any systematic fashion. Providing Latin and English contexts in which to view formations of the female Christian subject, each offers a richly complex and different site for the liaison of the ideological, the literary, and the historical. The anonymous Old English *Mary of Egypt*, included in the *Lives of Saints* manuscript but not written by Ælfric, broadens our perspective by bringing to the fore the peculiar dynamic surrounding the old naked body of Mary in this hagiographical discourse. Aldhelm and the female lives in the *Lives of Saints* collection frame Anglo-Saxon culture (from its early flourishing in Latin to its later West Saxon emphasis on English), enabling the assessment both of developmental models of history and of the implications of the frequently cited "golden age" of Anglo-Saxon women. As this chapter demonstrates, there is dramatic change between the sociopolitical criteria for and representations of female saintliness between the early and the later periods of Anglo-Saxon culture. By comparing Aldhelm's strategies for female representation with Ælfric's and with those of the anonymous translator of *Mary of Egypt* in the later period, we offer another way of framing the so-called "golden age" hypothesis of women's history.

Our final chapter recapitulates a recurrent theme: how the female body is repeatedly used as a site for signification, the ground for patristic metaphors (of, for example, learning, literacy, creativity) throughout the Anglo-Saxon period. We address the rhetorical means by which metaphors of the female or the feminine body are sustained, and the use of these metaphors as signifying categories both within the Anglo-Saxon period and within our scholarly accounts of it. Whereas our entire book pays close attention to language, hypothesizing and acknowledging its power to perform subjectivity and create or mystify agency, in this chapter we will concentrate on a few specific examples such as the figure of woman as wisdom or philosophy, the metaphorical afterlife of the dead female saintly body, and its passage into relic.

Our five chapters adopt both linear and nonlinear chronologies. Chapter 1 begins with Bede, but our purpose is to question the originary nature of his narrative (there is no beginning before an origin). Chapter 2 starts in the middle of the period, and then moves backward into the earlier evidence and forward into the critical present. Chapter 3, in its apposite discussion of the later Anglo-Saxon period, and Chapter 4, in its deliberate engagement with beginnings and endings, directly address the issue of linearity as an issue. Chapter 5 complicates the entire question of linear chronology by pointing to patterns of continuity throughout the period. And we end in the middle of the period.

We thereby resist any premature use of a developmental model from the early to the late Anglo-Saxon period. There *is* change, certainly, as well as difference throughout the period in the configurations of representational and restrictive practices concerning both women's and men's bodies and their control over them. But there is a danger in using the apparent decline of the status of women at the end of the Anglo-Saxon period to posit and celebrate a "golden age" for women in the early heyday of monasticism. The before-and-after model, while validated by certain legal and historical developments, obscures difference as well as aspects of continuity. Indeed, some of the patterns of continuity that we look at in this book persist well beyond the Anglo-Saxon period; we agree with Judith Bennett that, in many cases, women's history is characterized far more by continuity than by change.[21]

This book attends to aspects of continuity and change, but equally important is the role of difference in our understanding of historical periods. Engaging the dialectic of continuity and change with its co-production of class as one aspect of historical difference is crucial to our project. We cannot comprehend women as a category without considering the historical imbrication of class and gender. We return to our initial premise: this is a book about women, but we cannot think about women as an ahistorical category.

Chapter One

Patristic Maternity:
Bede, Hild, and Cultural Procreation

In this chapter, we discuss two events in Old English literary history, both of which originate with Bede in his *Ecclesiastical History*. According to Bede, Hild is worthy of memory at least in part because, as celebrated Abbess and Mother of the dual foundation of Streonæshalch or Whitby, she created an environment of spiritual instruction that produced five bishops. Twentieth-century historians, following Bede, also remember Whitby as a virtual "nursery of bishops," to borrow, as others have, Frank M. Stenton's evocative phrase of maternity.[1] The second event recalls an even better known literary moment when Bede bequeaths his society, and subsequent scholarly readers, the account of the so-called first English poet, Cædmon, often known as the father of English poetry. Allen J. Frantzen describes this in an equally evocative phrase as the "birth" of Christian Anglo-Saxon poetry.[2] So we can't avoid maternity in Frantzen's phrase either.

The two events are, of course, connected in this trio of names—Bede, Hild, Cædmon—but their connections reveal an unequal hierarchy. Bede authors and creates both moments, but it is Hild who is the Abbess of the monastery that produces Cædmon and five bishops. Yet scholarship tends to remember these two events separately. Putting Bede's two moments side by side (as they appear in *EH* 4. 23–24), we examine the cultural activities represented in the two accounts, and re-presented by the institution of Anglo-Saxon scholarship, as gendered ones. We might express this as follows: Bede (the man) fathers Cædmon (poets/poetry/sons) while Hild (the woman) mothers bishops/men.

The gender asymmetry suggested by the events of Hild's *Life* and Cædmon's miracle is a familiar binarism of patriarchy: women reproduce, men produce. This fundamental binarism (one that might be fruitfully added to those proposed by Frantzen), moreover, still informs much Old English scholarship.[3] When literary history remembers Cædmon as the originary event of English poetry, it tends to forget Hild—as a direct consequence of Bede's structuring of the event. Three critical expositions by Kevin S. Kiernan, Martin Irvine, and Seth Lerer have contributed to our rereadings of Bede's account; however, they do not address Hild's active participation in the miracle.[4] Historians, on the other hand, remember Hild but equally fail—though for different reasons—to examine her role in Cædmon's miracle. Indeed, Hild has been enjoying something of a renascence in academic circles. There has been one detailed study of her *Life*, by Christine E. Fell, and she often features in works on women in Anglo-Saxon England as well as in studies of the role of women in early monastic history.[5] In this way, Hild qualifies as one of those "exceptional individuals" (see Introduction) that we recontextualize in this book. The principal source of our information about Hild is of course Bede, but in recent feminist studies we see Bede's role in shaping her history downplayed in favor of a focus on women.[6] The all too obvious conclusion is that the different research paradigms of traditional historiography, literary history, and feminist scholarship shape the subjects the paradigms purport to investigate.

It is not necessary, however, to choose between silencing Hild and hearing Bede or vice versa. In our own capacity as critical double agents, we wish to avoid a duplication of binary choices that set critical paradigms in a competitive relationship. We are not concerned with chastising Bede, critics, or historians for selective amnesia or partial recall. Instead we reinvestigate the dynamic of Bede and Hild by connecting these two figures within the larger framework of their relation to cultural production. We remember what conventional (nonfeminist) scholarship and patriarchal authors (Bede) forget, silence, or erase and we suggest a different model for feminist scholarship.

Our understanding of the relations of cultural production is squarely within a Marxist tradition of cultural materialism. Britton Harwood offers us a useful definition of these relations "in which means of production (both the objects upon which labor power works and the instruments that work on these objects) stand to the agents of production (individual human beings, institutions, corporations etc.)."[7] We explore how this dynamic may be modified and specified to describe both cultural production in the Anglo-Saxon period, and the ways in which scholarship produces and reproduces that culture. "Culture" in our period involves a variety of means and forms of agency, and degrees of access to, alienation from, and control over these: it concerns, for example, developments in literacy and education; production of manuscripts; production and maintenance of a scribal labor force, a church bureaucracy, and personnel.[8] It also concerns the founding, building, and managing of a monastery—from its layout to its work force (ecclesiastical and secular). As the history of the lay laborer-turned-poet Cædmon makes abundantly clear, "culture" encompasses the provision made for those laborers and the stories told about them. Who sustains Cædmon, and whom, or what, does Cædmon sustain?

We begin, therefore, with an examination of how women are represented in originary moments of cultural production, using Bede, Hild, and Cædmon as a test case, and raise some theoretical questions and issues prompted by this example.[9] We then use our reconstruction of these literary events as paradigmatic narratives that offer the possibility of theorizing the relations of gender in the production of culture in early Anglo-Saxon society, and of outlining some questions and directions that will concern us in subsequent chapters. We historicize such originary narratives in order to situate their power *and* to theorize the continued production of their meaning in contemporary critical discourse. In other words, we have one eye firmly on the past and the other firmly on the present: we wish to appropriate the patriarchal myth of the origins of Old English poetry and suggest alternative ways of understanding this origin. Our emphasis is not so much on new information (the stories of Bede, Hild, and Cædmon are, after all, often rehearsed), but on new ways of interpreting it as we develop a feminist patristics (outlined in the Introduction).

Engendering Originary Narratives

and all who knew her piety and grace called her mother (*EH* 4. 23)

(quam omnes qui nouerant ob insigne pietatis et gratiae matrem uocare consuerant)

It is not hard to see how Bede's account of Cædmon has been invested with all the power of an originary narrative by institutional Anglo-Saxon scholarship: both Frantzen and Kiernan have drawn attention to the critical paradigms through which the account is conventionally read. As Frantzen points out, Bede himself presents the narrative as one of origins and, to judge by the reception of the *Hymn* in Anglo-Saxon England, the Anglo-Saxons also invested it with considerable power.[10] But these three moments—the "original" authorial moment, the evidence for its reception in Anglo-Saxon England, and its subsequent reception by Anglo-Saxonists—are not synonymous, though there is a discernable tendency to map one on top of the other (the critical approach on top of its "history"). Each moment is invested with particular desires which are themselves part products and part producers of contemporary concerns and issues: that is to say, literary events are complex and over-determined. What has been neglected by recent analyses is the significance of such events for our understanding of the interplay of gender and desire in the production of their meaning.

Above all, Bede's desires are those of the Christian writer who interprets the human history of the Church in England according to the paradigm of sacred history. Cædmon's story, as an account of the origins of sacred poetry, is incorporated into, and embraced by, the Word. The social power of this narrative derives from the ways Bede's account makes manifest the Word of God in a Christian community, emblematized as the monastery of Whitby. Bede's sacred desires are necessarily mediated via literary genres, and his story thus discovers an intersection of sacred master narrative, generic form, and his own desire and talent as narrator. One obvious way to make manifest the power of God is to use the miracle narrative, and the narrative of Cædmon stresses the miraculous. Cædmon is the vessel through which God's ways are revealed to men, but Cædmon is no saint in this not quite hagiographical narrative. Nor is his story that of the first poet's first inspiration and the first poem. Cædmon's song is divinely inspired, as Bede emphasizes, and he draws others to the faith by singing Christian songs that have the power to move, perhaps even to convert. This is a powerful originary moment in the history of English Christianity—the moment when the native (Germanic) traditions of oral song-making are allied with the subject of Christianity and harnessed for the faith. Others could sing before Cædmon, but only Cædmon, divinely inspired and remaining illiterate, sings *Christian* songs.

Bede's narrative certainly shaped, even produced culture. The combination of the status of Bede as a native Anglo-Saxon *auctor* and the *Hymn* as a product of Christian and native traditions seems to have been highly influential. Bede's Latin *EH* was translated into Old English in the ninth century and is conventionally associated with Alfred's court, while the Latin continues to function as a source of authority for later Old English writers such as Ælfric.[11] More importantly, the *Hymn* enjoyed a wide dissemination. Old English versions of the *Hymn* date from shortly after Bede's account, copied into the margins of *EH* and elsewhere a total of 21 times (with some significant variations between the copies)—a figure that speaks for itself when the majority of Old English poems survive in only 1 version.

The manuscript copies of the Latin and English versions of the *Hymn* offer some explanations for this popularity. As Katherine O'Brien O'Keeffe has demonstrated, scribes gradually find ways of assimilating this oral poem to the highly literate textual culture of the later Anglo-Saxon period by developing methods of formatting and punctuation unique to Old English poetry.[12] These scribes, in other words, preserve and commemorate the poem by reversing the processes of its oral composition. Bede is, after all, very precise about Cædmon's methods of composition. He is a song-maker who relies on his memory to transform a sacred text into poetry with a Christian message. Many of the Old English versions are separate from their context in Bede, written in margins or in one case at the end of the manuscript (a nice post scriptum). Thereby, they acquire a quasi-independent status—materially severed from both authors, Bede and Cædmon. The reception of the *Hymn* in the Anglo-Saxon period is thus one that recuperates the poem linguistically for the vernacular: to Bede's Latin paraphrase is added an Old English version (or versions), marked in the manuscripts as textually separate from the Latin narrative. The Latin and Old English are contiguous, not projected one on top of the other.

Bede's celebrated remarks about his individual stylistic preferences and priorities in refusing to translate the poem ("for it is not possible to translate verse, however well composed, literally from one language to another without some loss of beauty and dignity," *EH* 4. 24) underline an authorial honesty, or perhaps self-consciousness, that marks his narrative as a particular instance of a master narrative. His paraphrase is a Latin graphic trace of an originally vernacular oral song. For all its power as an account of the first moment in Anglo-Saxon Christian poetry, however, Bede's narrative is simultaneously one of loss. The Latin paraphrase—the prestige language of Christian culture—only makes the reader more aware of the vernacular poem that it supplants and that the Old English versions seek to redeem. Bede identifies ancient traditions with emerging institutions and his text produces a re-ordering, a re-membering, in terms of his priorities and desires, which inevitably involve a forgetting.

Historians and literary critics also bring their own desires to Bede's account of Cædmon. In reconstructing this story of English Christianity as an event of either English literature or history, certain lacunae in Bede's account gain prominence. To the traditional historian testing the authenticity of Bede's miraculous narrative, the Cædmon story offers the challenge of history or hagiography, fact or fiction. This is a laudable enterprise: time and again, Bede has been demonstrated to be, in modern terms, a reliable historian using scholarly methods of documentary or witness testimony wherever possible. But reading for "facts" only exposes the lacunae of this particular text. For who was Cædmon and where is the rest of his poetry? We know nothing of Cædmon save that his name is probably British. In spite of Bede's long list of

Cædmon's compositions, we know nothing of his poetry save for the copies of the *Hymn*, which Bede does not even give in the original language. Since the only means of verifying this problematic narrative is via the author (just who is Cædmon without Bede?), Bede ensures himself a place at the originary moment, which is an a priori moment of cultural production—enacted between Cædmon and God, channeled through Bede. This is also a classically patriarchal moment, where poetry is exchanged between men and the Father (God) via the human father (Bede). Although, as we have already said, maternity seems to be inescapably evoked by this narrative, the myth of origins turns out to be an ideological myth of masculinism.

Where the historian is frustrated by the paucity of evidence, the literary critic has a field-day. To judge both from the regular critical output on the story and the *Hymn* and from the number of times the *Hymn* has been anthologized, Bede's story of Cædmon and his poem is a critical bestseller. The attractions are self-evident. The structure of Bede's story resembles mythical accounts of the beginnings of poetry from different cultures (Scandinavian, for example) to add to his mythical story of Hengest and Horsa and the origins of the Anglo-Saxons (*EH* 1. 15). The literary critical story begins with this premise and emphasizes that the origins of English poetry are coterminous with a repositioning of the relationship between a Christian Latin culture and a Germanic oral one. The paradigm reads Bede's story using, in microcosm, the binarisms of Anglo-Saxon culture and Old English literature—Christian/Germanic, literate/oral. This story is familiar: the scene is staged between the old (the Germanic or British illiterate laborer, Cædmon) and the new (the Christian scholar, Bede). The new triumphs by incorporating the old within its ideology just as Pope Gregory recommended to Augustine (*EH* 1. 30). Embedded in this paradigm of successive stages of conquest and domination, made palatable by myths of progress and voluntary cultural submission, are many ambivalences, deceptions, and remetaphorizations. These attend and disguise the violence of the overlay of one order of cultural representation upon another.

In mapping critical desires for origins on top of a text that is itself concerned with origins, Bede's narrative neatly becomes the site for many treasured assumptions about Anglo-Saxon culture and Old English literature. The literary critical story acknowledges Bede's narrative as originary, and it therefore depends on the interrelatedness of narrative and poem. The popularity of both text and poem derives in large measure from the simple fact that we cannot go beyond the text: *there is nothing before Bede; we do not know who Cædmon was.* The role of the reader is that of witness to the beginnings of

English poetry, blessed by the Church, and authored by one of the greatest scholars of the Anglo-Saxon period. In short, the reader is required to stand witness to a miracle. It is therefore not surprising that this is also a story which gives priority to Bede and to the mysterious Cædmon embedded ineluctably in his account. This is the power of originary narratives. But, as we have already argued in our discussion of the *Hymn*, such moments are also moments of loss. What is omitted in the conventional literary reconstruction of Bede's account is Hild.

Bede's originary moment is fraught with apparently competing narratological agendas (the sacred, the literary genre, the cultural/political) that displace and overlay each other in a series of successive accommodations and appropriations. But, while the master narrative is rewritten and its elements rearranged by those who follow Bede, its trajectory remains unchanged in that the demands of all these narrative structures offer no place for a different conception of agency.

Bede's originary moment is also, as we have seen, a political instance—then and now. Frantzen explores eloquently how Bede presents a "cultural thesis" that privileges, by a series of appropriations, literate Christianity as a consolidating cultural force over the pagan oral past. The power of Bede's originary significance, Frantzen also points out, "is entirely the creation of those who came after him."[13] As culture is produced and reproduced in this redrawing of oppositions, it is not surprising that Hild's absence is simply reconfigured and female agency unaccounted for, but this absence does offer a new perspective on the so-called dichotomies of the period—Christian/pagan, oral/literate—and the myth of a "barbaric" past replaced by, even gracefully (i.e., with God's grace) assumed into a more progressive future. These patterns of realignments of oppositions assume a decidedly nondichotomous, even unified force from a feminist perspective.

However literary readers have chosen to re-create the drama of Bede's moment, whatever critical methodology they use to elicit a reading, the principal actors—Bede, Cædmon, and God—remain the same. What is striking about these readings is their masculinity: Bede's drama lays claim to literature for men as well as for Christianity. His is a patriarchal myth of literary creation that imitates the first Christian myth: the first song created by Cædmon is a *Hymn* of Creation sung to the Father of Creation—Bede's account fathers the first Christian poem. The feminist reader is required to stand witness to a miracle whose very grounds for belief are an exclusively masculine model of authorship. Striking too is the weight of critical silence that is complicit in reconstructing this patriarchal myth. The fourth actor in Bede's narrative is

Abbess Hild, the abbess in charge of Cædmon's monastery, the woman who acts as the ultimate arbiter for the veracity of Cædmon's miracle, the woman responsible for advising Cædmon to take monastic vows and for facilitating his continued work as a Christian poet by ordering him to be instructed in the events of sacred history. But Bede does not name Hild in his account of Cædmon, nor does the Old English translation, and in fact she is already dead in the narrative logic of *EH*, since her life ends as his begins.[14] Hild's death issues the moment of the birth of poetry and is itself a direct product of Bede's twinned desires in writing—as a Christian man and as a Christian hagiographer.

In fact, Hild is twinned with Cædmon in a number of respects. Her Life, a more pronounced hagiography than Cædmon's, prefaces and parallels his, and like Cædmon, although to a more radical extent, she is displaced by Bede in the miraculous account of Christian poetry. Elided in Cædmon's history, she is, however, given her own, but here she is displaced by the trope of mother of the monastery and by the genre of hagiography. Bede's narrative is framed by Hild's decision to dedicate her life to God at the age of thirty-three (perhaps a purely symbolic age), and the manner of her death in 680, which is duly accompanied by a number of premonitory visions. Within this hagiographical frame, the key details of Hild's life, according to Bede, emerge. Born of noble, perhaps even royal parents (Breguswith and Hereric) in Northumbria, and also related to the royal house of East Anglia, Hild was baptized by Paulinus at the same time as Edwin, the first Christian Northumbrian king. She seeks monastic life in exile at Chelles with her sister, Hereswith, but is recalled before leaving by Aídán. Her first position as abbess is at Hartlepool, but thereafter she founds and presides over the influential double monastery of Whitby, "teaching them to observe strictly the virtues of justice, devotion, and chastity, and other virtues too, but above all things to continue in peace and charity" (*EH* 4. 23). She directed the nuns and monks in a careful program of scriptural study—Bede tells us that five monks later became bishops while a sixth, Tatfrith, died before he could be consecrated—and acted as advisor to kings and princes.[15] So remarkable were her achievements, Bede tells us, that all who knew her called her "*Mother*" (*EH* 4. 23).

We have already pointed out some ways in which Bede and successive critics have cast the myth of origins, literary and divine, as an ideological myth of masculinism. When Bede insists on Hild's ubiquitous maternity (perpetuated by twentieth-century critics), we are prompted to examine this construction of the maternal role more closely. After all, the critical insistence of this maternal metaphor, amounting to "citation" in the Butlerian sense (see Chapter 4) is overwhelming. Bede theorizes the maternal here as nurturing, which is paradoxically synonymous with Hild's active production of the clergy.[16] But the power to translate reproduction into cultural production is denied because Hild is alienated not only from her labor, but also from her gender and her clerical "progeny."

She is alienated too from her own mother, Breguswith, whose dream predicts her daughter's subsequent spiritual achievements. Although the best-known dream in the narrative of Hild and Cædmon is Cædmon's, it is by no means the only one. Hild's life includes three dreams, beginning with Breguswith's, which predicts her daughter's exemplary life:

> This was bound to happen in fulfilment of the dream which her mother Breguswith had during the child's infancy. While her husband Hereric was living in exile under the British king, Cerdic, where he was poisoned, Breguswith had a dream that he was suddenly taken away, and though she searched most earnestly for him, no trace of him could be found anywhere. But suddenly, in the midst of her search, she found a most precious necklace under her garment and, as she gazed closely at it, it seemed to spread such a blaze of light that it filled all Britain with its gracious splendour. This dream was truly fulfilled in her daughter Hild; for her life was an example of the works of light, blessed not only to herself but to many who desired to live uprightly. (*EH* 4. 23, 410–11)

In an asymmetrical parallel to Cædmon's dream, this dream underscores the spiritual relation between Hild and Breguswith at the cost of obscuring any other relation between the two as mother and daughter. The comparison with Cædmon's dream is instructive, for, while Breguswith's is the first and female annunciation dream of the narrative, Cædmon's is its masculine counterpart, and assumes the more novel role in this variant of the annunciation (he received news not of a child but of a song). Breguswith by contrast, in the role of the soon-to-be mother Mary, is produced in the service of familiar hagiographical convention. Leoba's mother, Æbbe, has a similar dream when childless, pulling from her breast a ringing bell of the church, which is interpreted by her nurse as a sign of the impending birth of a daughter, Leoba, who must be accordingly dedicated to God.[17] Maternity does keep circling sacred narratives.

Conventions are products of processes of naturalization; it is easy enough to read Breguswith's dream as mere hagiographical convention. Whence, perhaps, the fact that neither Bede, nor the Old English translator, nor subsequent readers have registered the unfamiliar in Breguswith's dream. But there is more than a touch of the uncanny about the dream: the maternal Breguswith looks under her garment ("sub ueste") and finds a symbolically female object—a necklace—in a blaze of light. A Freudian would relish such a wom-

an's dream, given its enticing romance of absent father/husband and sub-
stitute object—the necklace/child found under the woman's clothes. But such
an analysis of female sexuality is refused by the text. Both classic psycho-
analysis and patristic hagiography demand that dreams be paths to fulfillment
in one way or another (a point repeated by Bede twice in this short passage),
but the subject of the wish of this particular dream is obscure. It is Bede who
interprets Breguswith's dream retrospectively as a sign of Hild—the wish is
thus generalized by the conventions of Christian hagiography—and we have
no evidence at all of Breguswith's own agency, her subjectivity or consciousness, and therefore no royal road to her unconscious, however much we might
infer that her wish is for a child.

Breguswith's prediction of Hild's life is complemented by a visionary
apprehension of her death, by the nun Begu, in the same chapter. Begu dreams
that she sees the roof of the monastery open, the room fill with light, and
Hild's soul carried up to heaven in the midst of the light, accompanied by
angels. Begu interprets this as a vision of Hild's death and reports it to Frigyth,
the nun in charge of Hackness, who commands prayer and the singing of
psalms for the rest of the night until news of Hild's death reaches the community. When it does—brought by monks from Whitby—all the nuns confirm
they already know of her death.

Begu's vision takes place at Hackness, founded by Hild, and therefore in
Hild's absence, just as Breguswith's did in the absence of Hild's father, Hereric.
There are, however, other parallels with Breguswith's dream. The explicit
connection between the two dreams is the figure of light—always a sign of
divine presence. Begu's dream in fact confirms Bede's interpretation of Breguswith's, since here too light is associated with Hild. Yet Begu's vision is
reiterated three times: first by Bede, in indirect speech; second by Begu herself
to Frigyth; and third by the entire female community as they receive the by
now narratologically redundant news of Hild's death. In case the reader has
not grasped the significance of this "beautiful harmony of events" (as Bede
puts it)—news of Hild's death spreads through Hackness at the moment she
dies at Whitby—he reports a third dream as a postscript. A nun at Whitby
dreams she sees Hild's soul ascend to heaven, wakes her companions, and
begins praying with the novices until the news of Hild's death is announced. It
is by these processes of reiteration, or visionary witnessing, that Hild's sanctity
is ensured for the religious community at the moment of her death and at the
cost of obscuring the real conditions of her life (and death), or indeed those of
Breguswith's and Begu's.

Relations between mothers and daughters, and between nuns and maternal abbesses, are traced instead by the narrative trajectory of the dreams and their interpretations. Bede interprets Breguswith's dream; by the time of Begu's dream and that of the nun at Whitby, the women themselves are good interpreters. With this glimpse of agency, we might say that they have begun to own their dreams. Even so, Bede notes, it is only when the male monks from Whitby report the news of Hild's death to the community at Hackness that it is confirmed that Begu's vision was revealed at Hackness at the moment of Hild's death at Whitby. The framing of Hild's life and death by dreams, the number of times Hild's death is reported both in terms of visionary and of factual knowledge, together with the structural parallels of all the dreams, are strong indications of the entire religious community's desire to underline Hild's spiritual significance.

Bede explicates Streonæshalch (Whitby) as "quod interpretatur sinus fari" (*EH* 3. 25), which means "bay of light" (not "bay of the lighthouse," as Colgrave and Mynors translate it). Hunter Blair associates Bede's exegesis of the place name and the bay with the blaze of light and the necklace in Breguswith's dream (and, we might add, the light in Begu's).[18] The place name can thus be read as a proleptic, and condensed, sign of Breguswith's dream, while the light in effect anchors relations between Breguswith and her daughter. Hild's light, her saintliness, is located in the landscape—via the place name—and is also associated with the maternal body, since it is under Breguswith's garments that she sees the shining necklace. Located in the specifics of place, Hild's saintliness is thus also firmly associated with family.[19] The pious mother is of course another hagiographical convention, ultimately rooted in Scripture, but this mother's "place" is marked by a material convention—the necklace. The necklace is a specifically multivalent, female sign. We note Ælthelthryth's tumor on her neck, which she interprets as punishment for her youthful pleasure in wearing costly necklaces (discussed in Chapter 4). Here, however, the necklace is a symbol of Hild herself; its wealth is a familar Christian metaphor of her pricelessness (this point is made clearer in the Old English Bede, where the necklace is a "gyldenra sigila").[20] As a material sign, however, the necklace is a symptom of the processes whereby aristocratic wealth, displayed on female bodies, is absorbed into the Christian monastic economy. The charter evidence we examine in Chapters 2 and 3 and Aldhelm's negotiation of the wealth and status of the Barking nuns in Chapter 4 reveal a continuity here: the wealth of high status women appears to be a persistent interest of the Church. Hild herself belongs to the earliest generation of aristocratic women who "found" monasteries. The dreams in Hild's life perform the necessary cultural work to produce a female saint, whose own body—like that of her mother's—has been fully translated into this ecclesiastical economy symbolically by the time of Begu's dream, where her soul departs into heaven.

Maternity is doubly appropriated when it is thus emptied of its gendered force and specificity and reabsorbed into the masculine economy as a means of production under masculine control. In fact, Bede effectively "gets the birth out" of this double construction of maternity (Hild as mother, Breguswith as mother), removing the specifics of female presence, experience, and agency: maternity is sterilized, as it were, for clerical metaphorical use. Moreover, we stress Hild's own participation in this dynamic: the procreation of culture may be remetaphorized as masculine, but in producing clerical "progeny," indeed, in "appropriating" Cædmon's poetic talent in the service of patriarchal Christianity, Hild is also reproducing patriarchy and producing the means that alienate her from her labor.[21] We are confronted with one of the paradoxical aspects of Hild's relation to cultural production (a point we take up at greater length later): the more actively she participates in the production of patriarchal culture, the more passively she is constructed by the cultural record. We might note too that Breguswith's actual maternity is similarly appropriated; Bede's narrative leaves us with no sense whatsoever of her agency. We trace this fascinating dialectic of absence and presence as it plays out in other cultural instances in later chapters.

That Hild had in reality both access to and a degree of autonomous control over the means of cultural production has been well documented. "We cannot think of Whitby without thinking of Hild," states Blair, discussing the importance of Whitby as a center for learning in the seventh century.[22] Blair's article, though posthumous and partly reconstructed from his notes, is a fine example of traditional historical research, which carefully re-creates Hild's life and the foundation of Whitby by piecing together information from Bede with other historical sources. He then considers the famous Synod of Whitby, the story of Cædmon, and the role of Whitby as a "nursery" for bishops. In other words, Bede's narrative in *EH* 4. 23 is supplemented by information either found elsewhere in *EH* or by other sources—as in the case of Hild's royal successors, Ælfflæd and Eanflæd.[23] Blair fashions a narrative of Whitby in which Hild figures as important in the major institutions and events of her age; his article is complemented by that of Christine E. Fell, who offers the kind of detailed story paradigmatic of contemporary historical research into Hild. Scholars such as Jane Chance or Joan Nicholson develop another story by uncovering Hild's relationship with other exemplary aristocratic women, nuns and queens, in early Anglo-Saxon society.[24]

This valuable research is an important way of remembering Hild, but let's be quite clear about Bede's biography. Neither Eanflæd nor Ælfflæd—the two royal women and nuns closest to Hild—are mentioned here. Nor is the Synod of Whitby, which is arguably the most important event in Church history in the seventh century and discussed by Bede in *EH* 3. 25. Even in the context of the development of the English Church, these "omissions" are startling: the continued prosperity of Whitby after Hild's death is largely due to Ælfflæd (who was dedicated to the monastery by her royal father, Oswiu of Northumbria, at the age of one, *EH* 3. 24) and her mother Eanflæd. (We talk further about both of these women in Chapter 2.) In fact, Bede's narrative of Hild's political contacts mentions only her relationship with men—her connection to the so-called first English nun, Heiu, remains mysterious, since the Heiu was dead before Hild's appointment to Hartlepool. Hild was certainly present at the Synod held in her own monastery where she voted for the pro-Celtic side, as Bede and the *Life of Wilfrid* suggest, but Bede does not refer to the Synod in the narrative of her life in *EH*.[25] Strictly speaking, of course, these are not "omissions" since Bede covers them in other sections of *EH*, but the structure of his *Life* here excludes them—suppresses them, perhaps—in favor of a focus on her piety and her spiritual worth to the religious community as predicted by all those dreams.[26]

Conspicuously absent from Bede's *Life* is any trace of what we may assume with good reason to be the forceful physical and verbal presence of this politically prominent woman. This silencing of voice and presence, which resonates even more profoundly in the case of her mother, raises issues similar to those in the development of literacy, suggesting that the "disappearance" of the oral trace of Cædmon's *Hymn* and of female presence might be usefully jointly theorized, a more general observation to which we return later, both in this chapter and the next. Hild's specific disappearance, however, is clearly a matter of Bede's desires in re-creating her story. Bede credits Hild with influence in the political events of her time but only with an unspecified reference to the fact that kings and princes as well as "ordinary people" sought her advice. *Which kings, which princes, we might ask?* What Bede stresses instead is Hild's fostering of learning at Whitby. Again, the nurturing element of the maternal role is highlighted, displaced from her own "real" mother onto the daughter, but this "real woman," Hild, similarly is nowhere to be found: her actual connection to political power, social change, and the realities of cultural production are unidentified and unacknowledged. The proof of Whitby's excellence is the fact that it fostered five bishops, all of whom are named unlike those aristocrats who sought her advice—Bosa, Ætla, Oftfor, John of Beverly, and Wilfrid of York—and two of whom are given their own narratives in *EH* 5.

2–7; 19. Mother, founder, educator, *not* principal agent: this is how Bede chooses to remember Hild.

Just how influential was Bede's *Life* of Hild in the Anglo-Saxon period? Unlike other saints, both male and female, in the early Anglo-Saxon church—Cuthbert, Oswald, or Æthelthryth, for example—there is little evidence for a wide spread Anglo-Saxon cult. She is commemorated in only one calendar (Willibrord's), included in only one martyrology (the ninth-century *Old English Martyrology*), and her death briefly noted in the *Anglo-Saxon Chronicle*.[27] Evidence for a lost *Life* of Hild, presumably written at Whitby, is suggested by the wording of her entry in the *Old English Martyrology*.[28] Otherwise, bearing in mind the fragmentary and accidental nature of material that survives, Hild disappears without trace to reappear post-Conquest in a few regional liturgies and calendars.[29]

It is clear, therefore, that Hild deserves to be rescued from Bede and afforded her own place in history. The question is, just what kind of place? In rewriting her history, we should beware of silencing the patriarchal desires of her hagiographer—desires that are equally evident in Bede's account of Cædmon. A comparison between the two accounts sharpens our point: removed from the "primal" scene of cultural production in the account of Cædmon, Hild is given a different nurturing role in the production of Christianity in her *Life*. Metaphorically at least, Bede produces, Cædmon reproduces what the monks produce for him (Christian poetry), but only Hild reproduces. Bede, after all, goes out of his way to stress Hild's role as "mother" in her *Life*. But as "mother to all," emptied of female presence and political force, Hild may be creator/originator of none: her power to create and to produce is initially dissipated and then specifically forgotten.

The gender asymmetries present in the reconstruction of originary events are replayed out by scholarship, literary and historical. The conventional historical account argues that Cædmon's story, with Hild as his patron, demonstrates that Whitby *must* have been a center of vernacular as well as Latin learning.[30] Leaving aside the essential mystery of Cædmon at the heart of this narrative, several other questions remain unasked, even by those historians writing about women: what was Hild's role as patron? what does it mean to call Hild the patron of Cædmon? how does Bede write of Hild's participation in Cædmon's story? In contrast, the conventional literary critical account reads *as* Bede, bearing witness to his miraculous story of Cædmon and ignoring his story of Hild. In each case, Hild suffers: only partially remembered by history; repressed by literary critics. There is no better example of the implicitly gendered stance of originary narratives than Bede's silence about Hild.

She is granted the status of supporting role in his account, giving center stage to Cædmon, but contemporary critics have been reluctant to grant her even this. It is all too easy to forget Hild when thinking of Cædmon. Women have no place at the beginning of English poetry, it would seem. Nor do they have much of one in the institutionalized narratives of contemporary scholarship on this subject.

Crudely speaking, those scholars who remember Hild reconstruct her history, her *historia*; those who remember Cædmon, reconstruct the literary myth of Christian poetry in which Hild is given little role to play. But Hild bridges these two worlds, revealing and questioning the inadequacies of our own disciplines that sever the literary from the historical. For the feminist reader, the historical approach to Hild might appear to be the most fruitful. Hild has at least a place in the historical record, even if it is a place that needs to address the patriarchy of her hagiographer. But this methodology risks diminishing her agency in the Cædmon story, as Bede does, and leaves unanswered our questions about her role and agency as cultural patron. Moreover, Bede does not just relegate Hild to the margins by refusing to name her, he silences her textually by the more radical method of "killing" her. To be sure, Bede praises Hild in her own story, but the Mother of the monastery is only the Abbess of poetry. Can we recuperate, or rather revive, Hild as a literary figure *and* a historical figure?

The Gendered Paradigm of Cultural Production: Complicit Mothers, Implicit Fathers

Without Hild there would be no Cædmon. Without Bede, however, we would remember neither Hild nor Cædmon. In the patriarchal world of the seventh century, the three figures of Bede, Cædmon, and Hild are more inextricably intertwined than in modern rewritings. Hild is a woman of her age and there is no indication that she escaped it even as abbess. Frantzen calls attention to the alacrity with which Cædmon is "whisked" into the monastery by Hild, and to her ability to spot a new protégé, concluding that her role contributes to the appropriation of the artist.[31] Indeed, as we have suggested, her promotion of Cædmon in the interests of patriarchal Christianity invokes her complicity in her own appropriation, her own removal from the cultural record. Perhaps these are reasons why we have been reluctant to look too deeply into her story. At present, it seems that one branch of feminism seeks to recuperate and redeem the forgotten women of history; a second seeks to define and, thereby, redefine the representation of women in the arts; a third addresses the equally important project of understanding patriarchy. A feminist patristic offers an interpretive framework that can embrace all three projects and realign the narratives of Hild, Bede, and Cædmon: we need to look more closely at the theory of cultural production embedded in Bede's account.

In the masculinist myth that is Cædmon's story, the process of creating songs is doubly suppressed in favor of the product, the *Hymn*. First, the man who creates the *Hymn* does so in a miraculous dream, which names him. Second, the woman who facilitates this process remains unnamed throughout, defined only by institution (the "Abbess") and by nonanaphoric pronouns. The account thus privileges divine composition over human agency, product over process, Bede over Cædmon, and both Bede and Cædmon over Hild. The emphasis on divine production expels gender—this is a "birth" without a birth. We see the same movement repeated in Hild's *Life*. Hild's moral worth (as mother) is emphasized at the expense of her own mother, Breguswith, her fostering (as mother) of literacy *and* her evident political power (cf. Synod of Whitby); all are displaced by the metaphor of "mothering" bishops. Another "birth" without a birth. These narratives of culture, in other words, emphasize product over process as examples of how birth/nurture is appropriated and downplayed by Bede. The question then arises of how we can recuperate the *processes* of cultural production to understand a specifically female agency and reconstruct the business of these women's lives: is there a way to put the "birth"—the physical realities of women's experience—back into the paradigm?

Here we want to connect the cultural metaphor of birthing to material practice. To locate the historical woman—the "exceptional" Hild or her unrecorded counterpart—in her sociocultural reality is to understand that relations of cultural production are fundamentally relations of labor. We could ask, for example, exactly what it means to say that a woman "founded a monastery": did she design it, dig the foundations (as Saints Seaxburg and Landrada did according to their *vitae*),[32] or raise the money to buy the land (as Hild did apparently)?[33] Similarly, what is implied by the title of abbess? What does it mean to say that a woman "ran a monastery"?[34]—did she teach, produce manuscripts, fundraise, oversee the necessary agricultural and domestic systems?[35] How involved was she in the legal and financial transactions so common in the history of monasticism? Did she witness land charters, for example—an issue we take up in Chapter 2. Some women, it appears, did many of these things, and much historical work outlines the individual contributions of "exceptional" religious women, but the larger issue of how these

contributions to the production of culture were valued in a masculine economy remains to be addressed: at what points and for what reasons are wom-
en's apparent control over and access to the means of production subsumed
within and replaced by patriarchal modes of production.

In sum, we are asking different questions about women's work, about
women's relation to their labor and to the social economy in which it is
exchanged, and about the forms of cultural representation, especially those
which "write" material culture, via which we construct this historical relationship. Jane Tibbetts Schulenburg provides a starting point for our enquiries
with her examination of female religious life from a variety of sociopolitical
viewpoints that range from the conditions of female sanctity to policies of
cloistering and patterns of monastic donation. She usefully summarizes:

This early period in Frankish Gaul and Anglo-Saxon England was an especially positive age in the development of women's monasticism. It was a time when royal and
ecclesiastical authority was weak and decentralized. Political and economic power was
situated within royal and aristocratic households and easily accessible to women.
Society was essentially "open" and fluid. It was an era of relative peace and prosperity.
It was also an age of new beginnings—a time of necessity during which the Church was
becoming established and was not yet highly organized, reformed, or right-minded. In
this milieu, women's practical assistance was especially valued. Female religious were
accepted as partners, friends, sisters, and collaborators in the faith. . . . Unfortunately,
with the reform movements and their emphasis on ascetic piety and clerical celibacy,
the initial appreciation of women's active participation in the Church was lost and
replaced by an atmosphere of heightened fear and suspicion of female sexuality.[36]

Although we question the implications of a "golden age" of female monasticism, Schulenberg outlines key aspects of the broader cultural discussion
in which we aim to contextualize Hild and her work: the connections between
women's status and labor and stages of social development, and the developing distinctions between public and private from the point of view of both
gendered labor and domain.[37] England in the seventh century was still loosely
comprised of individual kinship-based aristocratic kingdoms, awaiting the
later development of a centralized monarchy and movement toward a civil
state. Marxist historians and feminist anthropologists would agree, overall,
that the rise of the civil state leads historically to a substantial decrease in
the power and the visibility of women, whether they are placed in monastic
or secular spheres, and to the devaluation and privatization of the domestic sphere.[38]

Many developments in female monasticism in the Anglo-Saxon period
neatly and illuminatingly parallel this anthropological theoretical overview.

The changing requirements for female sanctity, for example, document how the early emphasis on the public presence and political acumen of the saint later gave way to the promulgation of her domestic virtues. Consider too the specific effects of policies of strict active enclosure on female monastic communities.[39] While we might examine more closely the degree of female autonomy within the double monastery, the abbess's more literal domestic confinement increases her answerability to the abbot and provides an instance of the consolidation of kinship-based (whether matrilineal or patrilineal) societies under the advancing civil state.[40] The new isolation of and emphasis on the "household" as social unit, as opposed to the more problematically diffuse (and harder to tax) kin-group, gives the male head of household, whether social or religious, power to control female production.[41]

Studies of material culture offer clear spatial images of a similar pattern, but raise additional questions about the relative status of monastic women within the overall development of restrictions on women as a sex and as a class. In her analyses of male and female monastic household layouts in the later medieval period (which raise the possibility of analogous work on the Anglo-Saxon period), archaeologist Roberta Gilchrist argues that spatial organization and design layout of the household "are both generated by and active in perpetuating a societal ideal" and that "In this model, gender domains would be formulated by the kinship structures specific to a social and economic mode of production."[42] In general, nuns' cloisters were more difficult to access from the surrounding precincts than were the male counterparts, but Gilchrist also notes a specific difference: "In nunneries the *dorter*, the communal sleeping area of the nuns, was the most secluded. In the monasteries, the chapter house, the heart of the community where daily business was transacted, was the most inaccessible to the external secular world."[43] Although the seclusion of the male monastic place of business might be variously theorized, the inaccessibility of the female sleeping quarters suggests an analogy to the restrictive privatization of the domestic sphere. Gilchrist argues against one contemporary feminist view that celebrates the monastic life as freedom from sexualized domestic oppression, asserting that "medieval nuns were contained within a private domain, not dissimilar to that of their secular counterparts, which emphasized their chaste fidelity as Brides of Christ."[44]

Clearly, the archaeological analysis of gender domains has much to contribute to expanding our literal and symbolic understandings of women's movement and activities, but it can also help to diagram the developments in their connections to modes of production. The spatial containment of women, Gilchrist contends, is an indication of rank and status, and here we might place the active female monastic cloister on a par with the middle-class Victorian woman's parlor: in both cases their architectural segregation demonstrates the "surplus labour of women who are alienated from their role in economic production."[45] Schulenburg also reminds us that denial of access to certain spaces is parallel to denial of access to cultural production when she catalogues the Carolingian reform councils' strict exclusion of women from "sacred space," now designated as "public." This exclusion from the public sphere contrasts with the purported freedom of the "undifferentiated space of the great hall."[46]

As we map out and attempt to understand the cultural and economic terms of a hypothesized decline in women's rights and freedoms in the Anglo-Saxon period, we must also try to describe the "height" from which they fell, and return to the "golden age" hypothesis (see Introduction for further discussion). What, if anything, was materially different in the condition of women and their relation to cultural production in the early period, when Hild apparently ruled at Whitby, traveled freely, and voiced her opinions in public at important religious and political events? What of the situation of female religious in the tenth and eleventh centuries? We discuss these issues of change and development more fully in Chapters 3 and 4.

Schulenburg, for example, makes the point that the transitional social "fluidity"—that is, when lines of power have not yet been rigidly drawn up—and the decentralization of political and religious authority in early English society allow women greater access to and control over means of production, whether cultural or agricultural.[47] Public and private spheres coalesce in the "undifferentiated space" inhabited by the politically powerful family and women moved freely within this space. This view is supported by anthropologists Stephanie Coontz and Peta Henderson, who emphasize class as well as gender distinctions in describing the developing civil state's cooptation of forms of authority: "The new public, hierarchical nature of authority put an end to the informal and delegated powers that aristocratic women had exercised by virtue of their family position."[48] Aristocratic status and operational kinship ties are here assumed to be necessary bases for women's realization and exercise of power, and could bear greater emphasis. Any discussion of female monasticism throughout the period should, but too rarely does entail consideration of class. This is a point that cannot be said often enough (and we have said it before in our Introduction). Hild and her peers are not only women: they are, for the most part, high-ranking women.[49] Moreover, the specific status of the aristocratic woman within a patriarchal social system has been variously theorized by feminist critics interested in the coincidental developments of gender and class oppression. Broadly speaking, the aristocratic woman may be perceived as having different interests and hence consciousness that separate her from lower class women, and this obscures the commonality of oppression of both men and women of the lower class; or, rather, the lines may be drawn somewhat differently:

the contradiction is between some men and *all* women as a social group. There are no contradictory interests among women in either kin-corporate or aristocratic class society. Aristocratic women do not share the socio-economic status of aristocratic men, as they do not have independent access to the means of production. . . . Like high-ranking servants, aristocratic women are artificially attached to the class of their husband or father, while in fact they belong to the dominated classes of society, even if they are not conscious of this.[50]

As a female double agent, Hild's own consciousness of her specific relation to, and degree of complicity in, patriarchal modes of production and how she might have valued and perceived her own labor are, of course, the most mysterious questions in our inquiry. And the best answer we can give is to keep questioning the cultural record. Instead of celebrating the aristocratic woman's exercise of power, we can critically examine the conditions of the exercise and remember the contradictions and tensions generated by the very conditions of her status. Such tensions are vividly illustrated by Bede's account of Breguswith's dream of the shining necklace.

Kinship, therefore, is one area of research where we can continue to question the cultural record and define more particularly the parameters of female monasticism.[51] We can, for example, look at some of the royal mothers represented by Bede and review the series of conversion scenarios that are scattered throughout *EH*. The conversion of the Kentish kingdom provides the first and perhaps most fundamental example. Augustine, arriving in Kent to convert the English, finds a royal family already sympathetic to Christianity to the extent that Bertha, the Frankish wife of Æthelberht I, is a Christian (*EH* 1. 25). Bede, however, does not stress the importance Bertha might have had in this Kentish court, in spite of the fact that Bertha and Æthelberht are the parents of quite a remarkable dynasty of Christian saints—mainly female saints—that link Kent with Northumbria and Mercia.[52]

A similar process is evident to a more marked extent in Bede's account of the conversion of the Northumbrian kingdoms. Edwin's conversion was certainly facilitated by his marriage to Æthelberht's daughter, the Christian Æthelburg, who brings Paulinus with her and whose daughter Eanflæd was one of the first to be baptized in Northumbria (*EH* 2. 9). Bede takes pains to record the two papal letters that urge conversion on Edwin: one written to the king and the other to Æthelburg, which emphasizes the importance of true Christian marriage and her role in Edwin's conversion (*EH* 2. 10–11). Yet the real drama of Edwin's conversion—the well-known accounts of Edwin's dream and of the advice of the high priest Coifi—excludes Æthelburg altogether (*EH* 2. 12–14; see also Chapter 5 for further discussion). The conversion of kings, as we might expect, is of far greater importance than the conversion of queens—however much we might wish to speak of the "power of women through the family."[53] In the case of the conversion of the West Saxons, Bede tells us that Oswald of Northumbria was present at Cynigils's baptism and cemented the alliance by taking Cynigils's daughter as his wife, but Bede does not tell us her name (*EH* 3. 7). Similar dynamics are present in the subsequent accounts of the conversions of the Middle Angles (*EH* 3. 21) and the South Saxons (*EH* 4. 13), where both queens were already Christian—facts of lesser importance to Bede than the dynastic allegiances cemented by these newly Christian kings.

It has become conventional among feminist historians to point to the kinship ties of the royal women who, as abbesses, nuns, and saints, achieve a considerable degree of prominence in this period. Hild herself is closely associated with the royal families of both Northumbria and East Anglia, and her monastery of Whitby even more closely tied to the royal house of Edwin (the church there provides the royal burial ground, Eanflæd retires there, and Ælfflæd succeeds after Hild, *EH* 3. 24). Since Whitby seems to have taken some pains to tie Edwin to their other benefactor, Gregory, it is not hard to see why his cult may explain the lesser importance of Hild's.[54] Royal monasteries do indeed stay in the family (in more ways than one), and the connections we seek between these remarkable women may in fact obscure the evident political interests of the royal families. It is possible to piece together a considerable network of female contacts and kinship affiliations for the early period of Anglo-Saxon monasticism, but each needs examination on its own merits. While we may balk at the description of "high-ranking servant," the status and power of such aristocratic women is clearly coopted in the service of patriarchy.[55]

Female monasticism is above all a partnership between royal and ecclesiastical interests—at least as it is presented in the historical accounts. The royal women, we might assume, derived considerable benefit from their kinship affiliations, not simply to protect property interests, but perhaps to cement an alternative female caste, principally comprising mothers and daughters. Given the patriarchal structuring of such accounts, however, the aristocratic caste may be a ghetto.

By looking more closely at women's writing in the period, this issue of an alternative female caste/ghetto can be defined against patriarchal versions of women's experience. Texts written by women are few and far between in Anglo-Saxon England, but there does exist a notable series of Latin letters written by women both in England and on the continent, the majority of whom are addressed to Boniface. Critical discussion has mainly concentrated on the (often held to be inferior) Latin rhetoric of these letters, although it has largely neglected the complementary issue of the extent to which female voices and experience may be obscured by such institutionalized forms of writing.[56] We address issues of voice, agency, and literacy more fully in Chapters 2 and 3. More important in this context, however, is the fact that these letters constitute a body of evidence for female attitudes toward kinship relevant to our understanding of a female dynasty of mothers and daughters. The women in these letters are often concerned about the loss of kinship ties and seek to replace them with spiritual ties, using virtually the same language.[57] In one (Ep. 13), Ecgburg laments her separation from her sister, Wetburga (who is in Rome), and the death of their brother, Oshere: she turns to Boniface for spiritual consolation. In another (Ep. 14), a letter jointly written by a mother, Eangyth, and her daughter Bugge, to Boniface that discusses a possible voyage to Rome (eventually undertaken by Bugge, after the death of her mother), the alienation of women from kin is even more pronounced: the letter stresses that the women have neither son, nor brother, nor father, nor uncle. Leoba's first extant letter to Boniface (Ep. 29), shows her to be in a similar predicament and offers an interesting solution. This letter, which also shows Leoba keen to have advice about her poetic skills, recounts how she has lost both father and mother and is therefore writing to her distant relative, Boniface, to claim fraternal as well as spiritual ties. Leoba in fact subsequently joins Boniface's mission. The contrast with Berhtgyth's correspondence with her brother Baldhard, from whom she is apparently permanently estranged, is pointed.[58] It is hard to escape the conclusion that women, exiled from their kin for whatever reasons, seek the solace of real exile and the life of the ascetic, or *peregrinus*.[59] In fact, several of the women who did join Boniface in such an exile were actually related to him, like Leoba.[60] Hild too originally wished to join her sister at Chelles, and it would appear that this was the closest kin she had.[61]

The evidence of these letters, however tentative, suggests an alternative way of interpreting the notion of a separate female caste within Anglo-Saxon monasticism and its evident patriarchy. The saintly royal women *maintain* the family, even within their cloistered environment, and their family maintains them, with an eye firmly on dynastic interests. These monasteries and the cults of royal women were supported financially by their families and descendants, within the ideology of the Christian ruling family—be it Northumbrian, Kentish, Mercian, or West Saxon. They remain Anglo-Saxon mothers, whether literally, spiritually or both, and they mother patriarchal dynasties that in many cases promote the spread of, or help maintain, Christianity. (For the continued symbolic and actual importance of mothers in the later Anglo-Saxon period, see Chapter 3.) Interpreted in this light, it is possible to understand the cultural importance of suppressing mothering. What we witness in Bede's account of Hild's role is an appropriation and a *rewriting* of mothering, a reinscription of the feminine within the parameters of patriarchy.

Hild's specific situation once again raises larger general questions when we consider the implications of this reinscription, and the many places that we may find "mothering" or literal and metaphorical forms of female experience rewritten throughout the period (points we develop in later chapters). Whether we read Bede's gendered accounts of Hild and Cædmon as unique or as paradigmatic of the ways Anglo-Saxon writers constructed events of cultural production, we can ask the same question of men's writing that we asked of women's: to what extent do institutionalized forms of rhetoric condition and require the reinscription of the feminine? Asser's celebrated account of Alfred learning vernacular poetry from his mother, Osburh (which is itself paralleled by the continental example of Theodoric's daughter, Amalasuntha, and her plans for the education of her son, Alaric) offers an important counterpoint to our discussion of Hild.[62] Structured according to the masculinist enterprise of emphasizing Alfred's precocious mental skills that are revealed in competition with his brothers, Asser omits Osburh's name, a process we consider further in Chapter 2.[63]

The formal demands of the hagiographic genre where women's deaths take precedence over their lives can be addressed in similar fashion. Saints' lives say as much, if not more, about the spiritual and cultural preoccupations of their hagiographers and intended readers as they do about their ostensible subjects, and Bede's *Lives* of Æthelburg and Æthelthryth are cases in point.[64] The narrative process of isolating (in cloister or on pedestal) the female saint obscures, as we have already suggested, her relationships with other women, which in turn obscures the possibility of reconstructing women's experience of kinship. In her discussion of the later Anglo-Saxon royal female saints, for example, Susan Ridyard notes some ways in which the hagiographer casts saintly mothers and daughters or sisters in a competitive relation to each other, vying for greater degrees of piety, as in the cases of the mother, Werburg, and the daughter, Eormenhild, or the sisters, Seaxburg and Æthelthryth. Working from these hagiographical sources, Ridyard herself construes the mother/daughter, sister/sister relationship as either political or spiritual, paying little attention to other ways of constructing kinship and connections between women, as her discussion of Edith and her mother, Wulfthryth, indicates.[65]

Recent feminist theories of maternity can be very helpful here. According to Julia Kristeva, for example, the hagiographical emphasis on virginity and spiritual maternity conceals and devalues real connections between women. It also minimizes the value and reality of physical maternity—including its threatening aspect to both men *and* women. Kristeva calls particular attention to the arrogation of the maternal function by male mystics as a basis for cultural forms of arrogation of the maternal principle, and other forms of appropriation of the female body for the cultural and political purposes of patriarchal religion have been well-documented by recent research in the later medieval period, especially by Karma Lochrie.[66] In the light of these symbolic frameworks, which theorize the appropriation of the female body, we ask in Chapter 5 what happens to the bodies themselves. We might reexamine the implications of, for example, the eminently "displaced" body of St. Edburga, one of the most famous (i.e., recorded) women of our period. She is not only disinterred on several occasions but also divided up, the parts of her body signifying equally political and divine protection—the edge, however, goes to those who host the greater part:

Although she has been divided into two shares in her relics, yet her virtue abounds in every particle: it offers a superiority to the nuns of Winchester, since the greater part of her body is there, while the oft-recited glory of her heavenly miracles gives lustre to the monks of Pershore.[67]

Ridyard questions the veracity of this account, suggesting that it was written "to provide the Pershore relics with a history."[68] Whether or not this is in fact the case, it is precisely our point that such stories and such metaphors comprise the cultural record, and *do* contribute to writing the history of women's agency—their bodies and experiences.

We return, finally, to a question we raised in the first part of this essay and consider further in Chapter 2: to what degree might the suppression and rewriting of feminine process parallel the "disappearance" of the oral trace?

The complexity with which accounts of the cultural record are overdetermined is evident from the ways other Anglo-Saxon male writers represent the act of writing. In many cases—Asser, Alfred, and Ælfric spring to mind—the product that is the text takes precedence over the process of composition.[69] Masculinity is associated with, and subordinate to, the finished product, it would appear; a point that bears out Bede's structuring of Cædmon's account. How far is it the case that Anglo-Saxon accounts of the production of texts suppress process and can we usefully conceptualize these forms of suppression or absence in similar ways?

"But every technology exacts its price," O'Brien O'Keeffe writes. "The power to preserve is gained at the cost of the intimacy of words. Through writing, words, divorced from oral source and substance, are conveyed by silence and absence. Writing becomes a technology of alienation."[70] While we do not want to fall prey to either a privileging of, or nostalgia for, voice and presence, nor would we want to isolate or victimize the feminine, such images and accounts resonate with our discussion of the *processes* by which the "disappearance" of Hild is culturally enacted. When we struggle to hear or reconstruct Hild's voice at the great Synod of Whitby, for example, we might remember O'Brien O'Keeffe's suggestion that "In the oral world, knowledge is gained and displayed in verbal struggle."[71] It has been our aim to introduce and initiate questions in this chapter, which we follow up in the rest of this book. We also offer a caveat: if contemporary scholars and historians, following in the wake of all who knew her in Bede's time, continue to call Hild "mother," then let us do so with a heightened sense of the term, and of the complexities of its cultural determination. Let us name Hild, and her social role, advisedly, within the context and confines of the cultures that produced her and continue to produce her, and let us continue to construct a broader understanding of relations of cultural production in the Old English period and subsequently that would seek to hear how she might name herself.

Chapter Two
Orality, Femininity, and the Disappearing Trace in Early Anglo-Saxon England

These next two chapters started out as one, but grew longer, and ever more central to our project, as we moved through the various stages of collaborative writing. While we realize that not all readers will read in an exactly linear fashion, nor even from cover to cover, we do urge that these two chapters be read in sequence. As we said in the Introduction, our argument and our choice of material are apposite and continuous.

Paradigms of Absence in Anglo-Saxon Culture

When we began asking questions about Hild's absence from Bede's account of the "birth" of Christian poetry in Chapter 1, intending to use this well-known story to build hypotheses about the relations of women to cultural production in the Anglo-Saxon period, we came up against the problem, the fact, indeed the *creation* of absence in many forms. In addition to the basic problem of the lack of "hard" information, critical paradigms which either exclude or simply "add on" gender as opposed to making gender central to those paradigms are a consistent part of the Anglo-Saxon critical landscape, from Bede's historical perspective on through to the present. One aspect of absence, then, is manifest as a lack of both coherence and specificity in the ways we have asked questions about women's lives. The compounded problem of absence is not only one of realizing and theorizing it, but also one of coming to terms with it as feminist scholars. We insist on the validity of framing questions about women's lives in the face of apparent lack of information, and of interrogating the cultural record by means of a revised and expanded critical paradigm in which gender is a fundamental variable. When we include the world of orality and theories of both presence and absence in the equation, however, it might appear that, to use a deliberately mixed metaphor, we are entering a hall of ever receding mirrors, lined by echoes and traces. But these are the very haunts of the double agent.

How to begin theorizing the twin disappearance of the oral and feminine trace as we outlined in Chapter 1? The "absence" of evidence about women (and, indeed, the accumulated evidence calling our attention to women's absence) neccessitates a willingness both to speculate and to withhold judgment and occasions a certain scholarly discomfort. Such discomfort is productively imaged in the manuscript page, as analyzed by Katherine O'Brien O'Keeffe in her study of transitional literacy; she argues that "a 'text' has a material reality intimately dependent upon the transmitting manuscript."[1] A manuscript provides a place to "read" a variety of cultural activities and oral processes: scribal, monastic habits of glossing, notetaking, borrowing, prioritizing information, literate ways of "hearing," to name but a few. As O'Brien O'Keeffe evokes the multivalence of the page, it becomes for us an echo chamber of sounds and letters, a mirror of voices and memories, exploding the boundaries of the "oral" and the "literate," attenuating and indeed disabling binary definition. Elements of the oral construct the written, and vice versa. And while we must read the page, and in so doing inevitably textualize the oral, the idea of the literate, written page as an echo chamber for voice sets us on the track of the female double agent.[2]

For us, and we suspect for many feminists, such multiplicity of conflicted meanings provides a site of both scholarly and ideological discomfort. To follow the analogy of the page as echo chamber and mirror—a place of aural and visual complexity—is also to look for the trace of the oral in the written and the feminine, then, in the masculine. This, in turn evokes a multifaceted and nondefinite subject, and also the uncomfortable prospects of female co-optation and/or complicity in patriarchal forms of discourse. Such a critical strategy also risks, and negotiates, simplistic or denigratory assumptions about the coreferentiality of the worlds of the oral and the feminine: the association is by no means a new one. We are aware of deep-rooted cultural and critical assumptions that on the one hand designate women as the bearers of traditional knowledge in oral cultures, but on the other consign women to that role in transitional literate cultures.[3] Such assumptions remain valid even as women have, and continue to be, the world's illiterates. This is dangerous territory, and although in traversing it in this and the next chapter, we risk betraying female agency, we also seek to recuperate it.

Anglo-Saxon scholars have been discussing orality for a good while, with recent discussions of the interface between orality and literacy adding to the

already substantial body of work on oral formulaic approaches.[4] There has yet
to be a comprehensive work on orality and literacy along the lines of Brian
Stock's, whose value for the earlier medieval period is limited: according to
Rosamond McKitterick, Stock's work "begins too late, and is too categorical
about the irrelevance of the earlier period."[5] Elisabeth van Houts's study,
Memory and Gender in Medieval Europe 900–1200, poses some important
questions about the connections of women to orality, though it does not
provide a sustained focus on the Anglo-Saxon period. Two recent collections
address gender and literacy but not specifically orality, and largely ignore the
Anglo-Saxon period; in *Women, the Book, and the Godly*, a religious emphasis
allows Bede into the conversation about monastic women's literacy,[6] while its
companion volume, *Women, the Book, and the Worldy* excludes Anglo-Saxon
women entirely.[7] Such exclusions recall the ongoing creation of difference and
absence from within the period discussed in the Introduction. Moreover, the
overall emphasis on religious and aristocratic literate domains sharpens another important aspect of absence: what of non-religious, non-aristocratic
women's (or men's) relation to literacy?[8]

Some scholars within the Anglo-Saxon period have inserted gender into
the orality and literacy debate, and some have left it out—with oddly similar
results, as we shall discuss later. To jointly theorize the oral and the feminine,
we propose initially to look at two critical models—that of the functionality of
literacy and that of the various guarantors of the symbolic—in addition to the
image of the manuscript page. It may be as difficult to codify the scribal
relationship to the text in an oral/literate transitional period as it is the actual
power or presence of women in periods of social transition as these are found
in our period, but our ways of thinking about each issue may prove profitably
interchangeable at the levels of both metaphor and process.

McKitterick's own work, though focused on early medieval Europe, offers
some valuable working premises for our purposes. By emphasizing the uses
and functions of literacy, she creates an interactive definition that engages the
oral, the particular complexities of the parallel vernacular and Latin traditions
in Anglo-Saxon England, and social and religious contexts for literate modes.
In addition to asking who could read, write, or memorize, and what is involved
in these processes, she asks who has access to literate modes of production,
what are the motivations for choosing literate modes, and how does the oral
function in conjunction with these modes.[9] Like O'Brien O'Keeffe's multivalent manuscript page, such a functional model makes room for the untidy
overlay of different factors, while it also values access to cultural production as
a controlling variable in both oral and literate disseminative modes. Moreover,

McKitterick's model immediately attenuates a masculine/literate, oral/feminine binary, introducing class and religious difference into the equation.

A second critical model is adopted from recent discussions of the multiple forms of transition from orality to literacy, which make much of liturgical developments surrounding the Eucharistic controversy and the elevation of the host. As we point out in our Introduction, the premises of a master paradigm that alienates cultural history before the twelfth century dictate one general assumption (among others): that somewhere around the thirteenth century a big change in the nature of representation took place.[10] The connection between representation and power, and the power of and over repesentation is clearly brought to issue in the political and religious debate over who gets to see the host and when, and who defines what is seen. This is by no means an originary moment in the history of representation—the debate about the Eucharist was well underway in the tenth century, as Ælfric's Easter Day Sermon on the Mass would suggest (see Chapter 3). The later medieval debate provides, however, a useful theoretical paradigm.

We borrow a rather simple footnote here from Kathleen Biddick's complex argument on the Eucharist: "It is as if the host functioned in the way in which the 'phallus' does today in contemporary psychoanalytic debate." Biddick casts the Eucharist as a "guarantee of the symbolic in medieval Europe."[11] As the host's representational valence and status is redefined, the problem in the twelfth century then becomes one of how to authenticate the signified that had now become the signifier; thus "notions of visibility and invisibility came to be redefined and reengendered."[12] As the Eucharist in its symbolic function accrues power from the invisible and now primarily masculine body (of Christ) *and* from the general development of literacy, the oral is correspondingly gendered as feminine, popular, visible as in "physical," and ambivalent. While we qualify this narrative from the perspective of the Anglo-Saxon evidence discussed in Chapter 3, Biddick's next move is particularly interesting. Although learned culture must then "recontain and reframe the feminine textually," first producing the female body as an effect and then recontaining it in the endless performativity of gender production, Biddick argues that the "feminist performance" of female mystics manages to disrupt the processes of this appropriation and to keep relations between the oral and learned culture in tension.[13]

Since women's history might be more productively and accurately analyzed from the point of view of continuity rather than change, might we not also examine these processes of containment and recontainment throughout the many transitional phases of orality and literacy in the Anglo-Saxon period? The authority of the Eucharist and its patristic exegesis are ways to "guarantee" representation, or the forms of the symbolic, within patriarchal discourse, and the literate enterprise of textual containment leaves a trace of its own process just as the oral leaves its trace in the text. Women's appearance in the cultural record, indeed any point of entry into the patriarchal symbolic, itself entails just such a suppression and a remaking, an overlay of absence with presence—or, indeed, vice versa, depending on how we ideologically configure the role of literacy.[14] While the later medieval women mystics' performances reveal sites of tension between the oral and literate, such tension is created and sustained by other means in the Anglo-Saxon period—perhaps less "visible" because of the ways we have sought them. This, then, is one aim of this chapter, to look at some of the many and repeated disappearances of the oral and feminine as produced by the literate and masculine functions of representational flux. To glimpse the irrepressible body that haunts the text is on a par with hearing the ineffable voice of the lettered page—we must countenance both visual and auditory hallucinations—but the illusory, chimeric quality of either need not distract us from the analyzable aspects of the textual, historical, and critical means by which these elisions are achieved, and such disappearances are controlled.

Phrases like "guarantors of the symbolic," or "patriarchal signifiers," invite an examination of the entire issue of control of representation; simply, who gets to say what, who registers meaningfully, or is assigned value within culture, and how, indeed why, "they" get to say so. These are the problems of detecting agency. Not to mention the forms of discourse, linguistic or otherwise, that enable this process. Where there's a voice there's a body. These strategies of discourse mutually and inseparably engage bodies—and texts— along a spectrum of containment, both rhetorical and actual. That we take rhetorical discourses seriously should be apparent from our introductory argument concerning Christian rhetoric and its performance of the psyche. Textualizing the body and "writing" the voice are not merely linguistic operations; they leave their mark on bodies as well as in texts.

What is emphasized by evoking critical models like the manuscript page, the functionality of literacy, or the various guarantors of the symbolic, is that it may not be possible to divorce the oral from the feminine from a point of view of patriarchal containment, but neither is it possible to divorce the oral from the masculine, or the literate. If the oral and the feminine are inevitably twinned as paradigms of absence, then their sites of interaction may be detected by other forms of presence, and sites of containment will leave traces, or better still, will enact the historical and textual detail of the process of (re)containment itself. This chapter on the early period of Anglo-Saxon culture will loosely designate and examine three such "sites," beginning with an exploration of the epistemology of naming, and then looking at riddles and charters.

What's in a Name?

In the spirit of nondevelopmental chronology and the continuity model for women's history, this discussion begins in the middle of the period, in the ninth century, working backward and then forward into the critical present. Naming is one of the most obvious points of entry into the symbolic and an evocation, if not an indication, of presence. This is ostensibly barren ground for those who seek to enumerate women in the genealogically obsessive world of patriarchal dynastic politics, sacred or secular, that characterizes much of the period. Anglo-Saxon genealogies are largely invested in fathers and sons. But when we don't learn a name, we sometimes hear a voice, a report if you like, of presence. When we learn a name in one instance, and hear a voice in another, we ask what makes the difference, or what else is being named and why. We may ask what is the communicative function of reported female voices, and how is it possible to discover the oral trace of the female teacher/confessor/educator in the written record; how to hear the public voice, the voice of authority, of communicative agency—the voice, in short, which does not bear a name.

One recent critic has couched the movement from orality to literacy in the Anglo-Saxon period in gendered terms and provides valuable points of departure for our argument. In his discussion of King Alfred, Seth Lerer characterizes the onset and development of literacy in terms of the consolidation of modes of masculine authority and paternity, and takes as a key instance the well-known tale of the child-king's intellectual precociousness. Asser, the king's biographer, describes a competition among Alfred and his siblings, instigated by his mother, for a book of "English poetry."[15] Alfred wins it by being the first to learn it, that is, to memorize it. Lerer offers an analysis of just what is meant by "reading" in this context, but also places the passage at an important metaphorical crossroads. When this story is read against the later account of the adult Alfred's becoming inspired to translate Christian texts, Lerer asserts that Asser's narrative of Alfred's development "gets the king to move beyond the language of the mother to the texts of intellectual Christian paternity."[16] The two scenes "juxtapose the English and the Latin, the maternal and the 'paternal' sources of textual authority for the king, as Asser will replace Alfred's mother in his new instruction in the language of the Fathers."[17] Alfred's literate, Latinate, paternal, authoritative understanding is qualitatively different from his superficial apprehension (fueled by adolescent desire?) of his mother's Saxon book; it involves a higher level of intellectual discernment and mature interpretive powers—a difference clearly outlined in Lerer's discussion of the verbs used in the different passages. While we question, as indeed does Lerer, Asser's own investment in this highly value-laden structuring of the development of royal literacy, Lerer also argues that the controlling metaphors of paternity and authority stamp the entire Alfredian enterprise—"if Alfred is a King, he is also a father and an *auctor*."[18]

If, as Lerer claims, these scenes from the King's biography are foundational moments in the development of literacy, carrying an "almost archetypal force, submerging the superstitions and genealogies of popular lore beneath an overall assertion of textual authority," then this binarily-constructed process should bear far closer examination.[19] If he is right, this Alfredian coup on behalf of literate modes, whether we see it as a rhetorical instance or as a function of political and cultural development in the ninth century, has important ramifications for those who would assert the masculine hegemony of literacy or the feminine erasure of orality, and those who would analyze both.

We have relatively good sources of information about Alfred and his reign, and much has been written about his multifaceted paternity, which Lerer reminds us is in part nonmetaphorical: having given "birth to an English prose" (necessarily a metaphorical task), he is also "quite literally, the father of English education, placing his own son in a school devoted to teaching in vernacular and Latin."[20] True, Alfred's youngest son Æthelweard is the star pupil, but it is worth noting that later in the same chapter Asser makes the point that the king's daughter Ælfthryth also receives a thorough education alongside her older brother Edward, although her skill in Latin is not specified (ch. 75, p. 90). In Lerer's scenario, however, Alfred's male-identified paternity arrogates the birth function and conditions concepts of literacy, authority and authorship, identity and genealogy, imprinting his own reign and beyond with the masculinist stamp. Simon Keynes looks at a similar progression, where we recognize gender by omission only. He examines the connections between the codification of royal authority and the development of literacy, from Alfred through the later Anglo-Saxon period. What Lerer has dubbed paternity, Keynes might identify as ideology:

But if King Alfred has used the written word to project his ideological aspirations, both he and his successors in the tenth century were no less conscious of the advantages it could bring in the more practical world of the publication and administration of royal law.[21]

Both critics discuss the exercises of power and their relation to literate modes. Gender is an unidentified variable in Keynes's argument, though present by default—his exemplary testators, for example, are usually referred to by the generic "he." Gender is overwhelmingly present in Lerer's argument, but nevertheless the two critics beg the same questions. The overarching concept of masculinity that conditions so many processes remains as mysterious as the unexamined or unspoken assumption of normative masculinity. Ubiquitous paternity, spoken or otherwise, is about as informative a concept as amorphous maternity.[22] Neither affords us a means of theorizing the complex relations of orality and literacy.

What of the "maternal"? We place the term in quotation marks where Lerer does not. What of the Mother, of Alfred's mother? She is also a parent, like Alfred, and is also used as a metaphor. Osburh is not actually named by Asser in the book competition passage, and not named at all by Lerer in any context. In Lerer's text she is cast as a passive participant in this classic Freudian move as the "idea of a 'mother tongue' is brought to life in the person of the King's mother and her Saxon book."[23] We say "classic," but while we may recognize this as a Freudian model of cultural development where the "civilizing" masculine forces of intellect and reason overcome the feminine forces of emotion and relative chaos, Lerer's critical move remains both unacknowledged and untheorized. Shall we assume, then, that Alfred puts away childish things—his mother and her little game with her Saxon book, along with the world of the oral and/or the feminine? With the disappearance of Osburh, we also lose sight of female agency, which is left completely untheorized in the either/or constraints of this rather rapid transitional model. And along with Osburh, we also watch the world of "popular lore" disappear. Just what is "submerged" in the "traditional," as Lerer puts it, world of the oral and the feminine? Are verbally inciteful Valkyries, royal mothers egging on their sons, magic spells and folkloric incantations, the world of the marvelous (as opposed to the Christian miraculous), and, indeed, orally-based histories that support female title to monastic lands[24] collectively dismissed from a frame of literate reference because these are somehow amorphously connected?[25] We consider some of these diverse items later in this discussion, but it is in this nondifferentiated, wholesale submergence that we can identify the creation of a paradigm for female absence. We recognize here how the employment of a gendered binary can lead to drastic oversimplification, and how it may work to further obscure that which is not being named.

The disappearance of Osburh, in both Asser's and Lerer's texts, is one site of textual (re)containment—or, more simply, a place to begin asking questions. And if we do not establish any hard facts, we may at least rescue her from the critically confused category of the maternal. Why would Osburh, a reasonably savvy noblewoman in the politicized dynastic environment of the mid-ninth century, not be fully aware of literacy as a vehicle for power and authority? We may not know the extent of Osburh's own literacy, but we might presume that she understands its implications, and that she has access to, and some control over, its modes of production—the book offered as a prize to her children is a supposedly beautiful object in itself.[26] Why would this mother not be fully aware, moreover, of the paternal, or ideological, nature of the authority she encourages Alfred to claim? She wants her son to want this book, albeit a book of homespun Saxon poems. Janet Nelson provides a counterpoint to Lerer's argument here, as she pursues the political uses of these same vernacular poems:

He [Asser] tells us that what Alfred memorized as a child were "Saxon songs"; that what he prescribed especially for his elder children's education were "Saxon songs"; and "Saxon songs" were what he encouraged his retinue to recite and learn by heart. It is no coincidence that this last reference comes in the context of Alfred's careful organization of his royal household and its upkeep: essential bases, as Asser saw, of the government of the realm. What these Saxon songs conveyed, and hence, presumably, what Alfred wished to stress, was a distinctive Saxon, vernacular and aristocratic cultural inheritance . . . a social order in which kinship is central and obedience brings it reward.[27]

Nelson's argument recasts the "maternal" in terms of its interplay with ideology, as a vital element in Alfred's social and national program—coopted or complicit, perhaps, but hardly submerged. Perhaps we might consider then, as with Hild, the degree of Osburh's cooptation or complicity in patriarchal modes of accessing and interpreting power by means of her access to literate modes. This is not to simply swap the passive maternal for the assertive paternal, but to continue to dismantle paternal and maternal as binary categories of analysis, and to introduce some of what we know of Osburh's familial and historical context.

Osburh *is* an obscure figure; although Asser does not name her in the book competition scene, he does name her in his enumeration of Alfred's maternal ancestors in an earlier chapter (ch.2, p. 68), but this is our only reference to her. We only know her name as a function of this genealogy and, as Janet Nelson argues, Asser's genealogies have a complex function within his text and within its dynastic context. Nelson offers a glimpse at Osburh's "story," working obliquely with Asser's narrative and a detailed historical context.[28] Her ancestry is both glorified and given a Scandinavian emphasis by Asser, suggesting "ninth-century fiction," but serving the purpose of making the King's mother (and the King) more acceptable to the increased Scandinavian element of Alfred's domain of the early 890s, when Asser constructs his narrative.[29] Osburh, however, was markedly not accorded queenly status, highlighted by the Frankish demand for this mark of honor to be accorded to Judith, the foreign princess who marries Alfred's father Æthelwulf in 856.[30] What happened to Osburh? Was she alive when "replaced," asks Nelson, making Alfred's father a bigamist?[31] And if so, how does Asser's narrative finesse the situation? Although Asser's chronology is not always reliable, the book scene with Osburh comes after Alfred's father's marriage to Judith, after which Osburh exits the narrative. Osburh's elevated lineage is perhaps contrived as compensation for her lack of queenly status—as well as providing a consolidating tool for royal authority.[32] A fictional past is traded for a non-existent (i.e., nonrecorded) present and future. We know nothing more about her, and what we guess at must remain subject to revision. In a telling comment on the politically volatile conditions for women's entry into the symbolic, Nelson states that Asser's vagaries "suggest that Osburh's story was in a process of reconstruction at the time he was writing."[33] In a decade where succession became a divisive issue for Alfred, his son Edward, and grandson and nephews, the king's wife's stock was variable. And a mother might be up- or downgraded in proportion to the fortunes of a wife (see Chapter 3). Osburh and Alfred's wife Ealhswith (also barely named) may be counted as "prime victims in the 890s of his (Edward's) ambition, and of the historian's silence."[34]

What else is not named or textually (re)contained in these accounts of Osburh? Lerer's metaphorical maternity obscures other denominations for Osburh, such as educator, teacher, mentor, aristocratic mother with access to literate modes and motivation to employ them. We could even push the question and expand its frame of reference: how might Osburh's situation comment on the role of women as mentors and educators, a role so obscure in the Anglo-Saxon cultural record and so much more clearly accessible to historians of the Carolingian period? (Recall that not only Osburh, but female teachers as such, disappear in Alfred's literate trajectory; his earlier attempts at coeducation for his own children apparently forgotten, the king exhorts his illiterate nobles to acquire learning however they may, from their own sons or even from a servant—"whether freeman or slave," ch.106, p. 110.) The relative absence of mentoring, educating female figures in the Anglo-Saxon cultural record, and their relative presence on the continent—Dhuoda and the *Liber Manualis* that she wrote for her son come to mind—prompt some intriguing though highly speculative questions. Dhuoda writes her manual in France between 840 and 843, within a decade or two of Osburh's recorded tutelage, and is one of a substantial literate cadre of noble mothers responsible for their children's education.[35] Although there are not many named parallels to Dhuoda, Rosamond McKitterick offers evidence to suggest that she was not an exception, and places her in the context of a general level of basic literacy that prevailed among the nobility.[36] How might we similarly configure the connections between class and literacy, between women and literacy, in the Anglo-Saxon period? If Osburh's connection to literate modes is primarily to the vernacular, how might the unusual popularity and persistence of vernacular forms in Anglo-Saxon England figure into the equation? Were women more associated with "popular" literacy as an outgrowth of their connection to "orality"?

Some of these questions can be approached by looking at forms of discourse like the riddles or the charters and their connection to an oral world, and by looking at the more highly developed social and religious purchase on the vernacular in the later part of the period. However, Osburh's double agency—traceable through her marked absence from the cultural record and through the assumption of presence we have outlined here—and the submergence of her voice and function into hegemonic literate modes, have a history of their own. Osburh's story emerges as a repeated version of textual (re)containment if we reach back into the period and pursue the metaphor of voice as a means to evoke the presence of women as teachers, mentors, educators, and confidants, both royal and ecclesiastical. The particular silences occasioned by ninth-century West Saxon secular politics find ample parallels in church control of access to literate modes and in the cultural record by which control is enacted and reflected in the seventh and eighth centuries. Here again Hollis's valuable work on church history and its relation to women offers a range of examples of the process we designate as textual (re)containment. She charts the means by which women's voices, those of authority, learning, and wisdom, are progressively silenced, from the early heyday of the mid-seventh-century double monastery onward; her study concludes with

Leoba (as indeed will ours), the last of several generations of learned Anglo-Saxon churchwomen to "make it" into the cultural record, again within a couple of decades of Osburh's intimated role as educator.[37]

Hollis looks at the careers of influential aristocratic and monastic women such as Eangyth, Hild, Cynethryth, and Æbbe and provides some wonderfully detailed analyses of the textual means, some subtle and some egregious, by which their lives are rewritten and their presence minimized or erased. One example, however, particularly recalls the issue of voice. The late seventh and early eighth centuries offer plentiful examples of monastic women who retain a public voice, although the degree to which we may feminize the oral (or vice versa) here is attenuated by these women's usually aristocratic status and function within and on behalf of an increasingly patriarchal church hierarchy. One such woman was Ælfflæd, whose story Hollis examines in lucid detail, much abbreviated here. As Hild's successor as abbess of Whitby, one of the most important monastic centers in the north, she occupies a position of "quasi-episcopal eminence."[38] Like Hild, she acts as advisor to kings and princes, only this time we know who some of these potentates are (see Chapter 1). We have names. Ælfflæd is embroiled in one of the biggest episcopal and dynastic controversies of her time centering on the enigmatic figure of Bishop Wilfrid. Lauded by churchmen as a pioneer of the episcopal restructuring instigated by Theodore—an enterprise involving sizable expansion of both church bureaucracy and domain—Wilfrid was less popular with the North-umbrian royal family upon whose domain he encroached. He was exiled by Ælfflæd's brother Ecgfrith of Northumbria, and, following the king's death, Theodore writes to both Ælfflæd and Ecgfrith's successor, his illegitimate brother Aldfrith, on behalf of Wilfrid's reinstatement. Ælfflæd, confidant of kings, is present when her half-brother Aldfrith is on his deathbed; she reports his dying wishes for reconciliation with the problematic prelate, and those concerning his succession. (She even testifies verbatim to an oath taken by the dying king—another dimension of orality taken up in the discussion of charters in this chapter and the next.) Earlier, she appears as the confidant of holy men, discussing the Northumbrian succession of her childless brother with the reclusive and also dying Saint Cuthbert.

Ælfflæd's status and these events are generally attested to in different sources, Stephen of Ripon's *Life of Wilfrid*,[39] the Anonymous *Life of Cuthbert* and Bede's *Life of Cuthbert*,[40] which Hollis holds up as mirrors to each other in terms of style and content.[41] In Stephen's *Life* Ælfflæd's words are publicly heard and effectual, her presence is felt; she is at the heart of the political and religious life of her time, "always the comforter and best counsellor of the whole province."[42] In the Anonymous *Life of Cuthbert* she shares scriptural wisdom and deep spiritual knowledge and kinship with this most venerated of saints. In Bede's *Life* these attributes are rewritten almost beyond recognition. In Hollis's reading, Bede removes all functional power from her words; in her discourse with the saint her presence and power of speech are so reduced that she becomes a "species of comic butt . . . an unwitting spectacle of female stupefaction for the edification of a knowing audience."[43]

Of course, each of these texts is written with its own purpose more or less sympathetic to the secular and monastic milieus jointly inhabited by Ælfflæd, but even this truncated summary indicates that what is being textually contained/recontained in all of these accounts is Ælfflæd's public voice, her communicative agency as mentor, advisor, teacher—her effective oral functioning in sacred and secular spheres. These sites also belie tension between oral and literate modes, for which Ælfflæd's reported public performances are but one focus within the text, and in which gender is but one variable among several. The simple misogyny of Bede's account is complicated by the question of reception:

That Bede indulged in this form of polemic in a work composed for a monastic audience, but made no use of it in the *History*—intended for a wider audience and dedicated to the Northumbrian king—suggests that the misogynist undermining of royal women that was cultivated in ecclesiastical circles was not well-received in secular society.[44]

In Stephen's text, Ælfflæd is perhaps "heard" more in her secular context, her royal connections supporting her credibility: "these words were heard by most faithful witnesses and told to us. Of these, one is the abbess and most prudent virgin Ælfflæd, who is indeed the daughter of a king."[45] Stephen also allies (coopts?) her verbal power to the pro-Wilfridian, pro-Roman church cause. (Earlier in his career, she had been counted among Wilfrid's former enemies.[46]) The reported voice of the nonmonastic noblewoman, however, is also a function of the same set of coordinates, differently configured. The "poisoned arrows of speech" of Jurmenburg, Ecgfrith's second wife (his first was the famously virginal Æthelthryth) turned him against Wilfrid, as she voiced her misgivings about the prelate's power to her husband—perhaps with some reason:

She eloquently described to him all the temporal glories of St. Wilfrid, his riches, the number of his monasteries, the greatness of his buildings, his countless army of followers arrayed in royal vestments and arms.[47]

If we may not clearly identify the connection of orality and femininity in the textual rendering of the abbess's or the queen's voice without the intervening factors of class and dynastic concerns, both episcopal and secular, neither are literate modes clearly allied with the masculine, the hegemonic, or the authoritative. Indeed, in Stephen's text, authority has an uneasy relation to literate modes. Ecgfrith, apparently, is no respector of the written word:

With all humility he showed the king the written judgement of the Apostolic See with the consent and subscription of the whole synod, and delivered it to him with its bulls and stamped seals. Then he summoned all the chief men who lived there as well as the servants of God to the synod's meeting place to hear the wholesome counsels sent from the Apostolic See for the sake of the peace of the churches.[48]

Yet, no amount of papal bells and whistles, nor Wilfrid's oral performance, which is both duplicate and extension of the written document, can persuade Ecgfrith of the legitimacy of Wilfrid's claims; he flies into a rage and throws the bishop into prison. Ecclesiastical literate authority is dismissed in this instance; not so elsewhere in Stephen's text. Other kings show more deference. Æthilred of Mercia (a supporter of Wilfrid) literally bows to the written word, and then seals its authority with an oral declaration:

As soon as the writings from the Apostolic See were opened and read, the king bowed himself to the ground and obediently made a promise in these words: "As for the writings of this Apostolic authority I will never in my life disobey one single jot or tittle in them nor will I consent to those who disobey them; but I will do my best to get them fulfilled."[49]

While the first quarter of the eighth century is bound to present a picture of oral and literate modes in flux and overlay that are specific to the sacred and secular politics of the day, this particular array of tensions, indeed, contradictions, suggest that we cannot extricate the feminine from this process, or align it unambiguously with the oral. The Wilfrid affair and its textual redactions offer a case in point for McKitterick's questions about communicative functions of literate modes, about control over and access to those modes, and about their collaborative, cooptive or oppositional relation to the oral.

We hear the voices—verbatim, reported, echoed, constructed—of the often-named Ælfflæd and the barely-named Osburh in their distinct historical registers: the greater volume of Ælfflæd's is explicable in some measure by the institutional window of opportunity afforded high-status women within late seventh- and early eighth-century church hierarchy, and Osburh's sotto voce conditioned by secular politics that muted high-status women, especially queens, in ninth-century Wessex. Somewhere in between, incidentally, Ælfflæd disappears. Along with many other notable/noted women that we can identify in the late seventh and eighth centuries, there is no record of her in a later church history, Alcuin's *The Bishops, Kings, and Saints of York*, written in the last two decades of the eighth century.[50] While the solidification of church hierarchy and sacerdotal and episcopal authority offer clear directives and rationales for such exclusions, Alcuin's forgetting is noteworthy for several reasons: he borrows heavily from Bede's *History* and other works, which do name and give "voice" to a good many royal and monastic women, however we assess this identification.[51] Alcuin's work, written in "competent, if undistinguished" Latin verse according to Godman, his editor, has greater value as an idiosyncratic commentary on Northumbrian history, in which we know Ælfflæd had both secular and monastic key roles.[52] The poem was not circulated in England until a long time after its composition, but such omissions are quite telling in the context of Alcuin's Carolingian base; the French court, as we have seen, was hospitable to high-status women's literacy, and whereas monastic women in England were increasingly less visible, the continental missions offered plentiful examples of prominent, learned churchwomen.[53]

Naming is above all a textual process, revealed by both omission and identification. In closing this discussion, we juxtapose a remembered name, one of many reappearances in the cultural record, as a brief commentary on Ælfflæd's disappearance: Ælfflæd's brother Ecgfrith's first wife, the recurrently noteworthy and ever virginal Queen Æthelthryth, does retain her name in Alcuin's text—a trajectory of identification that bears a separate investigation (see Chapter 4).

Riddling and Renaming

Where there's a voice, there's a body. Textual containments produce women's bodies and voices according to the demands of the symbolic and its current guarantors, and such containment becomes readily visible in learned riddling and its rhetorical means of renaming experience. Or rather, it becomes visible if we look at the *process* of textual containment itself as a riddle, and the oral, the feminine, the masculine, and the literate as a conundrum of rhetorical definition. Some riddles, of course, have traditionally been seen as a source of information about bodies. The association of vernacular riddling with sexuality is a critical commonplace. Critics claim that within the Anglo-Saxon corpus some of the vernacular riddles offer a rarefied glimpse of the "real" world of earthy sexuality: no lofty arguments certainly, but all human life is there, and "nothing human is deemed too high or low for treatment."[54] John Tanke calls these critical topoi into question and convincingly demonstrates that these riddles are far more complex. He questions "the rhetoric of the lower class," which includes the critical assumption that vernacular forms address and construct "lower-class" subjects; Tanke argues that these riddled bodies, especially that of the "dark-haired servant-woman" (*wonfeax wale*) of Riddle 12, so liberally displayed, in turn reveal the ideologies that construct them and the interdependence of cultural assumptions about gender, race, and ethnicity.[55] Lerer, too, revises the critical stature of the riddles by asserting their dependence on literate modes of composition and perception, and by aligning them with the parallel momentum of literacy and authoritative discourse launched by Alfred. The question of audience is as always a sticky one, but, whether composed or collected by or for a literate elite as Lerer argues, the vernacular riddles do repeat and rehearse earlier, designatedly literate and Latinate form and content, and the bodies thus displayed will appear (or disappear) in some relation to oral, literate, Latinate, or vernacular purchases on the symbolic. That relation is our riddle.[56]

Aldhelm's Latin *Enigmata*, compiled at the end of the seventh century, and the vernacular riddles of the Exeter Book, collected at the end of the tenth, provide a doubled commentary on literate modes of textualizing the body within our period. Lerer argues that the earlier Latin collection stands as a systematic model for the later vernacular one in terms of shared classificatory principles; the form of the riddle is cast as an essentially literate intellectual enterprise which seeks to "rename the objects of experience," and to offer "the range of experience filtered through textual understanding."[57] Nicholas Howe recalls the biblical significance of rhetorical acts of naming: to create, and to solve, the riddle is "to participate in the initial act of identification . . . to remember the first act of riddling in Christian history, Adam's naming of the animals in Eden."[58] The riddles thus affirm a coalition of divine and literate authority and reiterate the processes by which they are enacted. On the other hand, Tanke's cultural understanding of the process of classification keeps our eye on its object and product; both viewpoints will be useful in asking how the riddles contain the body and produce it as textual effect, and how oral and literate modes are held in tension in both genres.

Aldhelm's Latin works, as we shall see further in Chapter 4, exemplify high artifice and artistry. Moreover, the number of extant manuscripts, commentaries, and glosses imply that his work was "required reading" for clerics and that it contributed to the formulation of an ideal of literate Latinity current throughout the Anglo-Saxon period and beyond.[59] If Aldhelm has been taken to epitomize a certain mode of literacy, some of his debt to the oral world in terms of metrical composition and the introduction of vernacular elements has also been acknowledged.[60] Andy Orchard encourages a reevaluation of the "Old Englishness" of Aldhelm, in that "Aldhelm's concerns were Cædmon's."[61] Cædmon, as we have argued, embodies one of the most dense conflations of oral and literate modes and is present at the "birth" of their means of dissemination. It may be that the literate churchman participates in some of the same textual processes as the unlettered lay laborer.

We look briefly at a few of Aldhelm's riddles; the objective here is not thoroughgoing analysis but broad observation of representational process. Initially, "birth" seemed as good an entry point as any other in order to look for an oral/feminine/literate textual nexus, but it subsequently emerged as an unavoidable preoccupation within the metaphorical purview of the *Enigmata*. Michael Lapidge and James Rosier note that "nearly one-third of the Enigmata contain an explicit reference to birth," while references to *viscera*, "womb," or "innards" are also frequent.[62] This is not unusual. Metaphorical metamorphoses of birth and of its femaleness are stunning in their power and variety in patristic writing in general. That arrogation of birth is a repeated and remarkably consistent trope need not diminish our interest in its specific instantiations—and to give Aldhelm his due, he occasionally came up with a new twist apparently all his own: witness the "vulva of regenerating grace."[63] Moreover, Aldhelm's status as curriculum author and the later recurrence of the *Enigmata* in a vernacular context suggest a more pointed connection to the formation of a cultural symbolic. Add to this the parallel of the tenth-century renaissance of literary Latin with the political dimensions of the Benedictine reform movement and we might see textual process and performance of the body in a more codependent historical relation.[64]

Riddles 30 (Alphabet) and 89 (Book-cupboard), quoted in full, bear special scrutiny for our purposes:

We were born seventeen voiceless sisters; we say that the six other bastards are not to be counted in our number. We are born of iron—and we die once again by iron—or of the feather of a bird flying swiftly in the sky. Three brothers begot us of an unknown mother. Whoever in his eagerness wishes earnestly to hear our instruction, we quickly produce for him silent words.[65]

Now my inwards are filled with holy words, and all my entrails support sacred books. And yet I am unable to learn anything from them. Unfortunately, I am deprived by fate of such a gift, since the deadly Parcae [the Fates] take away the illumination [which] books [provide] (Lapidge and Rosier, p. 89).[66]

Katherine O'Brien O'Keeffe focuses on these riddles in her persuasive discussion of speech, silence, loss, and their relation to literate modes.[67] Although Aldhelm does inherit a "corpus of dead metaphors," O'Brien O'Keeffe points to what may be distinctive in his use of them:

> The images of violence, however, are to the best of my knowledge an English contribution to the Latin *enigma* tradition, and the metaphors of sad transformation, common to these *enigmata*, appear as well in the Old English riddle tradition on writing. The use of mouthless speakers, dead life-givers, dumb knowledge-bearers, clipped pinions—all metaphors of loss—reflect an Anglo-Saxon understanding that speech itself is not a *thing*, but that writing, as it alienates speech from speaker, transforms living words into things. The technology that preserves also kills.[68]

This is a compelling analysis of forms of cultural melancholia, modes of nostalgia, and the dissociation attendant upon literate process; we would add to O'Brien O'Keeffe's evocation of violence, sadness, and loss in this passing oral context the contingent element of the feminine, and the associated silencing, even unto death, of the oral and the feminine.

There is much begetting in both riddles—Riddle 30 even classifies birth as legitimate and illegitimate—but little identification of birth as a feminine process, not to mention some serious confusion in its images for masculine generation: "Three brothers begot us of an unknown mother."[69] While her daughters are silent and their mother is "unknown" (or possibly "uncertain," *incerta*), the hand and the pen doing the begetting (and the silencing) in Riddle 30 are masculine. In Lapidge and Rosier's gloss, "the iron that begets them is the stylus; the 'three brothers' are the three fingers that hold the stylus."[70] The alphabetic "sisters" mouth soundless words, mimes of meaning for a masculine literate audience;[71] the pregnant book-cupboard (*gestant praecordia*) of Riddle 89 is sterile, an image of ignorant instrumentality, a mere vessel of meaning.[72] Also worth noting here are the images of birth and violence played out on another form of vessel, the feminized visage of the writing tablet in Riddle 32: "Now the iron point cuts into my comely face with its wandering movements, and carves furrows in the manner of a plough; but the holy seed for the crop is brought from heaven, and it produces abundant sheaves from its thousand-fold harvest. Alas, this holy harvest is destroyed by fierce weapons!" (Lapidge and Rosier, p. 76).[73]

Clearly the female body is somewhere present at these sites of riddling representation, even given the added dimension of grammatical gender (explored in further detail in Chapter 5). Present as a condition for signification, as a metaphorical ground, the body's meaning and functions are contained—indeed alienated—and produced as textual effects that depend upon that body's absence to signify in Aldhelm's rhetorical system. How seriously shall we take language here, and what power to perform a subject shall we acknowledge? As exercises in interpretation and classification of experience, learned or vernacular riddling contributes to the recurrent disappearance of the oral and the feminine from the literate formulations of the symbolic. That is, neither the oral nor the feminine means or produces anything—without the aid of some masculine literate midwifery.

Not only does the literate path create its own birth process, it also leads to salvation in the best Augustinian exegetical tradition, as suggested by Riddle 59 for "quill pen": the "trail [of letters] proceeds in a thousand directions and takes those who do not stray from it to the summits of heaven" (Lapidge and Rosier, p. 82).[74] Literate and divine authority appear to coalesce in effacing the oral and the feminine.[75] Perhaps a more interesting issue here, however, is the odd disjunction of content and context; these riddles' profound silencing of the oral and the feminine occurs in a late seventh-century learned milieu inhabited by prominent churchwomen, usually well educated and often highly vocal, and easily able to compose and read Latin verse. The same disjuncture is writ far larger in Aldhelm's *De virginitate*, as we shall see in Chapter 4. The riddles' minor rhetorical contradictions speak to a greater paradox characterizing the early church, and to the disparity between evolving doctrinal and institutional policies and the roles of monastic women in the seventh and eighth centuries, an evolution so well documented by Hollis.

Before taking up the tenth-century vernacular riddles, we call attention to a curious interim example from the *Collectanea Pseudo-Bedae*, a text discussed in more detail in Chapter 5. The provenance and principles of selection of this remarkable compilation bear extensive scrutiny, as do questions of its audience and reception, but for our present purposes one oddly truncated riddle stands out. Item 198 in the *Collectanea's* assortment of *dicta*—possibly the contents of a monastic "personal notebook"[76]—obliquely recalls our themes: "I saw a girl weeping and muttering, her ways are the paths of life."[77] Citing other parallels to this as a riddle, the editors explain that "the weeping denotes the flowing of ink, and the murmuring in the pseudo-Bede version the scratching of the pen."[78] The feminized pen is once again the instrument of literacy and the vehicle of enlightenment and salvation, absent as subject yet still the necessary ground for representation. But this pen weeps as it births words; curiously, metaphorical violence has given way to metaphorical sorrow—suggesting what manner of rhetorical shift? And for whom is the sorrowing subject performed, what audience does this rhetoric identify?

Aldhelm's seventh-century rhetoric performed its subjects before and for a different audience in the tenth, given the probable decline in female Latin literacy and the rise of Aldhelm's reputation in scholastic circles. The nature of a literate audience, or just who had what kind of access to vernacular or Latin literate modes, is, as we have suggested, a sticky question, which becomes stickier as the period progresses and there appears to be even less evidence of women's (either monastic or noble) access to literacy. We have to ask the question in its later historical context and will do so in the next chapter. Here, we limit our remarks on vernacular riddling to a few comparative points and to issues of contemporary reception and patterns of learned representation.

Whether composed by and for the commonfolk or understood as a verbal playground for a literate elite, the vernacular riddles offer a rich conflation of oral and literate elements and a concomitant glimpse of the feminine trace. The disappearance of the feminine in process in Aldhelm's text and in the isolated example from the *Collectanea* is completed in the Exeter Book collection and only identifiable by comparison. Riddle 49, for example, cited as an analogue of Aldhelm's "book-cupboard," shows no rhetorical trace of the feminine. The vessel in this case is simply dumb and stupid, but not recognizably female.[79] Riddle 51, "pen and three fingers," has elements reminiscent of Aldhelm's "alphabet," "writing tablets," and "quill pen" riddles, but the tropes of birth and violence are gone (violence remains only in association with the heroic)—as well as the path to heaven:

Ic seah wrætlice   wuhte feower
samed siþian;   swearte wæran lastas,
swaþu swiþe blacu.   Swift wæs on fore,
fuglum framra;   fleag on lyfte,
deaf under yþe.   Dreag unstille
winnende wiga   se him wegas tæcneþ
ofer fæted gold   feower eallum

(I watched four fair creatures
travelling together; they left black tracks
behind them. The support of the bird
moved swiftly; it flew in the sky,
dived under the waves. The struggling warrior
continuously toiled, pointing out the paths
to all four over the fine gold.)[80]

Our question remains how to register such disappearances within the specific historical formulations of the symbolic, and whether there is a correlation between women's rhetorical disappearances and their decreased participation in literate modes.

As literacy takes hold, literate modes continue to textualize the body and to shape and rename experience. Indeed, to efface it. Seth Lerer concludes his discussion of literate process in the vernacular riddles with a detailed analysis of Riddle 42, the cock and hen riddle. He argues that this riddle, perhaps more than any other, is about the process of interpretation itself, the nature of which is in turn reinterpreted in the specific terms of literate, monastic under-standing. The riddle is one of the most dense, though perhaps not among the most successful, of the Exeter Book collection—"the poet was perhaps strain-ing too hard after effects."[81] It begins with two animals openly copulating and concludes, via some elaborate runic conundrums, with a challenge to name them:

Ic seah wyhte   wrætlice twa
undearnunga   ute plegan
hæmedlaces;   hwitloc anfeng
wlanc under wædum,   gif þæs weorces speow
fæmne fyllo.   Ic on flette mæg
þurh runstafas   rincum secgan,
þam þe bec witan,   bega ætsomne
naman þara wihta.   Þær sceal Nyd wesan
twega oþer   ond se torhta Æsc
an an linan,   Acas twegen,
Hægelas swa some.   Hwylc þæs hordgates
cægan crafte   þa clamne onleac
þe þa rædellan   wið rynemenn
hygefæste heold   heortan bewrigene
orþoncbendum?   Nu is undyrne
werum æt wine   hu þa wihte mid us,
heanmode twa,   hatne sindon.

(I watched a couple of curious creatures
copulating openly, out of doors;
the fair-haired one, flushed
beneath her garments, was filled with life
if that effort prospered. I can tell men
in the hall—those who are well-versed—the names
of these creatures with runes. There shall be
Need (N) twice over, and one gleaming
Ash (Æ) on the line, two Oaks (A)

and two Hails (H) also. With the key's power,
who has unlocked the treasury's chained door
that, firm in intent, denies runemen
access to the riddle, covered in its heart
with cunning bonds? Now they're exposed
to men drinking in the hall—the proper
names of this lowly pair.)[82]

Lerer argues that "put one way, then, the riddle deploys a hermeneutical vocabulary drawn from learned criticism to encode a barnyard joke. Put another way, it rephrases the potentially obscene in terms of the patently religious."[83] He diagrams the ways this riddle reveals the processes of learned culture's "recontainment" of the physical, with the resounding conclusion that "Riddle 42 exemplifies the power of the written text to name and codify the range of living and imagined things."[84] Not only are they codified, they also, to a degree, simply disappear as the animals eventually "copulate nowhere but in the solver's mind."[85]

Just what is happening in this riddle, and what is being claimed for what is happening? We can begin by naming what is happening and, in the round robin of critical interpretation surrounding Riddle 42, naming it differently and challenging, even disinterring, the reality that grounds patriarchal metaphor. In the riddle, a group of men are enjoined to use all their book-learning and rune-lore to name what happens when two animals have sex, and then to figure out how they figured that out. Many years later, another member of the learned culture contemplating the riddle interprets their intepretation of their interpretation in order to continue and affirm their interpretation. As we interrupt this round robin, we call attention to the process of textualization per se, where the world of experience disappears regularly under the heavy blanket of patriarchal metaphor. This cycle suggests the need for a critical strategy which takes in some degree a more "literal" path to the "literate," but which refuses to reidentify the oral/feminine with the inarticulate and the physical.

John Tanke's reading of Riddle 12 does just this, even as it also points to a certain slippage in language, to the fissure in the symbolic occasioned by paradox. One of the "obscene" riddles of the Exeter Book, Riddle 12, engages slavery, ethnicity, sexuality, and femininity in a "complex series of conceptual oppositions."[86] The result, Tanke argues, is both subversive and liberating; the *wonfeax wale* ("dark-haired servant-woman") offers a spectacle of drunken and sexual performance, which is watched, contained, and condemned within the controlling context of riddling interpretation, but she also somehow elides the trap of its definition. Within the rhetorical system of the riddles and our interpretation of them, this "literary figure" emerges as the "locus of an extraordinary and paradoxical fantasy: that of a subject so enslaved to the law that she is quite capable of toppling it."[87] Tanke's "renaming" of the textualized body and our intervention in the critical round robin in Riddle 42 demonstrate that, while "taking back" language, and focusing on linguistic slippage as a means of identifying the feminine trace are now premises of feminist critical theory in general, as rhetorical practices they have much to contribute to the specific location of the operation of paradox within the Anglo-Saxon symbolic. As the riddles provide an unusual window onto both vernacular and clerical culture, so too does the mass of documentary evidence in this period.

Chartered Territory

Anglo-Saxon charters provide a vast, if unruly, storehouse of information about many aspects of the period, including the complex relation between orality and femininity. The following remarks, far from aiming at any exhaustive study, are intended to raise questions and constitute directions for inquiry. Much valuable work has been completed or is underway on collating and assessing this complex material—the very designation of "charter" covers a variety of documents from church decrees to testimonials to wills.[88] But charter analysis is hazardous for reasons that are in themselves interesting and potentially informative. Accurately dating the existing charters presents a host of challenges, both diplomatic and historical, and scribal alteration and revision, as well as outright forgery, often reveal parallel or alternate provenances for extant and hypothesized texts. While a charter may be labeled "spurious" or "doubtful," it can nonetheless testify (among many other things) to a continuous literate effort to authorize the writing of space, and to the tangle of motivations attendant upon that effort.[89] In her discussion of the authenticity of the charters of St. Augustine's Abbey, for example, Susan Kelly shows how monks were "prone to tampering" and that two existing versions of a text demonstrate that "a charter in favour of a layman was altered to create a direct grant to the monastery."[90] Here the charter points externally to political aspects of the history of the monastery; in another instance, the charter might also internally narrate a struggle for landownership, as with the story of Cookham monastery.[91] These two brief examples from a multitude of others (Sawyer's edition contains just under 1900 entries) will serve to highlight an immediate emphasis, that the charter—as document and as narrative—tells a story, indeed several stories.

The charters' multivalence, moreover, resonates in both oral and literate registers, recalling the echoic manuscript page as mirror for voice (discussed earlier) and serving as a force for attentuating binary distinctions. The charter may be injunction, incantation, and documentation; it conjoins orality of performance, palpable ritual (like beating the bounds), threat of damnation, and security of ownership; it speaks to the living and for the dead—sometimes verbatim. Charters provide a history of passage, "of how the secular society of Anglo-Saxon England absorbed the ecclesiastical gift of the written word," and document the coexistent development of oral and literate purchases on the symbolic as these texts access and seek to embody forms of authority.[92] Given such multivalence, what might the charters tell us about the representation of women in the written cultural record, and what can these documents tell us about women's relation to oral and literate modes? Later medieval historians, such as Judith Bennett, have persuasively shown how documents such as court records and manorial accounts can contribute to our understanding of women's status and "real" lives; perhaps the charters can provide some access to the unrecorded places inhabited by Anglo-Saxon women.[93]

The demographics offer no surprises. Marc Meyer has looked at how many and what kind of women figure in the charter evidence and at the contexts for their representation. Women are certainly present in these documents, whether named or mentioned as wives, daughters, and so on, but it is important to distinguish how women figure in the legal structures that underpin these documents, that is, at what level they participate in the formation of a cultural symbolic. Religious and secular women as individuals appear as grantees or donees in only 7 percent of Sawyer's total listings, a slight percentage that both excludes religious communities of women and calls attention to their presence as unrecorded in monastic land transactions.[94] Other generalizations might also be predictable: early or late in the period, female recipients of charters were usually members of noble or royal households, or closely associated with them;[95] independent buying and selling of land and litigation of land disputes are similarly class-bound activities.[96] There were, of course, exceptions but, although women appear in various legal contexts in the charters (as sureties, witnesses, oath-helpers, initiators of judicial procedure), "the fact remains that by and large women were dependent on male guardians to fight a suit or defend a claim to family land."[97]

The numerical evidence can only tell us so much. Women's exclusion from and inclusion in public, symbolic forms of ownership, and their degree of participation in oral and literate modes are narrated by the charter evidence in some less direct ways, where the exception obscures the rule and reveals the site of contradiction. Having said this, our first such site of contradiction became apparent via further analysis of an initial head count. Meyer asserts that "well over two hundred signatures of women (although most of them were queens' attestations) appear in the witness lists of the charters."[98] First, let it be said that this is a tiny proportion. A single charter may have a handful of witnesses or several dozen (practice varies throughout the period), but on aggregate, given the high number of extant charters, female representation in this area is negligible. What does this negligible participation mean, or more important, what does it mean to "witness" a charter in terms of participation in or access to oral and literate modes? Susan Kelly details a peculiarity of the Anglo-Saxon charters in this respect:

> The most bizarre aspect is the complete absence of any outward mark of validation. There is no sign of the autograph *signa* or subscriptions of the donor, witnesses and notary which were normally found in the Italian private charter, nor of the autograph valedictions and monograms which validated papal and imperial documents. The Anglo-Saxon diploma certainly concludes with a list of the subscriptions of ecclesiastical and lay witnesses, but these are almost invariably written by a single scribe, usually the scribe of the text . . . There is not a single example in an Anglo-Saxon charter of a true autograph subscription. This should not be regarded necessarily as a reflection of massive illiteracy among laity and clergy.[99]

Indeed, it is hard to imagine why an Aldhelm or a Theodore or other famously literate charter witnesses would not individually sign their names, if the point emerging here concerns not deployment of individual literate skills but rather McKitterick's notion of access to and control over these skills. Moreover, the charters' peculiar anonymity, their lack of authorship, resists binary gendered associations with modes of literacy and authority. Male or female, literate or not, the charter witness participates in a developing consolidation of legal, authoritative, and literate modes—albeit one that is interrupted and complicated by the vernacular and oral features of these documents. Nonetheless, the attestation of witnesses structurally validates the content of the document; and as such we might assume that they "signify" within the cultural symbolic to a greater extent than those named *in* the document, whether they can sign their own names or not.

That queens should be represented, even so minimally, is perhaps to be expected, whether they are included by virtue of exceptional class status or exceptionality. The conditions of royal female representation are far from consistent, however: "Queens usually attest only in very rare circumstances in the early Anglo-Saxon period and not on a regular basis until the later tenth century."[100] Kelly exemplifies one such rare circumstance as a combination of force of personality and marital disposition. In the latter part of the seventh and early eighth centuries, Wihtred of Kent had three wives—"one hopes consecutively"—all of whom attest charters, and all of whom are exceptions to the Kentish custom of charter subscription.[101] Hollis, on the other hand, presents a list of royal couples appearing on witness lists in the eighth and ninth centuries to demonstrate the exercise of a "joint secular lordship over the monasteries they endowed, which reflected their joint rule over the kingdom at large."[102] The charter evidence contributes equivocally to an ongoing debate about the degree and nature of female royal power at any given point, or region, in the period. Our emphasis here is not to engage with this debate, but simply to point out that it is not surprising to find queens represented in the cultural record at this formative, structural level. In contrast, or odd juxtaposition, that high-status monastic women, many of whom were royal, some ex-queens, are almost entirely unrepresented in this area of the cultural record is an intriguing absence.

Kelly refers to the unusual practice of abbesses witnessing charters in a discussion of some exceptions to custom. She identifies three early charters attested by abbesses and one later ninth-century forgery of an early eighth-century document that includes abbesses in its witness list.[103] Kelly states that "this may reflect a change of policy, or perhaps simply re-working by the ninth-century forger who made use of the witness-list."[104] Such "policy" is suggested by another example: in a late seventh-century charter of Wihtred of Kent (the same whose wives are so well represented), granting privileges to the churches and monasteries of Kent,[105] four abbesses are listed in the document, three of them identifiable, influential, and eminently royal or royally connected.[106] That they remain *within* the document suggests "that it was not felt proper for them to attest a synodal document; their presence is mentioned prominently and with respect, but they do not subscribe."[107] The witness list contains a not unusual mix: an archbishop and a bishop (both of whom are also named in the document), an abbot, assorted priests, and a good supply of laymen. In such company it is a challenge to rationalize how and why Æbba (also known as Domne Eafe), for example, one of the abbesses respectfully mentioned in the document, founder of the preeminent Kentish monastery Minster-in-Thanet, herself the recipient of six charters, a decidedly interested party in the monastic and royal politics of her day—in other words, a player at the structural level—would not be judged a proper witness to a document concerning church-related business.[108]

In contrast, in two other early charters abbesses witness church-related land transactions.[109] This fact prompts some necessarily highly speculative questions about what aspects of church "business" monastic women might be party to or excluded from. Is there a difference between simple land grants witnessed by abbesses like those outlined in S168, where in the year 811 Cenwulf of Mercia grants land to Archbishop Wulfred, and S254, where Æthelheard grants land to the church at Winchester in 737, and a document like S20, where Wihtred grants privileges and tax-exemptions to the churches of Kent? Or do we see a formal difference in S20, an earlier document (699) that derives from a church synod, that indicates more hierarchical and institutional exclusions? As Kelly suggests, attendance at the synod might be one thing and participation in its formal "literate" rituals might be another.

If there is no immediately apparent rationale for excluding a signatory as likely as Æbba, there are certainly more material reasons for the relative absence of abbesses in this context. There are proportionately fewer surviving early charters corresponding to the heyday of female monasticism, when one could with some reason designate certain churchwomen as potential "players," in that they occupy the rank, positions, and roles that access or intersect with early Anglo-Saxon cultural formations. One isolated "crossover" case suggests a watershed point here: in 825 Abbess Cwenthryth, daughter and also heir to Cenwulf of Mercia, is the first witness of over sixty others (both unusual features) listed in a document (Sawyer includes it in his "miscellaneous" section) that chronicles her own loss of jurisdiction to Archbishop Wulfred.[110] This charter records a long-standing and bitter dispute involving the challenge of episcopal to royal authority. Cwenthryth, in her position as abbess and king's daughter, withholds land and rents from the archbishop, though she is finally forced to accede not only these but her own authority. A year later a further document shows Wulfred taking over land belonging to Minster-in-Thanet.[111] "It is a mark of Wulfred's final triumph," notes Kelly, that he "was able to act as the Lord of Minster without reference to an abbess."[112] Cwenthryth's mark as witness to this document is also one that attests her defeat: that she is represented here ironically signifies a form of erasure, even as the document details the forces that occasion her imminent absence. She was to become the last recorded abbess of Minster-in-Thanet.

This class, or more accurately, this small subgroup of monastic noblewomen, is certainly represented *within* the earlier documents, and the overall

decline of female monasticism later in the period might account for abbesses'
increasing absence from later charters. In this connection, the business of
naming once again raises questions about the conditions for women's entry
into the cultural record in the rare instances where monastic women are represented; titles, functions, and names—or piety, individuality, and nobility—
variously intersect later in the period. The abbess at Wilton is not named, for
example, in a charter granting land to the abbey in 955; the individual woman
is elided in the reference to the "holy community" (*sanctimoniale congrega-
tioni*).[113] Curiously, though, a certain Ælfgyth stands witness to this same
charter, calling herself "magistra" and expressing her delight at the royal
gift.[114] Almost twenty years later, Abbess Wulfthryth of Wilton is named
within a document confirming the abbey's privileges, but does not witness.[115]
To confound any emerging rule, however, Morwen, abbess of Romsey, attests
two charters and is named in another.[116] In the tenth century there is a flurry
of documents granting land to individually named women, distinguished by
their holiness, and perhaps rank, but not by their institutional titles, status, or
affiliation; women in these charters are designated as "matrons," "widows,"
"religious women," "faithful women," and "noble women" (sometimes in
combination).[117] The abbesses as such recede ever further from the cultural
record, even as the concept of female monasticism is revised, not to mention
enclosed, by the advent of the Benedictine Reform and the exigencies of
regional ecclesiastical and secular politics. Accounting for their isolated documentary appearances later in the period invites the same localized speculation
about personality and exceptionality that characterizes the study of queens.
Edgar, for example, is the donor in all but one of these later charters repre-
senting abbesses, a king noted for his prolific production of charters and his
particular attachment to monastic women—especially those at Wilton.[118] But
the equally miniscule evidence from early and late in the period prompts the
argument that it is precisely during the earlier period that we might expect to
see abbesses more represented at the structural level of the cultural record.

    The scarcity of evidence for the presence of abbesses remains intriguing,
and Kelly's notion of propriety perhaps brings us closer to the edge of a
paradox that reverberates throughout this period. This paradox centers on the
deep shift in hegemonic cultural paradigms taking place in the seventh and
eighth centuries, persuasively analyzed by Hollis in terms of religious, psychic,
and erotic change. Just what are the conditions of interaction of the monastic
noblewoman, the bishop, and the king? What does each see in the other, what
cultural metaphors shape how each sees the other, and what does each bring
to the interaction? These are questions we will take up in Chapter 4 when we

ask what message Aldhelm conveys in his *De virginitate* (or, what *did* the bishop say to the abbess?). Here, though, Æbba remains a convenient case in point, as she practically exemplifies the theoretical complexity of her own situation. *How* can she be in the document but not a witness to it, and what are the terms of her exclusion from this level of access to cultural production, a woman whose access would remain viable in so many other contexts? Does gender or class make this difference? The very negligibility of this aspect of the charter evidence brings us to this site of contradiction and prompts us to ask these questions.

In further contrast, some charters tell us stories about women and their families, or provide a means for women to narrate their own stories, and so prompt us to ask a different set of questions. In addition to the convoluted histories of land exchanged and promises made, changed, and broken that are chronicled by such charters as the group involving Archbishop Wulfred, discussed above, or the long dispute over the governance of the Cookham monastery[119]—where Abbess Cynethryth doesn't lose as abjectly as does Cwenthryth[120]—charters publicize family quarrels. As a rationale for his decision to grant land to Abbess Hrothwaru, the decree (another of Sawyer's miscellaneous documents) of Archbishop Nothhelm in 736 or 737 recounts the story of a dispute between Hrothwaru and her mother Bucge, a married laywoman, who allegedly tries to usurp her daughter's inheritance of monastic land. Hrothwaru's grandmother Dunne had deeded it to her by charter, on her deathbed, but her disgruntled daughter Bucge appropriates it: "when the grand-daughter asked that the charter should be given back, her mother, not wishing to give it back, replied that it had been stolen."[121] Lies, intrigue, and deathbed scenes notwithstanding, the document offers another perspective on ecclesiastical intervention in the affairs of privately-owned monasteries and their female rulers: sometimes it was the only way to handle one's relatives. Hrothwaru's is a shortlived victory, however, and her inheritance is no longer viable as such; it will revert to the church upon her death.

In rationalizing, or creating, histories of ownership these "narrative" charters are stories of the ways in which monastic women's lives intersect with existing power structures, and with the creation of a cultural record that perpetuates such structures. These stories also obliquely reveal women's presence in the process of the creation of that record—especially in those many instances where the document is motivated by dispute. With the obvious exception of a particular and particularly obfuscatory rhetoric, the charters share to some extent the mode and concerns of hagiography, when the narration of female saints' lives, and indeed their relations with their families, can operate to introduce, assert, and perpetuate myths of monastic ownership.[122] A further and still speculative analogy is interesting here, even as it brings us back to the intersecting worlds of the oral, literate, and feminine. In her recent essay on the Minster-in-Thanet foundation story and its several redactions, Hollis makes an important point about the history that Bede and later clerics "did not write."[123] She regards the "Mildrith legend" as a monastic myth of origins fostered, if not developed, at an early stage by monastic women. Complete with an introductory female genealogy, one version of the story, found in London, British Library, Cotton Caligula A. xiv (s. xi, med), 121v–124v, an eleventh-century manuscript also designated as a life of Mildrith, reflects most closely according to Hollis the interests of the Minster-in-Thanet foundation in its complex seventh- and eighth-century political milieu. Not only do we see the parallel between hagiographical and documentary/testimonial modes, but also how oral and literate modes coproduce the cultural record. What is most distinctive about the Caligula version is its deployment of folkloric, pre-Christian oral narrative for seventh-century monastic purposes, its use of the traditional "rash promise" story to establish clear title—documentary, genealogical, and moral—to monastic privileges and properties. Hollis concludes that the import and style of the manuscript, especially the inclusion of a genealogy, have more in common with chronicle than with hagiography, and assumes that the Thanet nuns were well capable of both creating and writing their own chronicles. The question of transmission, whether by lost written sources or by oral modes, raised by Hollis's argument is indeed a powerful evocation of what is *not* written, what does not "make it" into the cultural record, and also of how the oral world, motivated and engaged by monastic women, shadows the written record.

If the charters bring us to edge of recorded, literate culture and some women's relation to it, they also resonate with the oral world and with women's voices. Here those "superstitions and genealogies of popular lore" that Lerer argues are submerged in Alfred's paternal literate overthrow of the feminine are present in force and variety, and are inescapable functions of the *authority* of the document.[124] Addressing the question of how the written charter, an originally ecclesiastical form, accrues its legal force within a secular society, Kelly stresses the importance of ceremony and visible, palpable rituals: a literal movement of sod might correspond to a written transfer of land, witnesses might touch the parchment, the charters might be stored on altars as a visual reminder of divine sanction.[125] In fact, Kelly argues that the primary force of the written charter is *symbolic*; what the charter may or may not actually contain—she notes one occasion when blank parchment changes hands—is less important than what it stands for, a concept of ownership ratifed by forms of display, supported by communal historical opinion, often relying on verbal testimony of local witnesses.[126] The charter thus implies performance, physical and verbal; in its external and internal reporting of voices and oaths; it harnesses the force of performance and the oral speech act for its literate objectives, but does not silence them. And so we hear, sometimes resoundingly, women's voices within the charter, or detect traces of their presence without.[127]

The necessary world of oral performance that the charter evokes invites speculation on women's participation; the possibility of women's oral testimony might revise the paltry figure of 200 or so female charter witnesses in a more functional appraisal of women's access to literate modes. Moreover, such access is to a degree secularized by the charters' increasing use of the vernacular throughout the period, especially as a vehicle for conveying specific topographical directions. An analogous question is raised by the practice of "vouching to warranty," whereby local witnesses would be called in to substantiate ownership in trade disputes.[128] To what extent might women have participated in such oral-legal transactions, and, to push the argument further, to what extent might the development of urban and rural economic markets shape such participation?[129]

We conclude, as we began, with questions, and speculation. While such an approach may be numerically inconclusive, it helps us keep in focus the complex oral purchase on the literate, and to include the social, historical, and economic as variables intersecting with gender. And it may serve to check casual or dismissive assumptions about the amorphous world of the feminine and the oral. The situation is not that simple, and we continue to explore it in Chapter 3.

Chapter Three
Literacy and Gender in
Later Anglo-Saxon England

This chapter takes up three issues central to Chapter 2 and explores them in relation to evidence from the later Anglo-Saxon period. We begin with the world of the law, examining in detail one particular lawsuit from Hereford as a means of entering into the complex evidence of legal documents, land-charters, and female agency from this period. In so doing, we return to and extend our thoughts on the relation between female agency, naming, social role, and class on the one hand, and literacy and orality on the other. Naming is a hermeneutic issue as well as a social one, of course, closely related in its structure to that other major system of signification in the period—the mass. Accordingly, in our second issue from Chapter 2, we continue our exploration of the interpretive dynamics of both Latin and vernacular Exeter Book riddles by teasing out the homologies between the sacramental mystery of the mass and the mysteries—or enigmas—posed by the riddles. Such homologies help explain, structurally at least, the attenuated evidence for female agency and representation in literate evidence from this later period. Our conclusion examines the representation of the female lover in *The Husband's Message*—a case of a woman who reads—that dramatically underscores just how pervasive are patterns of female double agency in Anglo-Saxon culture. By reading for women's relation to orality and literacy (our third legacy from Chapter 2), we become even more aware of related patterns of absence and presence, and of agency and its mystification. These patterns are central not only to *The Husband's Message*, of course, nor even to these two interrelated chapters: they are fundamental to our analysis of the relation between women and the cultural imaginary throughout this book.

Women in Dispute

Sometime in the reign of Cnut, between the years 1016 and 1035, a shire court was held at Aylestone Hill, near Hereford, Herefordshire, to resolve an inheritance dispute between Edwin, son of Enniaun, and his mother. Present at the meeting were representatives of the Church (Æthelstan, bishop of Hereford) and the king (the powerful Tofig the Proud), the sheriff (Bryning), several prominent landholders in the region (Earl Ranig and his son, also named Edwin, Leofwine son of Wulfsige, Thurkil the White, Æthelgeard of Frome, and Godric of Stoke), together with "ealle þa þegnas" (all the thegns) of Herefordshire. With the exception of Æthelgeard of Frome and Bryning the sheriff, these men are otherwise known from documents of the period.[1]

As noted in the written record or writ ("gewrit," line 1), the procedures at the shire court begin with Edwin, son of the Welshman, Enniaun, who speaks ("spæc," 9) his suit for the estates of Wellington and Cradley against his own mother ("agene modor," 9).[2] Since his mother is clearly not present (as the list of those at the meeting indicates), Bishop Æthelstan asks who acts as her representative ("hwa sceolde andswerian for his modor," 11). Thurkil the White replies that he does, but he does not know the claim ("talu," 12). Accordingly, three thegns (Leofwine of Frome, Æthelsige the Red, and Winsige, the seaman) are appointed to ride to the mother at Fawley (about nine miles away) and to ask her what claim she has to the disputed estates. The record reports that she denies holding any of her son's lands ("þa sæde heo þæt heo nan land næfde þe him aht to gebyrede," 17–18). Expressing her anger, she initiates her defense by summoning Leofflæd, Thurkil's wife, and speaking her will in the presence of all of them:

Her sit Leoffled min mage, þe ic geann ægðer ge mines lands ge mines goldes ge rægles ge reafes ge ealles þæs ðe ic ah æfter minon dæge (21–23)

(Here sits Leofflæd my kinswoman to whom, after my death, I grant my land and my gold, my clothing and possessions, all which I own.)

She then speaks directly to the thegns:

Doð þegnlice and wel; abeodað mine ærende to ðam gemote beforan þam godan mannum and cyðaþ heom hwæm ic mines landes geunnen hæbbe. and ealre minre æhte. and minon agenan suna. næfre nan þingc; and biddað heom eallum beon þisses to gewitnesse. (24–28)

(Act well and like thanes; announce my message to the meeting before all the good men and tell them to whom I have granted my land and all my possessions, and not a thing to my own son, and ask them all to be witnesses of this.)

The thegns return to the meeting and report back her charge ("hwæt heo on heom geled hæfde," 29–30). At this point Thurkil the White reenters the narrative; standing up, he asks all present to grant to his wife (Leofflæd) the lands her kinswoman (the mother) had granted her. Resolution is swift. Thurkil is granted his request and rides to the cathedral in Hereford (St. Æthelbert's), where, with the consent and cognizance of the meeting ("þæs folces," 33), the agreement is recorded in a gospel book, and where it still survives (as Hereford Cathedral, P. 1. 2, f. 134).[3]

The Hereford lawsuit is one of the few documents in Anglo-Saxon England where a woman is recorded as not merely speaking her will, but apparently orchestrating her response to her son's suit in her own absence. This is remarkable (and dramatic) evidence for the imbrication of speech, writing, gender relations, and legal and ecclesiastical authority in a late Anglo-Saxon legal document. The "gewrit" purports to record a legal dispute resolved at a shire moot (court) conducted by spoken word; embedded within that record is an account of another meeting, whose business is also wholly conducted by speech. This second meeting, between the three representatives of the shire meeting and Edwin's mother at Fawley, provides the occasion for a third kind of oral event; the spoken will. The "gewrit" is a witness to all these speech acts—the shire meeting, the meeting with the mother, and the oral will. The belated nature of the written document as witness is neatly indicated by the fact that the last thing we read is where and when Thurkil had the account recorded.

Women are clearly not present at the Hereford shire court. The two women central to the dispute—the mother and her kinswoman Leofflæd—are both represented by the same man, Thurkil the White, Leofflæd's husband, while the three thegns represent the shire's business to the mother. In addition, Thurkil obtains the authorization of the will at the court and has the entire transaction entered into church records, in the gospel book. The mother's will, spoken and in the presence of witnesses, is legally binding in its own right. For those unfamiliar with the practice of willing in Anglo-Saxon England, it is crucial to note that the written document, or what we now call the will, is purely evidentiary; the document stands as a record of, as witness to, the spoken will. The spoken will (a particular kind of a speech act), by contrast, is itself binding, whether or not a written record is made.[4] By having the entire dispute recorded, what Thurkil has established is Leofflæd's right to inheritance. There is, however, no record of Thurkil's formal refutation of Edwin's initial claim on the estates at Wellington and Cradley on Leofflæd's behalf. In fact, Edwin recedes from view as the narrative unfolds. In that unfolding narrative, other voices—preeminently the mother's—come into focus as his past speech, reported indirectly at the beginning of the "gewrit," is overlaid by more present events. Despite this dominance of the maternal voice, there is no evidence that the mother's will was ever executed. It remains suggestive, however, that Wellington is listed among the estates subsequently owned by Thurkil, while Cradley appears among the estates later owned by the canons of Hereford.[5]

On the face of the evidence, then, Thurkil and his wife are the beneficiaries of this dispute, though the Church too has its interest in the suit. It would appear that Edwin's mother also gets what she wants—the successful willing of her property to Leofflæd in spite of her son's claim, which triggers the will in the first place. There are, however, a number of other factors that complicate our interpretation of the dispute when looked at from the interrelated perspectives of gender, agency, legal procedures, narrative structure, and speech and writing. For one thing, Thurkil's motives are far from transparent. He is happy to act as the mother's representative at the shire meeting, presumably on the basis of his relationship to her (although this information is revealed only after he has agreed to do so), and he initially denies all knowledge of the claim. Nor is Thurkil selected as one of the three thegns who represent the meeting's business to her. On the one hand, Thurkil's claim of ignorance may be genuine, which would explain why other shire-members are appointed. On the other, the appointment of the thegns may be a rare example of due process: Thurkil is the mother's representative at the shire meeting to discuss both claims, and local knowledge of the family might account for caution on the shire's part. Yet again, Thurkil's denial may be sheer opportunism or even good strategy: as we know, Thurkil and his wife stand to benefit from the dispute. While these kinds of interpretive ambiguities are certainly characteristic of the records of many disputes in this (or, indeed, any other) period, it is worth remembering that it is Thurkil who has the meeting recorded.

Every charter tells a story, as we pointed out in Chapter 2, and the Hereford dispute is very much a woman's story, however much that story also involves other stories such as that of Thurkil. As many have noted, the use of written documents generally in the upper reaches of government, both royal and ecclesiastical, increases in late Anglo-Saxon England. Simon Keynes elegantly argues that the royal diplomas of the reign of Æthelred II (the Unready) provide persuasive evidence for the centralization of writing in the royal court. Whether or not Keynes's argument holds and whether or not centralization is indeed a facet of royal administration, the fact remains that the writing of royal diplomas is exclusively in male hands.[6] As for the royal diplomas, so too for other diplomas and charters. Hazardous though it is to make generalizations on the basis of this evidence, the vast majority of legal documents from the later Anglo-Saxon period record transactions in which the main figures are not women but men. No woman below the rank of queen or mother to the king appears in witness lists of the royal diplomas after the mid-tenth century. Men similarly dominate as beneficiaries. During the reign of Eadwig (955–57), according to Keynes, the beneficiary of two of the royal diplomas issued to women is the same "nobilis femina," Æthelhild (S 600, 601); Edgar's reign (959–75) is remarkable for its handful of royal diplomas to noble women (e.g., S 737, 738, 754, 762, many of whom are associated with the early stages of the Benedictine reform); but Æthelred's reign (978–1016), which also witnesses the increase of religious institutions as beneficiaries (whereby nuns may indirectly benefit), sees virtually no individual female beneficiaries or witnesses other than Æthelred's mother, Ælfthryth (S 877) and his wife, Emma (S 925).[7] Striking in this group of religious institutions as beneficiaries is the slender evidence for female institutions—take the example of Ely (S 907, 919), no longer the great double house of the early Anglo-Saxon period. So too the marked absence of the female personal name at ranks below queen or queen mother, as institutions rather than individuals become beneficiaries.[8] As noted in Chapter 2, women tend to be identified in such documents by their rank, status, or function—not just or even necessarily name, but certainly rank and serial number, as it were. Moreover, the increased visibility of the queen and the king's mother in this period correlates with the increasing invisibility of other women and other classes of women—especially abbesses—in the later diplomas.[9] This dialectic of visibility and invisibility is worth pursuing (and we return to it shortly), especially when correlated with the increase in literacy. Visible, named, literate women identified in the cultural record fall readily into the category (indeed, cult) of the exceptional; such exceptional women—queens, queen mothers, wives of kings—are precisely those whom history subsequently recalls.

A wider view of the diplomatic evidence of the same period demonstrates that, as in the case of the royal diplomas, secular men gradually realized and benefited from the virtues of written evidence in their legal transactions.[10] Hence the increase in legal documents generally. Married men regularly represented their—frequently anonymous—wives in such documents.[11] It is also from this period that the vast majority of Anglo-Saxon wills survive. The overall number of such wills is proportionately high but hardly compelling— Dorothy Whitelock edits 39 out of a total of 57, 11 of which are women's, and a further 4 of which are conjugal.[12] Pauline Stafford argues plausibly that the rise of the written will in this period is due to the nobility seizing the opportunity to clarify their legal interests at a time when the king is capitalizing on his.[13] At stake here is the increasing claim of the king to the payment of wergild and heriot from the nobility: in consequence, both the nobility and the king have vested interests in the effectiveness of written documents. Thurkil, a member of the nobility, acting in his wife's interests (which conform with his own) and making sure the evidence is recorded in writing, fits neatly in the implications of the general picture for the male use of writing in legal transactions in the secular domain. Indeed, when looked at from the perspective of the structure of the lawsuit, Thurkil is the narrative's primary agent and subject: his role in the dispute frames that of the mother. What we have here is further evidence of a doubling of agency whereby to trace the man's role and agency is also to recover and be newly alert to that of the woman; we detected a similar doubling of agency in Bede's account of Hild and Cædmon in Chapter 1.

Diplomatic evidence also helps explain the Church's particular interest in the Hereford shire court beyond its regular and expected participation in local government.[14] To state the obvious as many have done before us, the reason why many diplomas survive from Anglo-Saxon England in the first place is because the Church benefits, whether immediately or ultimately. This profile of the Church similarly harmonizes with the evidence of the Hereford lawsuit, since Cradley subsequently is owned by the canons of Hereford cathedral (as noted above). Taken together, the roles of Thurkil and the Church (represented by Bishop Æthelstan) in this case indicate that in the legal documents, as in the other documentary evidence of the period, literacy in later Anglo-Saxon England can be characterized in a normative sense as masculine, clerical, and qualified by factors of class and wealth.[15] There are no surprises here, given our discussion of orality and the charter evidence in Chapter 2. Despite the increased use of diplomas, charters, and other miscellaneous written documents in the later period, the contributory factors of gender, specifically masculinity, and class remain relatively stable across the entire Anglo-Saxon period. Class and gender are intractable features of sociocultural life in the period. What is at issue in the Hereford dispute is the mother's considerable wealth (indicated by her land, gold, clothing, and possessions); so too it is the grandmother's wealth that is at stake in the 737 charter discussed in Chapter 2.[16] Thurkil and Leofflæd, elsewhere known as prosperous landowners, benefit from their relative's wealth. We note therefore with some irony that there is no need for the Hereford document to explain why Thurkil represents the mother, related to his wife: wealth will be kept in one branch of this upper class family, if not another. The maintenance of family affairs via the control of dynastic resources so prevalent in our discussion of the royal female religious in Chapter 1 is thus only one facet of a much wider social focus on the family.

What's in a Name, Indeed

A further complicating factor in interpreting the Hereford scenario is the mother herself. Prompted by our discussion of mothers in Chapters 1 and 2, let us follow the mother here too. We begin by taking the evidence on face value, as we did in our discussion of Thurkil. Far from reticent, the mother is—on the face of it—the most vocal figure in the document. But she is not named. This phenomenon is not new to us: we first met it in Chapter 1 in Bede's account of the poet, Cædmon, where Hild is referred to throughout by her titles (abbess, mother) or by pronoun, and we met it again in Chapter 2 in Asser's reticence about Osburh's name. To follow the mother here, however, is to follow a subject who is utterly without name (unlike Hild or Osburh), though apparently in good voice. Her status in the document is that of mother and relative. Asymmetries of gender, role, and status are in full play in the Hereford document. After all, we know the names of all the other principal actors—Edwin, Thurkil, Leofflæd, even Edwin's father (however garbled is his name).

If the mother is without a name, then the other woman is certainly named. Leofflæd is identified first as Thurkil's wife ("Þurcilles wif," 20) in the account of the mother's defense and subsequently as her kinswoman ("min mage," 20) in the mother's will. Leofflæd's status as wife of Thurkil appears to carry more weight in the legal procedures that result from the dispute, while her status as female relative to the mother is crucial to the oral will. It may even be the case that Leofflæd is the mother's daughter, though she is not identified as such. By contrast, the mother herself remains anonymous, wholly identified in relation to the status of her son and to the marital status of her female relative, Leofflæd. Disparities of gender are thus registered as dissonances between social rank and family affiliation, not only between man and woman, but also between woman and woman. Crucial here is the status of and distinction between women as mothers and wives—it is in these roles that women function before the law. While royal women in this period play a greater role in the legal record, Stafford points out that they too are identified as wives and mothers. Within the different strata of rank, in short, the legal import of women derives from their status relative to their male kin.[17]

A narratological analysis both supports and qualifies these issues of gender and affiliation. On the one hand, the mother's missing name renders her agency in the narrative more opaque than Thurkil's: his name signifies, her anonymity does not; her agency resonates against his. On the other, Leofflæd's agency is equally though differently hard to get at: as the object of the mother's oral will and the explicit beneficiary of Thurkil's actions in the lawsuit, she neither speaks nor acts herself. Leofflæd's name is crucial to the case; her agency, however, is obscured by that of her spouse. The best reading of the written evidence suggests, tellingly, that the mother's name—as opposed to her status and agency as mother—is simply not relevant. We might speculate that the mother's presence and known familial relationships are sufficient to preserve an oral memory of the will in her name. The discrepancy in the use of names may be an artifact of the interrelationship between orality and literacy encoded in the document—a revealing slip between the oral speech act of the will (which has no need for names) and its written account (which is, among other things, a record of names). If what slips away in this transition from the oral to the written is the mother's name, then, paradoxically, the oral memory of that name may continue to function in the interstices of the performance of the written. In short, there is an intriguing parallel between the ways women's agency resonates against that of men in written documents and the ways the female name may point to a functional resonance of the oral in the written.

Turning to the admittedly thin evidence for wills in the period confirms our surmise—a written will without the name of the testatrix is simply untenable. We have in the Hereford document, in other words, written evidence of the only will in Anglo-Saxon England where the testatrix's name is not recorded. Judged from the broader perspective of the documentary evidence, however, the mother's case begins to resemble those of the anonymous wives and mothers of conjugal wills and other legal transactions whose business is conducted in the name of the husband or her male relations.[18] In these cases, as in the case of the evidence of royal women, a woman's name might in fact be said to be wife, mother, or widow; her agency—a less vocal presence than the louder agency of her male relations—functions in ways that are elusive but not impossible to recover. Our consideration of female subjectivity and agency, therefore, assesses the personal name against the social, religious, and legal categories of mother, wife, and widow. In so doing, we examine cases that pose the questions of just what is in a name and when a name is not a name. Anglo-Saxon genealogical practices, for example, generally indicate a close relation between a man, identified by personal name, and his immediate male kin or patrilineage.[19] By contrast, the legal evidence suggests that female genealogies are alternate constructions; they regularly identify a woman by marital status and kinship affinities, but the name of the woman herself is more transient.[20] The identification of a woman by name is a contingent practice, thus accounting for the relative absence of female names in the record. To repeat, rank and serial number often signify more than name.

Indeed, the most plausible explanation for the reason for the inheritance dispute in the first place is not that the woman concerned is a mother, but that she is a widow. Here too the Hereford document is reticent: identified as mother, her marital status as wife or widow is but a surmise. Other forms of contextual evidence are again more helpful in teasing out the implication of this lawsuit. As the later Anglo-Saxon period becomes increasingly litigious in all spheres of life, so too Cnut's reign is known for its tightening up of legal provisions for widows, in part to protect them from precisely the kind of litigation over inheritance that Edwin initiates in the Hereford case.[21] The religious evidence of the period indicates a similar concern to clarify women's status not as mothers, but as widows, wives, or virgins, complementing legal efforts to define chastity, marriage, and widowhood.[22] Widows feature prominently in the slender evidence for female wills and in the miscellaneous documents of the period (this is especially the case where the Church stands to benefit from the transaction).[23] The Hereford case thus conforms to a more general picture of the social vulnerability of widows that the laws and religious evidence seeks to redress. That the Hereford woman is identified not as a widow but as a mother, however, points to a fascinating paradox in the evidence more generally—that of a tension between the roles of mother and widow. In the Hereford case, motherhood occludes the woman's probable widowhood, but in many other cases (and the laws and the religious evidence are particularly significant here) widowhood occludes motherhood.[24]

Widows are most vulnerable where issues of inheritance or remarriage are at stake. Remarriage is an opportunity for the renegotiation of wealth and property by the kin (however much that kin includes the widow herself) and by the larger social network in which the kin features. Widowhood is thus a liminal moment in women's lives when the interests of the individual woman, her kin, the king, and the Church can come into conflict. If the widow chooses or is forced to remarry, claims by her kin on her morning gift (her dowry), and her property from the first marriage are now potentially doubled (and potentially contested by the kin of both marriages); claims on inheritance are similarly complex. At the same time, the king, under whose protection widows now partly fall, stands to gain from the collection of heriot and wergild. The Church, generally interested in regulating marriage as a consequence of its theology, shares legal protection of widows with the king and has its own specific stake in the future of widows: it is in this period that the laws begin to protect the status of the vowess and (formerly married) nun, for example. The potential for conflict to which these various affiliations and interests point can be traced in the royal laws. V Æthelred (1008), for example, establishes not only that the protection of widows is a matter for both God and the king, but also specifies the elapse of a year before a widow can remarry, after which she can do as she wishes.[25] II Cnut (1020–23) considerably amplifies Æthelred's provisions: a penalty for remarriage within the year (forfeiture of the morning gift and all possessions the widow gained from her first marriage, even if her second marriage is forced and unless she wishes to return to her first family); payment of wergild by the second husband; payment of heriot by the widow within the year, if not sooner; a ruling against forced marriages for both widows and virgins; and a recommendation that no widow should become a nun too hastily.[26] All these provisions take place, of course, against the backdrop of royal serial monogamy, discussed further in Chapter 4. It is also against this contextual evidence of marriage and widowhood that the various stakes in the Hereford inheritance dispute begin to make greater sense.

Inheritance patterns indicate that property could be inherited bilaterally throughout the Anglo-Saxon period. The evidence for the later period alone demonstrates that some widows are at pains to make sure that they control the distribution of their lands and property to their daughters and female relations, sometimes in preference to their male relatives (as does the Hereford mother). Overall, however, inheritance patterns show a strong preference for the male line.[27] The evidence of the wills and inheritance patterns confirms that of the laws: widowhood was a stage in the life-cycle where women's status was fluid, open to exploitation but also, paradoxically, one of the few moments when women could act in their own interests. After all, the Hereford document indicates the extent to which inheritance is of concern to the mother. The catch, however, is that this concern was shared with her son and her wider kin as well. It is not difficult to construct a scenario for the Hereford document where Edwin seeks to capitalize on his mother's unspecified widowhood as do Thurkil and Leofflæd. Needless to say, in this scenario

Thurkil benefits from the mother's vulnerability as a widow as much as do his wife and the mother herself.

Further complicating our understanding of the mother's role in the Hereford document is the issue of her absence from the shire court, about which the document itself (predictably by now) makes no comment. The dynamic relation between absence and presence is a recurrent theme of this book and is homologous to the dynamic relation between naming and anonymity we have been exploring in this chapter. We have argued several times that these relations structure not only Anglo-Saxon women's relation to the cultural archive of their period, but also our modern critical interpretations of that archive. When we ask where or who is the mother in the Hereford lawsuit, however, we are not simply paraphrasing questions we ask more generally about Anglo-Saxon women: we are engaging with the pressing questions the document itself raises. No one bothers to name mother. The mother's absence is the condition that enables Thurkil's actions and her own behavior at Fawley, not merely in uttering her will, but in instructing the thegns how to carry back her defense. We will return to the dramatic power of her speech in a moment; for now it is sufficient to underline the importance of the mother's absence from the shire meeting at Aylestone Hill *and* her presence at the other at Fawley to any reading of the lawsuit.

No woman acts as a regular member of a shire moot in this period, while courts themselves were held usually only twice a year (a possible indication of the political significance of this particular suit to the Hereford region). "Negotiations between families, meetings of the courts of king, shire, and hundred were all in the public sphere and women were conspicuous by their absence," Stafford points out.[28] The point is particularly apt when applied to the Hereford dispute. Stafford's use of the term, "public," however, merits some qualification.[29] While the mother and Leofflæd are apparently barred from the shire meeting by virtue of their sex, the fact that representatives are sent to speak to the mother and that the mother is able to orchestrate her defense to the shire by virtue of her absence from it argue for a different interpretation. The Hereford case, resting as it does on the oral will, provides evidence of a model of public behavior for women that is socially and legally acceptable and that works to compensate for their general lack of representation at meetings such as the shire. In short, we have here evidence not of women getting around the law's public face in private, but of women using a different medium of social, legally acceptable transaction.[30] That transaction is an oral one, fully functional within an increasingly literate world.

Such modes of transaction may carry the weight of custom, but they are not part of the written legal apparatus in late Anglo-Saxon England. The Hereford suit is therefore strong evidence for the asymmetries of men's and women's relation to the law and its symbolic arenas. The more spectacular dispute between Wynflæd and Leofwine (c. 990–992) confirms our point.[31] Wynflæd establishes her ownership of the estates of Hagbourne and Bradfield, Berkshire, given to her by Ælfric (presumably Leofwine's father) in return for the estate at Datchet, Buckinghamshire, in the presence of Æthelred II and several of the most prominent earls and ecclesiasts of the period (including Archbishop Sigeric of Canterbury and Bishop Ordbriht of Selsey). Even Ælfthryth, the king's mother is present. Informed of this action by Æthelred, Leofwine refuses to comply unless the matter is brought to a shire meeting. At that meeting, Wynflæd names eleven men and thirteen women in witness of her ownership, including the king's mother, abbots and abbesses, royal officials, prominent landowners and "menig god þegen. ⁊ god wif" ("many a good thane and good woman"). Archbishop Sigeric and Bishop Ordbriht send their declarations as well. The dispute is settled amicably enough, which is hardly surprising given this high-status and unusually gendered witness list. Leofwine returns the disputed estate and Wynflæd is commanded to pay back his father's gold and silver, which she appears somewhat reluctant to do. Although the specific circumstances of the original dispute between Wynflæd and Leofwine remain unclear (as they do in the Hereford case), and the provision for Ælfric's gold and silver suggests that both Wynflæd's and Leofwine's cases have merit, one thing is clear: it takes a woman with considerable contacts among the powerful, both male and female, to successfully settle a dispute at a shire meeting. Further, it is precisely the *presence* of this unusually high number of high-status witnesses from both sexes, together with her own *presence* at both meetings, that Wynflæd needs to sway the case in her favor.

As we noted in our assessment of the charters in Chapter 2 and as is further confirmed by Wynflæd's lawsuit, women do act sporadically in their own interests and by means of their own presence in legal disputes, despite their relative absence from witness lists. Indeed, in Wynflæd's case the concluding witness list names only men (a striking contrast with the presence of both sexes as witnesses in the body of the document). This sporadic dynamic of absence and presence persists throughout the period: it is as evident in the relative absence of women witnesses to the royal diplomas, for example, as it is in their relative presence in Wynflæd's dispute.[32] Some women, usually prominent by virtue of their class, status (religious or lay), or family find ways to represent themselves. And they do so in spite of a general lack of specified legal power to ratify any transactions (demonstrated by their absence from witness lists). The evidence is far from overwhelming (as we keep saying), but it persists throughout the entire Anglo-Saxon period. It is significant indeed that such evidence does not support a developmental model for women's history (whether in terms of a rise in literacy or a fall in women's agency). We can only speculate as to why the mother in the Hereford suit is at Fawley rather than Aylestone Hill. Her absence from the Hereford shire meeting, however, is as central to the entire transaction as is Wynflæd's presence in both meetings in her dispute.

Present Voices, Absent Names

To the homologies of female absence and presence, names and anonymity, we can add a third, similarly compelled by the Hereford document—women's relation to orality and literacy. The mother is by no means the only figure in the Hereford law suit to conduct her business orally—the entire shire meeting is a speech act. Here, then, is no simple binary correlation between gender and either oral or literate modes of communication. This case is not analogous to Seth Lerer's scenario of a royal paternal domain of writing that triumphs over a chronologically and developmentally prior world of maternal orality (discussed in Chapter 2). The Hereford document leaves us in no doubt that in late Anglo-Saxon England (well over a century later than the royal Alfred's "primal scene," according to Asser), the exercise of law in secular transactions was still conducted primarily by spoken word and dominated by men, whether or not they were recorded subsequently.[33] Indeed, we have this insight into the case of the Hereford suit only because a man had these oral transactions committed to writing and placed in the keeping of the Church. Thurkil's actions certainly attenuate the kind of clear-cut binaries often evident in modern criticism about orality and literacy: he functions equally successfully in both spheres. The mother's own relation to orality and literacy, moreover, introduces a further nuance that brings into focus the narratological significance of her absence, presence, and anonymity in the same document.

For a reader teasing out the relationship between gender and literacy, the most striking component in the account of the Hereford suit is the mother's speech. (This alone might help explain why the text is anthologized in *Sweet's Reader*, though not why it has attracted so little critical attention.) Unlike other cases where a woman plays a significant role in a legal dispute, this woman's actions are recorded as direct speeches.[34] The power of her voice in the written document draws much from her absence at the shire meeting; in addition to this physical absence from the moot, moreover, her words at Fawley are recorded necessarily in her absence. This evidence alone might give us pause. Whence comes her speech? Can we speculate that, in the absence of other evidence, a written draft was made of the entire proceedings, including the mother's words, which Thurkil takes with him to the cathedral at Hereford, where the formal "gewrit" is drawn up? In support of this speculation, we might point to Keynes's interpretation of the royal diplomas, which suggests precisely such activity.[35] However different the world of the royal diplomas is from that of shire courts, it is significant that some thirty-six lawsuits from such courts survive from Anglo-Saxon England.[36]

On the other hand, the oral characteristics of Anglo-Saxon written wills might provide a precedent for the way the mother's words are recorded. Her will is spoken in the presence of Leofflæd ("Her sit Leoffled min mage," line 21), while most written wills by their very nature preserve the wishes of their testator or testatrix in their absence. Yet the mother's spoken will has features in common with the written will: the use of the present tense, the use of verbs of speech, and the common verb of granting, "ge-unnan." The written will in general frequently presents itself as a document of speech.[37] The mother's oral will is thus at best a series of legal formulas as her condensed listing of lands, gold, clothing, and possessions—precisely those properties so characteristic of written wills—indicates. Formulas are, moreover, mnemonic devices—and the mother's will is sufficiently "oral" in its characteristics and sufficiently brief to account for its passage from memory into the written document. Such interchanges between the supposedly oral and the supposedly written underscore McKitterick's point (discussed in Chapter 2) about the functionality of literacy: uses of literacy by the probably illiterate in fact involve access to literate forms of knowledge. Here, too, the Hereford document will not yield readily to a binary analysis whereby the mother is identified by her speech (an oral will) and her male relation with its written record. Her spoken will shares characteristics with written wills, which themselves have oral features.

Two possibilities present themselves. The mother's oral will may be simply that, an oral will. But it is also possible that what is presented as oral is in fact a literate construction—a back formation from the written to the spoken. Either scenario affects our understanding of the mother's agency in uttering her will. We may have evidence here of a woman making full use of the legal privilege of an oral will or of the same woman fully alert to the ways the oral and the written are coimplicated: that is, of a woman fully aware of the symbolic importance of both oral and literate modes to her dispute. A similar explanation is certainly plausible in the case of Thurkil's behavior. A useful analogy here is the evidence for both women and men owning chirographs or copies of various legal documents, including wills. Are the owners of such documents literate in the narrow sense of being able to read or are they in fact literate in the broader sense of having an awareness of the symbolic, in this case legal, authority of the written word (as McKitterick would argue and as Alfred's absent mentoring mother would suggest)?[38] The real point, of course, is that there is no simple choice between oral and written modes of communication and record—the oral and the literate are thoroughly coimplicated in the Hereford evidence and this evidence yields to no easy interpretation. There is no way to verify whether the mother's will is an oral artifact preserved, somehow innocently, by writing or one already influenced by literate modes. The situation, as we have said before, is not that simple. Given our assessment of the functionality of the oral in the literate world (exemplified by the mother's use of an oral will flavored with formulations reminiscent of written wills), it is perhaps time to revisit the conceptualization of the oral in the literate as a "trace," which was our starting point for thinking about orality and literacy in Chapter 2. One point to make here is the disingenuousness of this trace. Despite the fact that the oral trace is in some regards an aural hallucination produced by the written, that trace is nevertheless functional; it provides access to modes of knowing and acting otherwise not imagined by the literate document. In tracing that access, we find ways to access women's agency—the mother finds a way to make her will—despite the dominance of the written and its coimplication with the masculine.

However we interpret the mother's oral will, the fact remains that she is recorded as uttering two speeches. The second speech (lines 24–28) substantially reiterates the first, instructing the thegns to return to the meeting, convey her will to it, and act as her witnesses. This second speech, which also has the hallmarks of a performative speech act—of familiar words used in a given situation—coopts the representatives of the shire in the mother's defense. What the mother does, in fact, is initiate the authorization of the will taken up by Thurkil in the resumption of the shire meeting. As a result, we should not be surprised that the mother's words in this speech act echo those of her will: "cyðaþ heom hwæm ic mines landes geunnen hæbbe and ealre minre æhte" ("tell them to whom I have granted my land and all my possessions," 25–26). Added to these words, however, are her anger—"and gebealh heo swiðe eorlice wið hire sunu" ("and she became very angry with her son," 18–19) and her imperious appeals to class interest and responsibility: "Doð þegnlice and wel; abeodað mine ærende" ("act well and like thegns; announce my message," 24) and "biddað heom eallum beon þisses to gewitnesse" ("ask them all to be witnesses of this," 27–28). Given the general absence of women's voices in the legal record, the power of this classy speech act with its additional emotional charge is undeniable. Moreover, "and gebealh heo swiðe eorlice wið hire sunu" presents some interesting challenges to the translator: although we read "eorlice" as a form of "ierlic," "angry" (as does Whitelock), its echo in the common adverb "eorlic," "nobly" or "manfully," is highly suggestive of a masculine gendering of anger and class in a woman's voice.[39]

Given the relative infrequency of women's voices overall in the cultural archive, we might seize on the mother's words as long overdue evidence that some women did speak, forcefully, to men at the same time as their words were used by men. The evidence is most familiar to us from the vernacular poetry. We recall the powerful, equally formal and angry words of Elene to Judas, the ending of the Wife's Lament, or the ways Wealhtheow is both used by and uses speech in *Beowulf*, all of which present considerable interpretive challenges.[40] We note parallels too with Norse literature where women often spoke up, with authority.[41] In Anglo-Saxon England as in Iceland, however, women below the rank of queen or queen mother rarely speak up in the legal arena. Yet the Hereford suit suggests it was evidently appropriate and accepted for this mother to use her words, even as the more powerful Wynflæd (S 1454) has hers reported for her. No one challenges this mother's right to speak—and the silence of her son at the shire meeting is telling in this regard. At the same time, however, both of her speeches are uttered in her absence from this meeting; the document is inevitably a record of this doubly absent speech. (At how many removes does a woman's speech become safe?)

Analysis of the Hereford document overall suggests, therefore, that the argument that it encodes compelling evidence for the forceful agency of female speech in an otherwise literate world applies only superficially. Such an argument derives in part from a sensitivity to women's voices in an archive that otherwise pays scant attention to them, but it neglects the coimplication of the literate and the oral in her words and consigns the mother to that world of orality, whose dangers we outlined in Chapter 2. It also neglects the more problematic and contradictory evidence of her status as mother (rather than widow), her lack of a name, her absence from the shire meeting, and the ways her interests are inseparable from those of her family. The homologies of absence and presence, naming and anonymity, orality and literacy that we have been exploring help explain this complex phenomenon. The Hereford suit includes a written record of a female voice with considerable dramatic presence, but that presence paradoxically depends on the absence of its speaker, whose interests are undercut by her anonymity as an actor. If writing is a way to preserve a record of a disputed case and its players, as the diplomas are fond of pointing out, then the fact that one of the players is nameless suggests either that the record is inept (which is always a consideration) or that this particular player's name is insignificant. Since the Hereford dispute is apparently resolved successfully, the missing name of the mother is indeed significant: it points directly to the asymmetries of women before the law and to the instability of female names as an indices of identity and agency.

What then can we learn from the Hereford dispute? Above all, that orality and literacy are complexly interrelated in the social domain of legal transactions in late Anglo-Saxon England. Here is no unequivocal evidence for a triumph of literacy over orality. This simple point seems counterintuitive, given that this same period also witnesses the rise in written documentation in this sphere of social activity as in so many others. Indeed, late Anglo-Saxon England also witnesses a concerted effort to organize and capitalize on written law codes. The diplomatic evidence is, however, qualitatively different from that of the law codes or the better-known cultural evidence for a gradual transition from orality to literacy, for example. The diplomas and miscellaneous documents are ways to preserve in writing—or for posterity—prior transactions conducted by the spoken word (as so many of the charters state). The law codes in this period, however much oral in their origins, features, or application, are very much the product of literacy and govern subsequent exercise of the law in its many domains (such as shire courts).[42] The same holds true for other forms of social evidence like sermons and homilies, which are equally clearly literate documents even though they are composed for oral delivery. Every domain of sociocultural activity necessarily yields different evidence for the relation of the oral to the literate in the period. In the case of the diplomas and miscellaneous legal documents, we are wary of any argument for this period that posits a gradual transition from orality to literacy, with its unstated assumption that such a developmental model ultimately prevails, without careful consideration of factors of gender, class, access, and function. To repeat the end of Chapter 2 once more, the situation is just not that simple.

Further, the developmental model of the relationship of orality to literacy is homologous to the developmental model for women's history. While the written evidence of the diplomas signals a change more generally in the use of writing in the upper classes of late Anglo-Saxon society, there are also consistent patterns of continuity throughout the entire period where women's access to and use of writing is concerned. In short, we need to be alert to the specific dimensions of every record. Every document tells a story, we point out, or rather several stories. Our analysis of the Hereford suit amply demonstrates the multivalence of the written document and the multivalence of the voices it records (whether those voices are recorded in direct or indirect speech). It is precisely this multivalence that prevents an oversimplification of the evidence. The paradoxical image of the manuscript page as an echo chamber for voice, *and* as a mirror of the written word, explored in Chapter 2 is as appropriate to this document from the end of the Anglo-Saxon period as it is to documents from the earlier centuries.

Nor can we usefully construct an analysis of the relation between gender and power *and* literacy and orality for the Hereford case that accords either women or men with uncomplicated, self-transparent motives or agency. This is the position taken by Elisabeth van Houts in another modern account of the case, which concludes that "we encounter a case where on the surface only male witnesses are knowledgeable (or not, as in this case Thurkil displays his ignorance), but underneath the surface their knowledge depended entirely on what women had told them."[43]

Van Houts's interpretation is much briefer than our own, and there is much to applaud in its positive feminist spin. Our analysis is longer because we wish to address the multivalency of the evidence and thus not get around the question of Thurkil's apparent ignorance. It is this multivalency that forecloses the possibility of one synthetic interpretation of the document. It may be the case that Thurkil's ignorance of the dispute is genuine, as we pointed out earlier; it is also the case that he is one of the dispute's major beneficiaries. In addition, his knowledge does not entirely depend "on what women had told" him because his kinship with the mother, his putative knowledge of procedures at shire meetings, and his understanding of the importance of having the dispute put into writing are equally central. As we have also pointed out, it is also possible to construct a reading where the mother herself has at least a superficial (if not a considerable) knowledge of the legal procedures of both the shire meeting and the oral will that enable her to begin the defense which Thurkil completes. Van Houts's model of masculine surface and feminine depth is one example of the many ways multivalent evidence is forced into binary constructions.

Also crucial to our reading of the Hereford suit is that it is a record of a secular transaction of the upper class, though not of the uppermost reaches of that class (the contrast with Wynflæd's dispute is significant here). In this stratum, individual interests can be traced only through a complex web of family affiliations, obligations, personal circumstance, and status. Gender plays its role here too. Even a cursory reading of the diplomas indicates that women's agency, voice, and actions are the exception rather than the rule. How, when, and in what form such women's agency is recorded are the most pressing and recurrent questions of this book. It is worth remembering that, since the diplomatic archive is a masculine record for the most part, the evidence for answers to such questions in the case of men, of whatever reach of the upper classes, is bound to be more transparent.

The Hereford evidence is therefore rich in ways of thinking about women's relation to power, to family, and to orality and literacy in the late Anglo-Saxon period. Above all, however, this is a case of a present voice and an absent name. In Chapter 2 we ask the question of how to hear a voice that does not bear a name. Our analysis of the Hereford evidence complements our prior discussion: where we do not hear a name, we are offered instead insight into the signification of female status. That status—as mother, wife, or widow—is a means of tapping into what we call the alternate genealogies of the female line. These genealogies of status are more fluid, less firmly embedded in the sociocultural imaginary of Anglo-Saxon England than their better-known masculine counterparts. Sometimes we have a name (as in Wynflæd's case); sometimes we do not (as in the Hereford case); sometimes we see a name (Leofflæd's); sometimes we hear a voice (the mother's). What is interesting about these analogous structures of naming, status, and voice is the ease with which they are elided in the cultural record. To trace women's family affiliations through the cultural archive is to recognize the extent to which the naming of a woman and the identification of her status are contingent acts, dependent in large measure on the specific instance of the document. Female status is a complex phenomenon. A widow may wield more legal power when identified as a mother, yet the laws and wills of the same period suggest that widowhood is often a more recognizable legal category than motherhood.

What Matter What Name?

The tension between woman as mother and woman as widow is a fruitful point of entry into a more sustained meditation about the instability—the contingency—of female names and status more generally in the later Anglo-Saxon period. Those women most visible in this cultural archive are royal women, whose status is variously identified as "hlæfdige," "domina" (lady), "conlaterana regis," "coniunx regis" (king's wife), "mater regis," "cyninges modor" (king's mother), or "regina," "cwen" (queen). In her major study of this bewildering terminology, Stafford points out that "A Queen always remained a Wife or Mother."[44] These multiple identities of the queen are in fact not so different from the multiple identities of other, lesser ranked women in the legal record, named variously as "religiosa femina" ("religious woman"), "matrona" ("mother"), "fidelis femina" ("loyal woman") or "nobilis femina" ("noble woman"), discussed in Chapter 2. In many of these cases, status is at least as vexed a guide to a woman's identity as her name: both status and name are context dependent.

Even the woman who is the most prominent queen in the historical record of this period has two names, Emma/Ælfgifu, and a similar pattern of identification according to name and status prevails. In a document like the *Anglo-Saxon Chronicle*, for example, queens and royal wives are not normally identified by name, but by status. Æthelred's first wife, Ælfgifu, is identified as a "hlæfdige" ("lady"); so too the Anglo-Norman Emma—renamed Ælfgifu on her marriage to Æthelred II—enters the *Chronicle* in 1002 as the anonymous daughter of Richard, count of Rouen.[45] On her marriage to Cnut in 1017, the *Chronicle* refers to Emma as widow, queen, and wife, refers to her father and former husband (respectively Richard and Æthelred II), but does not identify her by name.[46] It was by the name of Ælfgifu, or less commonly by a combination of both names ("Ælfgyua Imma seo hlæfdige," for example), that she was known consistently until the second half of the eleventh century, whereupon Emma becomes the name of choice (a choice also reflected in the historiography).[47] Ælfgifu is a common Anglo-Saxon name, especially for royal women— Cnut's other wife is also called Ælfgifu, as is Æthelred II's first wife—and the Norman Emma appears to be renamed for Æthelred's grandmother and thereby integrated into her royal husband's family. This is a common enough practice for the naming of Anglo-Saxon royal women in the later tenth century, though unusual for foreign brides. Stafford points out that "Sons were increasingly given kingly names, daughters were more likely to be named for their mother's, grandmother's or great grandmother's families," thus accounting for the greater variety in female names than in male names in this period.[48] However much politically motivated is Emma's insertion into this Anglo-Saxon maternal legacy, it is clear that Emma's prominence in the record derives from the powerful roles of mother and wife as well as queen: it is as Cnut's wife and the mother of his sons that she is presented in the *Encomium Emmae Reginae*.[49] It is by means of status, in short, that Emma is distinguished from the other important royal wives of the period.

Motherhood, Stafford notes, "was the acceptable face of female power."[50] The point is well taken, but we follow Stafford too in emphasizing the multifaceted stylizations of Emma, the most prominent queen in this period. To paraphrase Stafford, it is by means of the many faces of Emma that she is rendered most visible. That visibility, however, is not simply an index of complexity per se; it is also an indication of the lack of an unequivocal status for the category of woman in the many different genres of the cultural archive in Anglo-Saxon England. Whatever women are (and they are many things), their identification as women is most elusive.[51] It is precisely this absence of an unequivocal status for women that lies at the heart of the multiple ways by which women—of whatever class—are named or unnamed, and which forces us to question time and again the significance of a name and a status. It is also the reason why women—whether as individual agents, mothers, wives, or widows—or maternal genealogies are so hard to reconstruct. The problem is acknowledged by Æthelweard, whose Latin chronicle is dedicated to his distant cousin Mathilda, abbess of Essen, and whose prologue charts their "common family" in "modern times," insofar as memory and their parents instructed them. In so doing, Æthelweard traces his family back to King Æthelred and Matðhilda's back to King Alfred—the paternal line thus dominates—but the line falters: remembering Eadgyth, sister of King Æthelstan and Mathilda's mother, he recalls too that he does not know what happened to Æthelstan's other sister and requests that Mathilda (both nearer and from that side of the family) supply him with the missing information. Æthelweard, then, is aware of his important connections to Mathilda, but not fully clear how the two families are related.[52] For every woman recalled, another is forgotten, as is so often the case in Anglo-Saxon England. Æthelweard's maternal genealogy can be said to take the form of a riddle—a test of memory and of association— because there is no formal symbolic mechanism by which women are recalled, no consistent means by which they may be invoked. Such are the dynamics of contingency.

The greater paradox, however, is this: late Anglo-Saxon culture is fascinated by names and by naming. In the heroic literature, names are the primary means by which the elusive legendary figures of the past are recalled, however much these figures are detached from their mythic contexts. Ealhild in *Widsith*, Beadohild and Mæhild in *Deor* are well known examples of elusive female figures included in the otherwise male itemization of the legendary past. In *Beowulf*, female names—like their male counterparts—may point to an allegorical significance or trace an unwritten history, as in the cases of Wealhtheow and Modþryþ. Spiritual etymologies are deeply embedded in the religious literature of this period; runic names are encoded in narrative verse and poetry.[53] Female saints are recalled by the common liturgical practice of the litanies of the saints, as well as by the foundations, churches, hymns, and

the other apparatus of the cult (such as saints' lives).[54] The ubiquitous Æthelthryth owes her continued prominence in the cultural memory to the more
powerful Æthelwold, who was so attached to her cult at Ely.[55] The Virgin
herself, Stafford reminds us, was known by a variety of terms and titles, which
trigger other forms of association—the Old English life of Mary of Eygpt,
which we discuss in the next chapter, depends in large measure on the close
association between, and occasional conflation of, these Marys. The many
faces of the Virgin are in fact the ideological means by which the many faces of
woman are guaranteed.[56] Naming is itself a riddle, as we pointed out in
Chapter 2; the naming of woman doubly so.

Riddles of Literacy, Riddles of Signification

If to think through the relationship between orality, literacy, and gender is to
follow a disappearing trace, as we argued in Chapter 2, then to rethink that
relationship for the later Anglo-Saxon period is to continue to follow a trace
that keeps on disappearing yet is oddly present and effective in spite of dramatic changes in the uses of literate technology. Oral transactions, however
hard to detect in literate modes of signification, nonetheless function socially
through those literate modes (as the Hereford lawsuit exemplifies). Our argument here is both a structural and social one or, to paraphrase a point in our
Introduction, it is both historical and literary. Questions of female identity,
agency, and literacy continually evade definition because of their complex
(and compromised) position in the social imaginary and in social practice. To
get at these questions we need to assess carefully how modes of communication are envisaged and practiced. The later Anglo-Saxon period witnesses a
huge upsurge in the use of vernacular literacy in all spheres of social and
cultural life—for poetry, prose, laws, and diplomas and wills, for example.
Latinity too is reinvigorated, as is indicated by the renewed interest in style,
systematization of the study of grammar and Scripture, and compilation and
composition of many genres of religious writing—from tracts and sermons to
saints' lives and homiliaries.[57] This upsurge in learning both in Latin and in
the vernacular is an aspect of the Benedictine Reform, which we consider in
further detail in Chapter 4. For our purposes here, it is sufficient to note that
the different—yet overlapping—domains in which Latin and English are used
makes it even harder to pose, let alone assume, any single overarching relationship between literacy, orality, and gender.

Like the charter evidence we discussed in Chapter 2, wills, diplomas, and the other miscellaneous documents from the period are a particularly useful index of women's use of the literate document, offering complex evidence for the engagement of literate modes with oral forms of administration and governance. An era of developing literacy and a climate of a revival of learning might lead us to expect more—not fewer—women to slip through the cracks of the cultural record even as men's access to literacy increases. Evidence for women's use of and access to the literate document, however, is substantially less than that for men, as we have already pointed out. Other evidence such as the copying and composition of poetry or the various genres of religious writing (which perform in large measure the work of belief), while proliferating, are less useful as indices of women's access to or deployment of literacy. In spite of the fact that the Benedictine Reform targeted women (queens and nuns) as well as men (kings and monks), we have slender evidence of a Hild in the tenth century; little contemporary evidence for the learning of religious women; no abbey singled out in contemporary evidence for its remarkable community of women scholars (such as Barking, discussed in Chapter 4, though the cultural power of the royal convent at Wilton is often recalled); no firmly identified female writer or scribe; and scant evidence indeed for women readers.[58] As forms of literacy become more institutionalized under the aegis of the Reform—via the monastic school, clerical and royal bureaucracy, and the patronage of the prominent and the wealthy—women's access to these institutions becomes harder to detect. (The absence of abbesses from witness lists from the mid-tenth century, discussed earlier, is telling in this regard.) Given the distinctive equation of gender with power—the increased masculinization of both clerical and lay institutions in the Reform period— it comes as no surprise that the texts most firmly associated with women in this period are also those that present their royal learned patrons in only oblique fashion.

The *Encomium Emmae Reginae*, written under the patronage of Emma in the 1040s, and the *Life of Edward*, written under the patronage of Edith shortly after the Norman Conquest, are both anonymous, probably male, Latin works of considerable learning.[59] Neither work, however, takes the learning of their celebrated patron as the uncomplicated subject of the text. In the case of the *Encomium*, this issue is particularly vexed because the prologue firmly announces its intent to praise Emma.[60] Although commentators agree that this intent is best read as a justification of Emma's political maneuvers from her marriage to Cnut onward, Emma herself is curiously absent. The work instead presents Emma through the political lens of her ruling family— her husband, Cnut, and her sons, Harthacnut and Edward. The many faces of this queen (to paraphrase Stafford once more) as wife, mother, queen, and widow fail to render any single one prominent. In its partisan account of the political life of this period, Keynes notes, the *Encomium* is clearly designed to be much more than an encomium for Emma.[61] The point is sharpened when we contrast the written text and its indirect praise of Emma with the prefatory representation of Emma the queen, centered in the image, receiving the work from the author, watched by Harthacnut and Edward. In this image Emma is unequivocally a royal patron, which paradoxically draws our attention to the complex ways she might be said to form the oblique center of a text written ostensibly in her praise.[62]

Similarly, the *Life of Edward* bolsters Edith's precarious position at court as a widow, but takes her husband, Edward, and father, Godwine, as its subjects. The work does explicitly praise Edith's fame and her learning, presumably acquired at Wilton abbey where she was raised, unlike the *Encomium*, which is largely silent about Emma's learning.[63] Yet although Edith forms a continuous link between the various episodes of this curiously disjunctive work, there is no sense in which she herself is its dominant subject (even taking into account the missing sections presumably dealing with her life). The stories of both women, Stafford notes, are told through the stories of men.[64] It is worth pausing on this long-lasting phenomenon whereby women's stories are recoverable only through men's; this is by no means exclusive to the Anglo-Saxon period and indicates patterns of continuity for women's history that extend far beyond the Middle Ages. For Emma and Edith, however, to be a patron means to patronize family as a means of promoting self, of creating a subject. There is no other coherent cultural script for royal women.

Emma and Edith are celebrated for their extensive and lavish patronage of religious foundations. The *Encomium* and the *Life of Edward* are better read, therefore, as attempts to extend that patronage into the political sphere, rather than as vehicles for any display of learning by literate women. While we might reasonably infer that Emma and Edith were well educated (like Abbess Mathilda of Essen, to whom Æthelweard dedicated his Latin chronicle, discussed earlier) and subtle political actors, the roles they assume in the world of learning are those of patron and not writer. Stephanie Hollis detects a similar process at work in the earlier female shaping of the stories of the Mildrith legend associated with Thanet: the imbrication of land, patronage, and female agency in promoting the legend are later overshadowed by male cult activities.[65] As competition for the Mildrith legend suggests, patronage is by no means an exclusively female activity; the patronage of Ælfric's writings by both clerics and lay aristocrats is well documented, while Æthelweard (as one of Ælfric's patrons) and Æthelwold set the pattern for patronage of religious learning in the period more generally. As examples from the ecclesiastical and lay spheres, Ælfric, Æthelwold, and Æthelweard, however, are writers *and* patrons, firmly embedded in the world of bilingual learning promoted by the Reform.[66] That there are no known female writers in either Latin or English from this period is a measure of how even the most prominent women active in the new world of literacy, like Emma and Edith, are in fact peripheral to it.

It could be argued that since there is no "author-function" for the Anglo-Saxon period and since most vernacular writing is anonymous, our quest for women's agency and identity via their writing and learning is doomed to fail.[67] Yet there are male writers. In addition to Ælfric, Æthelwold, and Æthelweard, we can also point to Wulfstan, Byrhtferth, and Wulfstan Cantor (perhaps even Cynewulf) as examples of men who write in Latin or English or both in the period.[68] That these men hardly represent themselves as authors in the modern sense should not distract us from the ways they are represented—as "auctores" working within the established patristic traditions of the Church. With the exception of the pious aristocrat Æthelweard (who retires to a monastery), all are priests and/or monks—roles from which women are barred—and all derive their motivation to write from the intellectual mission of the Church. Once again, the asymmetry of gendered access to and use of literacy turns on the asymmetry of culturally ascribed, class and Church dominated roles and expectations for men and women. Women in this period are patrons; men are patrons and authors, often priests too. We need to look carefully at the ways in which learning is represented in the patristic symbolic of the Church to understand this asymmetry more fully.

The primary, most culturally significant, and powerful role of those men now best known as writers—Ælfric, Wulfstan, Byrhtferth, Æthelwold, Wulfstan Cantor, for example—is that of the priest in the hallowing of the sacrament in the mass. We first suggested in Chapter 2 that the sacrament might be understood as a guarantor of the Christian symbolic in the Anglo-Saxon period, arguing there that divine purchase on signification is a major factor in assessing the relation between orality, literacy, and gender. That purchase continues and extends into the vernacular in the later period. Bede's story of Imma (*EH* 4. 22), subsequently rehearsed in English by Ælfric, whose fetters are miraculously loosed through the agency of his brother's recitation of the mass, points precisely in this direction.[69] In stressing the power of the mass to effect what formerly "releasing letters" ("litteras solutorias") in Bede's account (runes or witchcraft—"drycræft oððe runcræft"—in Ælfric's account) might achieve, Lerer correctly locates Christian appropriation of non-Christian literate signification in the very heart of its most sacred signifier—in the mass.[70] While Ælfric's version of Bede's story acknowledges patristic authority for elucidating the efficacy of the mass in the interrelated workings of books and rites, the miracle itself centers on the unspoken power of the ritualized words of the mass.[71] Ælfric's exposition of the mass in the Second Series Homily for Easter Sunday focuses on this purchase of the mass on signification more systematically.[72] In so doing, the claiming of the patristic authority of both Bede and Gregory for accounts of the efficacy of the mass so appropriate in Ælfric's account of Imma disappears from view in favor of an emphasis on the mystery of interpreting Scripture and the mystical nature of the mass itself. It is through an understanding of these mysteries that we can begin to understand the complex relationship between learning, signification, and literacy at the heart of Christian knowledge in the period.

In a delicate adjudication between the (unidentified) arguments of Ratramnus and Smaragdus over the signification of the mass together with excerpts from Gregory's *Vitae Patrum*,[73] Ælfric's lengthy exegesis of the Old Testament Passover and the New Testament Last Supper in his Second Series homily for Easter Sunday takes the mystery of the mass (a condensation of both Passion and Resurrection) and the problem of interpretation as its central subject:

Nu wille we eow geopenian þurh godes gife be ðam halgan husle ðe ge nu to gan sceolon. and gewissian eower andgit ymbe þære *gerynu*. ægðer ge æfter ðære ealdan gecyðnysse. ge æfter ðære niwan. þy læs ðe ænig twynung eow derian mage. be ðam liflicum gereorde; (Godden XV, p. 150, lines 3–7; emphasis added)

(Now we will open to you through the grace of God the holy eucharist to which you are now to go, and direct your understanding about its mystery, both according to the Old Testament and the New, lest any doubt may harm you with respect to that vital meal.)

Here, as throughout the sermon, "mystery" ("gerynu") is a key word. Ælfric draws on his authority as priest and exegete in revealing and elucidating this mystery in the vernacular, directing ("gewissian") the understanding of his audience in the face of a doubt that may harm ("derian") the believer and thus compromise the efficacy of the mass. Unlike the story of Imma, which identifies the doubting subject as pagan in opposition to Imma's priestly brother, the stakes in this Easter Day sermon are much higher. The beginning of the sermon (quoted above) locates a fear of doubt in the Christian believer—in those about to take mass ("lest any doubt may harm you"). In fact, the sermon draws a line between doubt and belief throughout. Belief, though prior to understanding, operates through it, and stands at the limit of that understanding. The mystery of the Eucharist remains intact, guaranteed by the gospels, patristic exegesis, its priests, and its miracles. This entire interpretive and symbolic system points to the ultimate signifier of Christ's body:

þeos *gerynu* is wedd. and hiw cristes lichama is soðfæstnyss; Ðis wed we healdað *gerynelice*. oð þæt we becumon to ðære soðfæstnysse. and ðonne bið þis wedd geendod; Soðlice hit is swa swa we ær cwædon cristes lichama and his blod. na lichamlice. ac gastlice; Ne sceole ge smeagan hu hit gedon sy. ac healdan on eowrum geleafan þæt hit swa gedon sy. (Godden XV, p. 154, lines 153–58; emphasis added)

(This mystery is pledge and figure. Christ's body is truth. This pledge we hold mystically until we come to the truth, and then this pledge will be ended. Truly it is as we said before Christ's body and his blood, not bodily but spiritually. You are not to inquire how it is done, but to hold in your belief that it is so done.)

Revelation of the Eucharist as a transcendental mystery confounding human understanding and depending on belief turns on the familiar exegetical distinction between the literal and the spiritual. This distinction is held in place by the mystical nature of Christ's body, which *is* truth and which signifies the limits of human—or at least nonclerical—understanding ("You are not to inquire how it is done, but to hold in your belief that it is so done"). In response to those who inquire how bread becomes the body of Christ and wine his blood, Ælfric stresses time and again the mysterious transformation from literal to spiritual that takes place through the hallowing of the Eucharist:

Hwi is ðonne þæt halige husel gecweden cristes lichama. oþþe his blod. gif hit nis soðlice þæt þæt hit gehaten is; Soðlice se hlaf and þæt win ðe beoð *ðurh sacerda mæssan gehalgode*. oðer ðing hi æteowiað menniscum andgitum wiðutan. and oðer ðing hi clypiað wiðinnan geleafullum modum. Wiðutan hi beoð gesewene hlaf and win. ægðer ge on hiwe. ge on swæcce. ac hi beoð soðlice *æfter ðære halgunge* cristes lichama. and his blod þurh gastlicere gerynu. (Godden XV, p.153, lines 100–107; emphasis added)

(Why then is the holy Eucharist called Christ's body or his blood, if it is not truly that which it is called? Truly the bread and the wine, which are hallowed through the mass of the priests, appear one thing to human understanding without and call another thing to believing minds within. Without they are seen as bread and wine, both in form and taste, but they are truly after the hallowing Christ's body and his blood through a spiritual mystery.)

Through the ritual actions of the priest (mentioned twice in this brief passage), the mystery that is the Eucharist can be revealed only to the believing mind ("geleafullum mode"), not to human understanding alone ("menniscum andgit"). In such a system of signification, women—barred from the mediatory role of the priesthood—are positioned as either doubters or believers. Indeed, one of the miracles of the mass reported by Ælfric (ultimately from Gregory's *Vitae Patrum*) concerns a doubting woman sent a vision of a bloody finger in place of the sacrament (Godden XV, p. 155, lines 167–74). By contrast, the priestly caste are instruments whereby belief itself is enacted and, as indicated by this caste's evangelical mission, are the ultimate human guardians of its mysterious knowledge: "You are not to inquire how it is done, but to hold in your belief that it is so done," Ælfric insists.

The mystery ("gerynu") of the Eucharist, which relates knowledge to belief, is a mystification of human learning, and is held in place by the sign of Christ's body. This mystery is central to all Christian ways of knowing. It is a small step, structurally, from the aura of mystery that accrues to the priest in the mass to that of learning that accrues to the priestly author. We might speculate, therefore, that the bifurcation of gendered roles where writing occurs—no women writers, women as patrons—is elucidated by this deep level of the Christian patristic signification from which women are explicitly excluded. We might even argue that this speculation is suggestive of an historical relation between the patristic symbolic and the Anglo-Saxon social imaginary. We shall return to this point shortly. First, however, let us tease out the cultural significance of the sacramental mystery a little further.

The Latin equivalent of "gerynu" is "mysterium" ("mystery"), and Ælfric is a good guide to its meaning:

For ði is þæt halige husel gehaten *gerynu*. forðan ðe oðer ðing is ðæron gesewen. and oðer ðing undergyten; þæt þæt ðær gesewen is hæfð lichamlic hiw. and þæt þæt we ðæron understandað hæfð gastlice mihte; (Godden XV, p. 154, lines 137–41; emphasis added)

(Therefore is the holy Eucharist called a mystery, because one thing is seen therein and another thing is understood. That which is there seen has a bodily form, and that which we understand therein has spiritual might.)

The structural process in operation here is a metaphoric exchange of outer for inner—the visible for the invisible—in which the Eucharist is explicitly called a mystery, "gerynu," a form of allegory. This central structure of inner and outer governs much of Christian theology; it also provides the form, or template, for much Christian metaphor (as we shall also see, preeminently, in the case of Aldhelm in Chapter 4). By the exchange of inner and outer, the mystery both of the sign (the body of Christ) and of its mysterious signifier (the Eucharist) are held intact. The meaning of the Eucharist is produced by this process: drawing a distinction between sight and understanding, form and significance, belief operates through spiritual understanding to name the Eucharist a mystery. In the Christian tradition, this act of naming is perhaps the most crucial example of a more widespread Anglo-Saxon cultural interest in names. As we have pointed out, the process of naming in Anglo-Saxon culture often assumes the structure of a riddle; riddles are, of course, preeminent explorations of the mysteries of naming. We have noted too that the practice of feminine naming follows a different, often arbitrary and contingent, logic to that of the masculine tradition. We can therefore relate the riddle of feminine identity to the sacred signifying structure of the Eucharist via an exploration of riddles and mysteries.

In his exposition on the Trinity, Augustine points out that "enigmata," or riddles, are tropes, a species of allegory "which signify one thing by another" ("quae sunt aliud ex alio significantia").[74] This is a conventional enough patristic definition of an enigma. Isidore and Cassiodorus say pretty much the same thing: a riddle is an obscure figure whose interpretation reveals the veiled truth of Scripture, as in the celebrated passage from 1 Corinthians 13:12, "Videmus nunc per speculum in *aenigmate*; tunc autem facie ad faciem" ("We see now through a glass darkly; but then face to face," emphasis added).[75] Aldhelm too follows patristic tradition in composing his own "enigmata." Training in the composition and interpretation of riddles is for Aldhelm one step toward more significant compositions (as he puts it in his prologue) as well as a revelation in verse of the "enigmatic nature of things" (verse preface).[76] Riddles sharpen a love for truth, Augustine points out in *De doctrina christiana*; small wonder that the clerical glossing and writing of Latin riddles (especially those of Aldhelm) is a popular exercise in the Latin schools of late Anglo-Saxon England.[77]

As tropes, "enigmata" are veiled mysteries, pointing to and naming a truth; the sacrament of the mass is similarly a mystery, "gerynu," but this trope names the mystery or symbol of Christ's body, which *is* Truth. These two mysteries are often presented as synonymous, as indicated by the Latin gloss, "misterium," to "enigma" in one copy of Aldhelm's prologue to his riddles.[78] As a result, we see how the mystery of the mass and the mystery of the riddle converge on a similar explanation: one thing signifies another (to paraphrase both Ælfric and Augustine). Modern English "riddle" derives from the Old English verb "rædan"—to counsel, advise, guide, explain, to read.[79] Interpretation and understanding, therefore, are means whereby the riddle and the mystery of the mass are revealed—means of access to a remarkably similar significatory process. That the mass and riddles are structurally related is also indicated by Ælfric's revision of Bede's account of Imma, discussed earlier. In Ælfric's account, the ealdorman asks Imma "whether he broke his bands through witchcraft or through runic letters" ("hwæðer he ðurh drycræft. oððe þurh runstafum his bendas tobræce," Godden XXI, p. 204, lines 159–60). Runes too are mysteries—secret letters—and Ælfric's substitution of runic letters for Bede's "releasing letters" lays bare the substitution of one mystery for another—the mass—the words of which, crucially, are mentioned neither by Ælfric nor Bede. As homologies, runes and riddles point to the mystery of the mass by which, in Ælfric's work at least, they are subsumed and indeed guaranteed.

The relation between runes and riddles—posed as mysteries analogous to that of the Eucharist—underlines the ways in which the mass serves as a guarantor of patristic sacred signification *and* as its signifier. Claiming both the process—the ritual of the mass—and its product—that of belief—the Church maintains a monopoly on meaning: the structural relation of definition to cognition is seamless. Understanding of the mass as the ultimate mystery and its truth, moreover, holds in place and structurally determines access to other, lesser mysteries. The vernacular riddles of the Exeter Book that explore the relation of knowledge, writing, and speech perhaps call greater attention to this sacred mystery of belief than do the Latin riddles of Aldhelm; in so doing, they remove the feminine from its already tenuous relation to spiritual signification in the Latin tradition. It is time, in short, to extend here our discussion of the vernacular riddles first begun in Chapter 2.[80]

Take the example of Aldhelm's enigma on the chrismal (Riddle 55), filled with divine gift ("diuino munere plena"), which is imaged first as a house and then as a body, whose belly or womb ("uiscera") holds the body of Christ, and thus uses the pregnant body as its metaphoric base. Neither Exeter Book Riddle 48, whose solution is variously a chrismal, chalice, or paten, or Riddle 59, whose solution is a chalice, draw on such familiar Aldhelmian bodily images. Instead, both riddles play on the mystery of mute objects that speak and in so doing stress another aspect of the sacrament—its mysteriously efficacious spoken words. The solutions to these riddles are sacred objects (chrismal, chalice, paten) that are not used to demystify other objects or actions in the world, as is so familiar in the Exeter Book riddles. Rather, these sacred objects confirm the authenticity of the sacrament as signifier: that mystery, which we might term the riddle of the mass, remains mystified. Nor are images of orality in the vernacular tradition associated with the feminine as in the Aldhelmian tradition; such images are associated instead with the paradox of sacred knowledge, and with its various modes of signification. The ring ("hring," chalice, chrismal, or paten) that speaks in Riddle 48 does so in strong words ("strongum wordum," line 3), silently ("swigende," 4), without tongue ("butan tungan," 2); through its red gold men can understand its mysterious ("ryne," 6) intercessory speech ("galdorcwide," 7). The golden ring ("hring gyldenne," 1), passed around men and reminiscent of the social cere-mony of drinking in the hall in Riddle 59, not only speaks though dumb ("dumba," 8), but names the Lord ("hælend," 6), bringing it to the eyes and minds of men for meditation and understanding: "Him torhte in gemynd / his dryhtnes naman dumba brohte / ond in eagna gesih" ("Dumb, it brought clearly his lord's name into mind and into eyes' sight," 7–9).

Like the famous name of the codex or gospel book in Riddle 26—"Nama min is mære / hæleþum gifre ond halig sylf" ("My name is famous, useful to men and sacred itself," lines 27–28), Riddles 48 and 59 have as their solutions a name that points to another riddle. Riddle 26 refers not to any book, but *the book*; Riddle 59 identifies a chalice, and the chalice explicitly names Christ ("hælend," "dryhten," 6, 8). Both riddles reveal the power of the transcenden-tal signifier, but they do so in its fully mystified state. So too in his Easter Day sermon Ælfric points out that to name the sacrament is to name a mystery, which is truth and the body of Christ. One thing is another, to recall the allegorical formulation used both of the mass and of riddles. Riddles 26, 48, and 59 also do their work in the realm of the visual, inviting us to see that which cannot be seen—the chalice, chrismal, and sacred codex are visual clues to the invisible world of the mystery of sacred knowledge and belief. In these riddles, as in Ælfric's sermon, the thematics of sight and insight are fore-grounded. By drawing on the same metaphoric process of sacramental signifi-cation as the religious prose, these riddles confirm the ways in which patristic signification dominates the field of the cultural imaginary.

Such riddling of sacred mysteries is also connected to a mystification of speech, writing, and knowledge more generally. Like the deaf and dumb bookcase of Riddle 49 that digests useful gifts (discussed in the preceding chapter), the book moth that swallows speech in Riddle 47 is an example of the way in which the vernacular riddles imbue, indeed confound, material form with a mode of knowing that transcends the material world. These riddles mystify learning in the form, in fact, the name of books, but they also mystify speech and understanding itself. Such are the privileges of a clerical monopoly on meaning, which in another register enjoys the fantasy of copu-lating hens as an index of learning (in Riddle 42, discussed in Chapter 2). The familiar convention of the riddle—that dumb objects speak—is given great force in both Riddles 47 and 49. Like belief, a mystery that speaks of the immaterial through material signs, learning speaks through the material object (a moth, a bookcase) to highlight the usefulness—and uselessness—of such objects.

None of the Exeter Book riddles of knowledge draw on a thematics of gender, however, as is so often the case with their Latin counterparts in Aldhelm's riddles. Nor are gender issues explicitly relevant to the mystery of the mass as explicated by Ælfric, which itself stands at another intersection between the oral and the literate (suggested by the riddling chalices as well as by Imma's story of the efficacious words of the mass). Given this system of signification, we might ask where does the feminine go in the vernacular imaginary? What kind of a place can woman or the feminine occupy in the Christian mystery of divine knowledge? Indeed, where is the feminine in this process of creation—of meaning, of understanding, of knowing? Since the relation of both the female and the feminine to the process of patristic signification is at best less clearly defined than that of the male and the masculine, and at worst contingent, we should not expect any single answer to these questions.

One such answer is suggested by Ælfric's Easter Sunday sermon, where an anonymous, doubting woman witnesses the miracle of the host as it transforms before her eyes into a bloody finger (discussed earlier), which indicates that women and the feminine confirm the significatory process, but do not enter into it. After all, gender—masculinity—is implicitly operative in the mass itself through the sacred figure of the priest and his body. It is the ritual actions of the priestly voice and his body that create the conditions for the "proper" deployment of the sacrament of Christ's body. Priests are central to the celebration of the mass, Ælfric reminds us; women are not, however much they may witness its efficacy. This asymmetry of access to the Eucharist is also central to the relationship between the priestly Zosimus and Mary in the Old English life of Mary of Eygpt, discussed in Chapter 4. But another answer to the question of how women and/or the feminine signify in conventions of signification, naming, and interpretation is offered by the riddles. In the prologue to his "enigmata," Aldhelm pays considerable attention to the question of voice. Riddles are, after all, ways in which "mute and insensible objects speak."[81] Following conventional interpretation of enigmas by the Church fathers, Aldhelm finds examples in Scripture where rational creatures adopt the persona of the irrational, and where the irrational adopt the persona of the rational. Citing examples of such voices from the Book of Judges, Psalms, and Ecclesiastes, Aldhelm also offers the common "mater" riddle as a poetic example: "mater me genuit eadem mox gignitur ex me" ("My mother bore me and then she herself is born again from me," Ehwald, p. 77). The prevalence of birthing images in Aldhelm's riddles already explored in Chapter 2 is underlined by his use of the "mater" riddle in this discursive preface: the metaphoric association between the sacred, the irrational, and the maternal springs readily to Aldhelm's mind. The maternal functions here at the level of metaphor in much the same way as the doubting woman in Ælfric's sermon exemplifies the power of the Eucharist: the "mater" riddle illustrates but does not guarantee the structure of the allegory, which is an enigma.

As already noted, such images of birth are not reiterated in the vernacular riddles of knowledge and writing. There are, however, other vernacular riddles where birthing offers a place from which a riddle may begin. Riddle 35 in fact begins when the metal of the coat of mail is delivered from the womb or innards ("innaþe," line 2) of the earth. Here the feminine (as "mother earth") is presented as the primary personification, even though the mute object that speaks (the coat of mail) belongs to the masculine world of the warrior: the feminine here stands before and is displaced by the masculine. As the site of signification, moreover, the feminine lacks any sustained relation to its referent (a phenomenon we explore in greater detail in Chapter 4 in the case of Aldhelm's prose *De virginitate*). Nor is the argument that grammatical gender serves as a prompt for gender personification adequate to explain the layering of female and male personifications in this or other similar riddles (an argument we pursue further in Chapter 5). What is clear is that the feminine can serve as a site or vehicle for the significatory process, but cannot serve as its guarantor. Part of the process of making meaning, the feminine is in danger of having no meaning herself.

Other vernacular riddles point in similar directions. Riddle 29 figures the moon as female, who steals away between her horns the treasure of the masculine sun—an interesting angle on the male-dominated heroic world of gift exchange. The bagpipe of Riddle 31 is a fully feminized object, a mighty kinswoman anxious to prove her skills in the hall, eager for fame, familiarly mute, but gifted with song. The bagpipe riddle thus offers an instance of the conflation of the maternal with the oral found more often in Aldhelm's Latin riddles. In Riddle 31, however, the maternal is the instrument of song waiting to be played; the silence here equated with the maternal is clearly at some remove from the violent, frequently feminized world of Aldhelm's riddles. In one instance, however, mother speaks. Riddle 33 presents an iceberg as a laughing, terrifying female warrior, who binds waves with a hateful charm ("heterune," line 7) and speaks her own "mater" riddle with artifice ("searo-cræftig," 8): "Is min modor mægða cynnes / þæs deorestan, þæt is dohtor min / eacen up liden" ("My mother, one of the most beloved of the kin of women, is my daughter, great and exalted," 9–11). So popular in the Latin riddle tradition, the Old English "mater" riddle serves to voice not the just the mystery of ice or, as Aldhelm uses it, the mysterious voice of riddles in general, but that of the feminine and of feminine genealogy in particular. We have here, in short, a riddle within a riddle, strongly reminiscent in its symbolic structure of the chalice riddles, that riddle the mystery of the mass. Yet these parallels only highlight the fact that the feminine does not signify as a sacred mystery, but signifies as a female warrior, who is a mother, her daughter, and an iceberg.

Riddle 33 is a particularly compelling example of how the feminine oper-ates in the vernacular riddles by generating analogies whereby the original ref-erent is modified. When the warrior speaks (and she is never explicitly named a woman-warrior or a valkyrie) her terrifying charm, she does so with the voice of the "mater" riddle—the voice of a domestic mother without a proper name. Here we find yet again the substitution of the social role for the proper name within the construction of a female genealogy. Indeed, confounding with a parodic genealogy, this mother is also her nameless daughter, whose greatness carries connotations of pregnancy ("eacen," 11). Ice is thereby dou-bly domesticated—known to those on land and welcomed with love ("lissum," 13). By the end of the riddle, the terrifying power of the warrior woman and her voice is naturalized via the domestic, anonymous voice that is the femi-nine genealogy of the "mater" riddle. The chain of feminine signification stretches into anonymity as does the feminine itself into the "natural" world of ice (there is no feminine referent in this riddle). Naming is here as myste-rious a process as it is in the case of the sacrament. Signifer and referent, however, are split. Absent from the unifying sites of sacred knowledge, belief, and writing evident in other vernacular riddles we have discussed, the associa-tion of the feminine with anonymity, the maternal, the familial, the genealogi-cal, and the oral—evidently forces to be reckoned with—is in full operation in the iceberg riddle. The parallels with the issues of family status (mother or daughter), naming, and orality that we examined in the evidence of the Hereford lawsuit are striking. This "woman," however, is no woman. Doubly riddled, the feminine is doubly absent from the riddle even as it forms the ground and presence of its figures.

The Lady Reads

We have noted that the riddle of feminine absence and its relation to processes of naming and modes of communication (oral and/or literate) is found in referential and representational genres—the diploma, sacramental literature, and the riddle. Through examining issues of female agency as well as forms of feminine symbolization in these genres, we pose questions of female voice, authorship, and patronage as instances of the relation of the feminine to the patristic imaginary. The same methodology enables us to get at the related questions of the woman reader and the woman listener. Representations of the woman who listens and speaks are far more common in the vernacular culture than are those of the woman who reads or, as we have seen, writes. Think, for example, not only of the mother in the Hereford lawsuit, but of the genre of female saints' lives, where the saint is so often represented as a learned speaker but not a reader or writer (a case in point is *Elene*), or, more classically still, of the two female-voiced elegies, *The Wife's Lament* or *Wulf and Eadwacer*.[82] Just because the woman as reader is rarely represented, however, does not mean she is not there. In fact, the Exeter Book elegy, *The Husband's Message*, and the riddle which proceeds it in the manuscript and with which it is frequently associated—Riddle 60, the reed pen or flute—invite meditation on the lady who reads.

There is no need to rehearse the critical arguments for and against the association of *The Husband's Message* with Riddle 60 here.[83] For our needs it is sufficient that both riddle and elegy (as they are commonly identified) present an artifact (a reed pen or flute, a rune stave) as a mode of interpersonal communication that is shared only between sender and receiver, at least fictionally. Riddle 60 in particular is replete with the usual markers of this topos of alienated communication in the riddles: the mute voice ("muðleas," line 9) that nonetheless exchanges words ("wordan wrixlan," 10); the masculine aristocratic association of sword, pen, and mead bench (contrasted with Symphosius's more feminine emphases in the Latin analogy to the vernacular riddle); the miraculous voicing of inner states ("eorles ingeþonc," 13) despite, or perhaps because of, its status as artifact; the value of this mode of communication for secrecy, solitude, and exclusivity—a message for just two, "unc anum twam" (15).[84] This use of conventions and their resonance with other models of masculine literacy sharpens by contrast the use of a similar topos in *The Husband's Message*.

The Husband's Message certainly shares many of the characteristics of the riddle genre, most notably its use of an inanimate object—here a rune stave or stick—as speaker. It is, however, the poem's specific use of the object as both message and mediator between sender and receiver that links it most closely with Riddle 60 and, by extension, with those other vernacular riddles (discussed earlier) that explore forms of knowledge produced by writing and speaking. Communication in absentia produces the fiction of a message shared only in secret, to the chosen few—a mystery played out in full in Riddle 60 and played upon in *The Husband's Message*. Since sender and receiver of the message are absent from the primary scene of communication, poem and riddle examine ways in which technologies can be exploited both to overcome alienation and social isolation and to benefit from it. In Riddle 60, the content of the message remains explicitly unknown: "swa hit beorna ma / uncre wordcwidas widdor ne mænden" ("so that no man wide in the world may ever know our words," 16–17)—an enticing and insoluble riddle for the reader. *The Husband's Message*, by contrast, gives clear instructions to the woman by her male lover (the "husband" of the title) meant only for her, putting the reader in the role of eavesdropper. The male lover's imperious tone in commanding the woman to join him ("Ongin mere secan," "Go seek the sea," 26) is softened by rhetorical persuasion, material wealth, and the promise of shared power. At the same time that both riddle and poem explore the possibilities offered by technology for private, secretive, even dangerous (in the case of *The Husband's Message*) talk, however, they revel in a more commonplace paradox of Anglo-Saxon written culture. Both are literate texts parading as oral ones to a meta-audience of readers and auditors—voice echoes off the written page precisely because voice and written word are so inextricably bound on and through it. In this way, voice triumphs over absence through the mediation of technology as both poem and riddle recognize just how complex is the imbrication of voice and word. Voice and word in fact defy decoding in Riddle 60, where none might hear a message meant for only two. Past and present voices are layered through the runic words of *The Husband's Message*: the voice of the male lover mimicked by that of the rune stave (which has, in turn, its own voice and history); the memory of earlier vocal promises between the lovers; the anticipation of future oaths or pledges. In this layering of voices past and present, known and unknown, we note the parallels to the Hereford lawsuit with its own use of voice and narrative. In the lawsuit the mother speaks; in the poem, however, the lady reads. In this context, we note that *The Husband's Message* is generally less favored critically than its close relation, *The Wife's Lament*. The latter explores the voice of a woman conveyed by the fiction of an oral song without the complexities of a runic intermediary with its own voice so central to the former. But where is the woman who hears and reads in *The Husband's Message*; the feminine in Riddle 60?

The utterly obvious answers to these questions are that the woman is not "in" *The Husband's Message*, nor is there any indication of the feminine used symbolically in Riddle 60. The referent of the female beloved or wife in *The Husband's Message* is an absent one, and her absence dictates the structure of the entire poem. By contrast, the feminine never seems to cross the trajectory of the riddle whatsoever. Both riddle and poem, however, thematize absence not only in modes of communication—oral or literate—and the forms of knowing attendant on such modes (a strategy familiar to us from other riddles of writing and speaking), but also in gendered models of reading and listening. The relationship between exiled lover and absent beloved intensified by the figure of the runic stave as go-between in *The Husband's Message* is one that explores heterosexual relations as a source of absence, nuancing the more conventional, elegiac theme of exile. Indeed, *The Husband's Message* considerably amplifies the figure of the estranged woman common to both *The Wife's Lament* and *Wulf and Eadwacer*. The woman for whom this runic message is intended is rich ("sinchroden," "treasure-laden," 14; the familiar image of the aristocratic lady), powerful (she is tempted with the promise of equal gift-giving with her husband), and educated. In the fiction of the poem not only is she invited to listen to her lover's message, but she reads it and, in so doing, reads runes—a skill firmly associated with the educated class in the later Anglo-Saxon period. Reading and hearing are thus enfolded one into the other—a strategy of representation we have met frequently in the interrelationship of word and voice in the riddles and legal documents. This poem, moreover, offers literary evidence for a sophisticated woman reader in the later Anglo-Saxon period—a reader who is only too obviously absent even as an idea from its companion poem, Riddle 60. The poem, therefore, can be put side by side with the equally rare external evidence for women readers in the later period—readers such as Emma and Edith. Such evidence represents no triumph for the feminist critic, however, since it is so heavily qualified, whether by its rarity (in the cultural archive) or by the nature of its representation (in *The Husband's Message*). This representation of the lady who reads depends utterly on her absence (we have no idea how the lady reacts to her message, no expectation that she writes too); indeed, her absence provides the conditions, the site, for the meanings of the entire poem. Furthermore, the lady—like her counterpart in *The Wife's Lament*—appears to be the passive object of male feuding. Similarly attenuating her representation as reader are the ways the poem constructs other readers, who are cast in the roles both of eavesdroppers on a "private" message and of the woman reader who is the recipient of that message.

Since masculinity is so thoroughly imbricated in modes of literacy and knowing, and thus naturalized, gender perhaps does not seem as formally thematized in Riddle 60 as in *The Husband's Message*, although the same mystification of reading and hearing is at work. In fact, the riddle's lexicon of "monna cynnes," "eorles," and "beorna" point strongly to a masculine, aristocratic milieu—a world of privilege that the reed enters and that the reader may recognize, even if she does not know the content of the message itself. If the privileged relationship explored in the elegy is that of estranged aristocratic lovers, then that of the riddle is the aristocratic male social mileu in which literacy and listening can be explored in social terms. The reed is at first isolated from the world of men (in the universal sense): "fea ænig wæs / monna cynnes, þæt minnne þær / on anæde eard beheolde" ("few were there of mankind who there beheld my home in that solitary place," 3–5). As artifact shaped by mankind, however, the reed subsequently enters the world of masculine relations at the mead-bench, and becomes a unique and exclusive marker of those relations—it can reveal the noble inner mind ("eorles in-geþonc," 13) as well as mediate between individuals in that world, creating a bond that only two can share. The rune stave in *The Husband's Message* performs a similar function, but mediates relations between man and woman. That the social world at issue here is the same in both riddle and poem—the mead-bench of Riddle 60 is a symbol of male aristocratic circles in the hall and finds its counterpart in the treasure-adorned woman and her exiled lover's wealth in *The Husband's Message*—is entirely to the point. Reading and listening, speaking and writing are functions of class, and in the poetry the idealized upper class of hall and meadbench, warrior and treasure-adorned woman, prevails.

Both poem and riddle, moreover, bring into sharp focus the concept of the alternate structure used throughout this chapter to name the ways in which women and the feminine are imbricated in patriarchal cultural structures central to late Anglo-Saxon England. Aside from its thematics of absence and presence—the woman reader who is simultaneously absent and present from the text—doubled structures are evident in *The Husband's Message* at several other levels. The poem in its manuscript context at least draws on the two genres of the riddle and the elegy; its dynamics of literacy and orality explore literate modes of communication that produce and anticipate voice (the rune stave records its own as well as the male lover's voice and looks to further performative acts—that of the oath); male talk finds its complement in female auditor; and representational modes are twinned with referential modes. Our argument here anticipates the layering of metaphoric mode, representation, and referentiality, examined further in Chapter 4 (especially in our questioning of the female audience for Aldhelm's *De virginitate*) in order to underline how widespread is this doubling of structures wherever women and the feminine are concerned in Anglo-Saxon culture. Indeed, we might argue that in the case of later Anglo-Saxon England, developments in the technology of writing help delineate this use of doubled structures, whereby we can understand more clearly the efficacy of female agency which otherwise appears so often veiled by more dominant masculine processes and structures.

We began this chapter with a study of a woman who speaks in the case of the Hereford diploma; we end it with the case of *The Husband's Message* and a woman who apparently hears and reads. The representation of both women is profoundly implicated in and presented by literate processes that privilege both the male and the symbolically masculine—the poem and the legal diploma. Dictated by these processes and by the logic of the alternate structure that precipitates out of them, the woman who speaks and the woman who hears or reads are profoundly absent as referents from that literate evidence. It is this dynamic that is at the heart of the dilemma of the female Anglo-Saxon subject.

Chapter Four
Figuring the Body:
Gender, Performance, Hagiography

We have traced the powerful dynamics at work in the representation of women's participation in religious and secular culture by paying particular attention to the language of that cultural evidence. Indeed, as we note in our Introduction, we take language very seriously. This has led us to explore in considerable detail women's relation to orality and literacy throughout the Anglo-Saxon period. As we explore women's relation to voice and text, however, we argue that it is equally important to attend to the rhetorical forms by which women and the feminine are represented in the period. Where there's a voice, there's a body, as we pointed out in Chapter 2. In this chapter we turn to the many ways in which the female saintly bodies are figured by Anglo-Saxon textual culture and their relation to issues of Christian subjectivity.

We chose Aldhelm's *De virginitate* of the seventh century and Ælfric's *Lives of Saints* of the tenth for our analysis.[1] Explicitly Christian works, they are seldom included in analyses of gender and subjectivity in any systematic fashion. They provide, however, Latin and English contexts in which to view formations of the Christian subject, offering richly complex and different sites for the liaison of the ideological, the literary, and the historical. The *De virginitate* and the *Lives of Saints* frame Anglo-Saxon culture (from its early flourishing in Latin to its later West Saxon emphasis on English), enabling the assessment both of developmental models of history and of the implications of the frequently cited "golden age" of Anglo-Saxon women. This linear approach nevertheless resists any premature use of a developmental model—from Aldhelm to Ælfric, from the early Anglo-Saxon period to the late. It is worth repeating what we said in our Introduction: there *is* change, certainly, and difference throughout the period in the configurations of representational and restrictive practices concerning both women's and men's bodies. But there is a danger in using the apparent decline of the status of women at the end of the Anglo-Saxon period to posit and celebrate a "golden age" for women in the early heyday of monasticism. The before and after model, while validated by certain legal and historical developments, obscures differences among women (like those of class), *and* aspects of similarity and continuity in representational practices that create women's difference as well as men's.

Body Politics in Aldhelm's *De virginitate*
(Or, What *Did* the Bishop Say to the Abbess?)

she was thrust—despoiled of her own clothes, to the infamous disgrace of her family— into the loathsome harlotry of a brothel, where the detestable wantonness of pros- titutes runs wild and the shameless impudence of whores is disgustingly flaunted, nevertheless, walled about by the shining splendour of a mighty light, she gazed on angelic faces and was covered with her Lord's robes. (Agnes, Aldhelm's prose *De virginitate*)

What possible liaison can there be between a text like Aldhelm's prose *De virginitate* and the "real" identities of religious women in the late seventh century? What conditions the entry of monastic women into such an elabo- rately rhetorical instance of the patristic symbolic, or, how is the body figured and what kind of subject is performed under such rhetorical circumstances? Aldhelm's "literary" text invites historicization. Eminently politicized, it de- mands consideration of gender and class, of women's access to literate modes, and of doctrinal issues such as virginity and their gendered sociohistorical context of Christian monasticism in the seventh century. It raises abundant questions about referentiality and representation, and it begs questions of audience that bring us to the same edge of paradox that emerged in Chapter 2 in our discussion of high-status women's actual access to cultural production, and in the uncanny correlations between women's social presence and textual absence. This discussion will therefore aim to situate the text rather than fully "read" or analyze it, to examine the conditions and processes of its reception and motivation—although we shall not be able to resist, or avoid, some of Aldhelm's metaphorical virtuosity.

Aldhelm specifically and at some length dedicates his prose *De virgini- tate*—which is our primary focus rather than the poetic version—to Abbess Hildelith and her nuns at Barking abbey, circa 675.[2] On the one hand, the author's dedication genders the issue of audience and reception. On the other, commentators have assumed a mixed audience for the text because Barking was a double monastery and because Aldhelm unprecedently includes male virgins in his list of *exempla* (Lapidge and Herren, p. 57). The implications of this gendered audience for notions of Christian subjectivity can be examined doctrinally, structurally, and rhetorically—from within and without the text. Before considering gender here in the issue of audience, however, let us look for a moment at some components of class—wealth, prestige, and clout. The Barking monastery was a particularly wealthy foundation. Cyril Hart's analysis of boundaries and placenames in the charter evidence suggests that Barking had extensive holdings, being endowed "with no less than eight gifts of land within two decades of its foundation" (c. 666).[3] The eight individual gifts are summarized in "Erkenwald's Charter," which Hart argues to be at least partially authentic; the charter, witnessed by no less an episcopal presence than Wilfrid (though by no high-ranking churchwomen), insists on the monastery's independence from episcopal intervention and on the nuns' right to choose their own abbess.[4] While this independence was not yet problematic or wholly unusual, the monastery held another clear claim to distinction, according to Hart: "the only female saint to whom English churches were consecrated in the seventh century was St. Mary, of which the church of the monastery at Barking is one of the very few examples."[5] This monastery had resources, and deployed them with a measure of independence.

Recent archeological evidence supports a description of a comfortable if not luxurious physical environment at Barking in the early days of its foundation; along with combs, jewelry, coins, manicure sets, parts of musical instruments, and weaving artifacts, traces of gold thread were discovered indicating the production of luxury clothing.[6] While gold thread may have been used in the production of ecclesiastical garments, Kenneth MacGowan concludes that overall there is no "direct archeological evidence to suggest that the Saxon phases of the site were ecclesiastic or that they are located within the precinct of the Saxon monastery."[7] (The later phase of excavation revealed high-quality glass production.) The picture of a wealthy and commercially independent community is therefore enhanced as these excavations "may not have found the nunnery itself but perhaps, more importantly, they found the workshops that provided the goods and services required by the abbey."[8] Again, Barking is not unusual; archeological finds at Whitby indicate "a comparatively luxurious pattern of life" according to Carol Neuman de Vegvar, who also pointed out that servants were not uncommon in the more preeminent monastic houses,[9] a situation that prompts some attendant ironies explored by Christine Fell.[10]

Aldhelm himself calls attention to the problem of luxury in dress and ornament toward the end of his introductory preamble to the list of *exempla*.

Make-up, jewels, and fine clothing are associated with sexuality in as much as it is the married woman who flaunts them: "Parading with the senseless pomp of her ornaments—in the likeness of that woman offering the lethal drink of the brothel in the golden chalice" (Lapidge and Herren, p. 73), but the problem is also one of display, both sexual and material. Elsewhere, Aldhelm uses a far more direct address to class consciousness, but the adorned woman presents her own ambiguities.[11] Hollis makes an important distinction between Aldhelm and Bede here, which also speaks to the earlier transitional phase of female monasticism when Theodore's misogynist orthodoxies had not quite the currency they were to achieve in Bede's day.[12] Bede's story of the infamous goings-on at Coldingham, hints of immorality coupled with much reference to indulgent fine living (*EH* 4. 25), has a different pitch from Aldhelm's attenuated admonition:

Aldhelm's warnings against the dangers of self-adornment are obviously not, like Bede's story, a thinly-disguised polemic against the double monasteries, but his promulgation of the view that nuns *as a class* are liable to be guilty of decking themselves out fine, with all that that entails, erects a countervailing force to the willingness to accept them as comrades-in-arms in the service of God which is implicit in his *Miles Christi* metaphor. By giving currency to the view that women embody the temptations of the flesh, he effectively adds weight to orthodox pressures for the establishment of monastic separation.[13] (emphasis added)

The "pressures" here are Theodore's rulings (although equivocal) on the impermissibility of dual-sex houses,[14] and Hollis goes on to detail the tangle of contradictions Aldhelm's authorial stance seems to elicit, from deference to didacticism.[15] But it is a markedly different tangle from that of Bede, who may see immorality where there is hedonism or less,[16] and it is one conditioned by the contemporaneous interplay of ecclesiastical and secular authority. Hollis's pointed conclusions are worth quoting in full:

But of much greater underlying importance as a condition of the conversionary period determining Aldhelm's attitude to the nuns of Barking is the fact that at the time he wrote, the church in England, and hence its ecclesiastical hierarchy, had no automatic and inalienable hold on the lives, inner or outer, of its members. Its authority was far from absolute and unquestioned, and in so far as baptism and entry to a monastic order was not an act of free choice, the compulsions were secular ones. Aldhelm, even as a bishop, was a member of a ruling elite only in so far as he was connected by birth to the reigning house of Wessex. It is one view of the medieval monastic orders that the involvement of their members in secular affairs, and flagrant disregard of canonical injunctions or the rule of the order, represents decadence, whereas automatic deference and obedience bears witness to the quality of religious life and manifests the voluntariness of religious vocations. There seems to me to be a case to be made that the opposite holds true.[17]

Hollis evokes the complexity of authorizing forces, the same that give credence to, and entry into, the cultural symbolic. While the adorned woman of Aldhelm's text may be a sexual liability, we cannot dismiss the fact that she is also a woman of means, that class might prove as strong a conditioning agent for metaphor as gender, and that wealth and a degree of political influence compound with gender not only in Aldhelm's conception of audience, but also in our attempt to reconstruct it.

The female audience for the *De virginitate* must have been aristocratic, royal, and *very* intelligent, so critics argue, in order to comprehend, let alone aesthetically savor the intricacies of Aldhelm's Latin. The much touted brain power of the Barking nuns affirms a certain level of female monastic literacy and is often used to mark a high point for those who would claim a "golden age" for Anglo-Saxon women. When the library holdings of Barking are tested against the sources of the *De virginitate*, however, there may be less to celebrate. Hollis points out that Aldhelm's texts assume the nuns' familiarity with scriptural, exegetical, grammatical, and some secular texts, but not with the newer astronomical and computistical studies.[18] Such curtailed access to certain areas of study raises crucial questions about the nuns' relation to the new Latin learning brought by Theodore to Canterbury. The extent of the role (pastoral or contemplative) of the Barking women at a time of an increasing orthodoxy attendant upon that influx of Latinity needs qualification as we examine women's (rich aristocratic women's) relation to church hierarchy and authority in this period. Moreover, the Barking nuns' specific access to Latin literate modes must be seen in the context of a fluctuating pattern of Celtic, Roman, political, and regional alignments. The anonymous nun who writes to Bede for a commentary on the canticle of Habbakuk may have been differently or "better" educated; Benedicta Ward suggests that her request indicates that she came from a foundation that was "up to date in Roman liturgical practice" and excludes Barking because it apparently was not, reflecting instead Irish influence.[19]

Any implication of the Barking nuns' developing exclusion from full participation in the monastic avant garde must also be seen in tandem with the assumption of the text as deferential, as intellectual compliment, and—a more pressing disjunction—as *produced* by the specifics of female reception. Crucial here is Aldhelm's doctrinal flexibility in creating a new, more inclusive category of virginity—one that encompasses those who have been formerly married. His audience—widows, "divorced" women, and probably those who had simply left their husbands, preferring religious life—represented different approaches to chastity.[20] This major reconceptualization of the chaste female body places Aldhelm's text at a crossroads of legal and patristic tradition (Lapidge and Herren, pp. 52–57), one that intersects with issues of political expedience and the demands of family and patronage. (Aldhelm is avowedly related to one member of his audience, Osburg, and addresses by name one Cuthberg who had ostensibly rejected her husband in favor of monastic life.[21]) The shifting legal dynamics of land acquisition and retention are also implicated in Aldhelm's doctrinal innovation. The Church offered "an alternate form of protection" to widows *and* to their property—provided of course that they did not remarry.[22] Hollis calls attention to these sociocultural conditions of this text's production and its concommitant production of the female "virginal" body: "His (Aldhelm's) treatise is of particular interest in demonstrating the manner in which the numerical weight of formerly married monastic women served to mitigate the high valuation of female bodily intactness."[23]

If this supply and demand model holds up—the image of "weighty" women shaping Aldhelm's text as a "stable column" of patronage (Lapidge and Herren, p. 131) has a persuasive symmetry—how does it intersect with literary aspects of the text's production? On the one hand, we have a politically, ecclesiastically motivated text, and on the other a language most often read by modern critics as "literary." At this end of the spectrum, critics suspect that Aldhelm simply loved the sound of his Latin. Orchard argues that Aldhelm was above all a stylist, interested in the "telling and not in the tale," whose prose, "can be described as a triumph of form over content."[24] The prolixity and difficulty of Aldhelm's text invites a tangled critical response of celebration and dismissal, both of which intersect with the issue of audience. Aldhelm insists on a female audience, and Lapidge asserts that his text is not only doctrinally but structurally "determined by this audience of noble ladies-turned-nuns" (Lapidge and Herren, p. 52). Such a structure, however, remains buried beneath the inscrutable workings of Aldhelm's rhetorical wizardry. If by "structure" we include the ordering of Aldhelm's list of virgins, then this point is even more puzzling. There are considerably more male virgins than female (34 males—if one counts all three youths Shadrach, Meshach, and Abednego—and 22 females), whose stories have to be "read through" and digested first; no mean feat if we recall the sheer difficulty of reading this text. Aldhelm diverges from his likely source (Ambrose's *De virginibus ad Mar-*

cellinam) in placing men before women and then adding more men at the end
of his list (Lapidge and Herren, p. 56), a curious restructuring if occasioned by
his female readers. Aldhelm's order is traditional, in that it follows the general
sequence of salvation history (Old Testament, then New Testament) and an
equally traditional sexual ranking: "Having, therefore, completed in a cursory
fashion the examples of the masculine sex . . . and moving on gradually with
verbal footsteps to the equally distinguished personalities of the second sex"
(Lapidge and Herren, p.106). Aldhelm's understanding of "cursory" is relative,
of course, and the one generalization to be made about the difference in
narrative approach is, as we shall see, that bodily torture is a more developed
focus in the women's *exempla*. Lapidge asserts that "one looks in vain, therefore, for any structural principle informing the catalogue of virgins" other
than perhaps simple availability of texts (Lapidge and Herren, p. 57). How far
these aspects of narrative choice and organization are *produced* by a female
audience thus remains at issue; perhaps the best way to approach the prose *De
virginitate* is "with no demands for coherent structure or concise expression,
but with a preparedness to be transported by Aldhelm's *verbosa garrulitas*"
(Lapidge and Herren, p. 58). Lapidge here aptly begs the question of how to
determine the nuns' relation, as embodied readers, to Aldhelm's rhetoric.

As a "double" of the later poetic version, moreover, the prose *De virginitate* invites us to include the specifics of literary techniques (and their ideologies—Aldhelm studied with Theodore[25]) in our analysis of the processes by
which his female bodies are produced metaphorically for an audience largely
assumed to be female. When Aldhelm transforms his text into poetry (a
common enough exercise in the period) we are squarely up against the performative problem of the body as function and trace of patristic rhetoric.
And not just of patristic rhetoric. Contemporary stylistic analyses reproduce
Aldhelm's own containment of the metaphorical female body. Orchard, for
example, comparing the prose and poetic accounts of Thecla and Eulalia,
notes that the poetic version offers such a "rich display of rhetorical (and
largely verse-derived) pyrotechnics" that it "is perhaps inevitable that the
rather thin narrative content of the passage is all but submerged."[26] The "thin
narrative content" here is the torture and rending of Thecla's virginal body:
"wicked men sought to torture her female spine with such exertion that each
bleeding bone in turn might be emptied of marrow, if it were possible."[27]
Calling attention to these gory descriptions as functions of poetic technique,
Orchard then dismisses them as "composed of a number of quite commonplace and scarcely specific details."[28]

Situated between the apparent poles of rhetorical tradition and historical

determination—between the commonplaces of patristic rhetoric and the "realities" of and for the Barking women—the *De virginitate* presents a complex
challenge to a reader interested in hypothesizing the self of the woman reading
about the body in the text, in tracing the entry of the female body into the
patristic symbolic, or perhaps less ambitiously, in *identifying* a body, any body.
Moreover, although disparities between textual and "real" bodies might indicate profound difference, before we try to find the body in the text it is worth
recalling how the body is indeed powerfully present in and central to the
learned reading process. This not only demands the profound integration of
mind, body, and text, but also evokes the inevitably alimentary nature of the
act of reading as it engages the reading eye and the ruminating body without
the text. In an examination of how the Anglo-Saxons read, M. B. Parkes
stresses such an integrated reading experience. In scriptural interpretation
"knowledge of the word of God had to be explored and felt . . . so that it be
stored deep within the senses," and patristic reading tradition encouraged
what we might now call total identification—"the fathers had also emphasized
the need for readers to recognize themselves in a text, and to apply it to their
personal situations."[29] To our broad enquiry about the nature of this communication—just what *did* the bishop say to the abbess—we might add the corresponding question of how did she hear it, or physically process it: as a
"chewing creature" in the tradition of Augustine and Bede's commentaries on
ruminative reading, how might she digest Aldhelm's verbal feast?[30]

Even a brief look at its specific images and metaphors reinforces the
complexity of the processes by which the *De virginitate* performs a female
Christian subject. Having initially praised the nuns' intellects and the "subtle
sequence" of their discourse (Lapidge and Herren, p. 59), Aldhelm launches
his preamble with a wholesale removal of female agency and body. He addresses the nuns as "adoptive daughters of regenerative grace brought forth
from the fecund womb of ecclesiastical conception through the seed of the
spiritual Word" (pp. 59–60). Aldhelm then suggests that the nuns think of
their *minds* as male athletes, and the exercise of learning Scripture as a wrestling routine. As they are exhorted to greater intellectual effort, Aldhelm fixes
their (and our) gaze on male bodies, panting, heaving with physical exertion,
covered with grease, "sweating with the sinuous writhings of their flanks" (p.
60). But these male, intensely physical activities are spiritual metaphors; they
indicate a complex exchange of outer for inner, stripping the metaphor of any
body—male or female. The strenuous exercise of the mind is the point, the
higher goal.

After "traversing the spacious racecourses of the Scriptures" (p. 61) as defeminized and disembodied mental athletes, the nuns are enjoined to see themselves as bees, full of embodied desire and appetite; they "struggle eagerly to fill the greedy receptacles of their stomachs," their thighs and hips are heavy with the "fertile booty" of scriptural gathering (p. 61). They consume; they give birth, fertilizing in the same manner as the Church, "through the chaste seed of the Word" (p. 62); their bodies, in a metaphoric sleight of orifices, make "honeyed sweetness" (p. 63); and they unquestioningly follow the orders of the "king" bee (p. 63). The bees' spiritually controlled alimentation exemplifies "spontaneous acceptance of devout servitude" (p. 63), an ultimate appetite suppression that is both physically involuntary and actively desired. The mixed metaphor gathers momentum, or rather spins out of control, via the attendant and increasing obscurity of any body.

Later the nuns are reconfigured as soldiers fighting with "muscular energy"—their bodily intactness displayed upon their chests as the protective "breastplate" of virginity (p. 68)—against the serpent of gluttony who vomits "the pestilent poison of trangression" (p. 69). Interestingly, though confusingly, bodily excrescences in this introductory preamble contrast with (or perhaps parallel) the many scatological images in the list of exemplary virgins, where outer bodily and inner spiritual processes are linked in a series of continual metaphoric elision, focus, and exchange. Chrysanthus (one of the male saints) is literally soaked in "reeking urine," which is changed into nectar by the power of faith (p. 98); Agnes scorns bodily adornment as if it were "the yellow-brown scum of the reeking sewer" (p. 112); and while Christina is literally oppressed by the "stinking filth of the dungeon" (p. 114), Eulalia's rejection of marriage enables her to escape from the "filth of the carnal sewer"(p. 113).

One looks in vain for any consistency or fixity of metaphorical referents. What kind of body is produced here? Sometimes you see it, sometimes you don't, and sometimes it is male. Sometimes it eats Scripture and excretes honey, sometimes it gives birth to words. Many of these images, of course, have long literary and historical traditions that warrant more detailed investigation than possible here. Figuring the female as male, as *miles Christi*, is a familiar means of allowing women into the heavenly community; the metaphorical metamorphoses of birth and its necessary femaleness are stunning in their power and variety in patristic writing in general; the bee is a commonly used figure of virginity.[31] We are clearly in the realm of the strikingly unoriginal, of the topos. Aldhelm's much vaunted *verbosa garrulitas* poses the unremitting presence of repetition as an ideological and rhetorical problem, as well as a physical challenge to the reader. This problem becomes especially apparent when that which is repeated, that which is commonplace, that which is "merely rhetorical," is a body in pain.

Aldhelm's list of female virgins, which, as we have noted, come *after* the male *exempla*, present the reader with a series of tortured, exposed women's bodies. Male virgins certainly experience a wide variety of tortures—burning, boiling, drowning, flogging, racking, immersion in a cauldron of tallow and pitch, for example. Female virgins share these experiences, but their bodies are exposed, via narrative technique, rather more and rather longer than male ones. The violation and destruction of the female body entails the added narrative dimension of exhibition, sexuality, and the threat of rape. The displayed body is inescapably female. We cannot forget what Christina looks like, for example, even though it is her mind that did not "shrink from the stinking filth of the dungeon; nor did it fear the rock tied to her neck and immersed in the waves of the sea; nor did it weaken when sticks were cruelly flogging her tender limbs; nor did the disfigurement of her pretty head, even though her golden hair was shaved off and she was dragged shorn in public, influence the state of her mind" (p. 114). This image of shaming and violation, an oblique description or intimation of rape, whether or not it carries the potential titillatory force of other medieval accounts of ravished maidens, focuses the gaze as forcibly on the violation present in the text as on that which hovers as an unrealized narrative possibility.[32] Consider the following scene from Thecla's life, where so much is left unelaborated:

Brought in front of the cages of the theatrical arena by the bloody bands of executioners striving zealously to deprive her of the prize of her virginity, with Christ granting his protection she nonetheless kept her token of chastity unbroken and the precious mantle of her virginity undestroyed among the fierce roaring of lions and the ferocious jaws of hungry bears. (p. 113)

Or consider Dulcitius's "lustful eyes" as he contemplates the bodies of Chionia, Irene, and Agape, whose nakedness remains graphically unrevealed in spite of his best efforts:

he ascended again the lofty tribunal seat, so that aroused by the filthiness of his disgusting lechery and inflamed by the fires of titillating enjoyment, he could feast his lustful eyes on the holy virgins stripped of their own robes; but the garments of their apparel, tugged at, one by one, by impious hands, could not be removed from the holy limbs at all. (p. 118)

The rhetorical elaboration Orchard notes in the later poetic version of the *De virginitate* further intensifies this narrative "gaze." Compare, for example, the terms of Lucy's martyrdom, where "poetry" equals more, and more sexualized, violence. A closer examination of first the prose and then the poetic Latin texts points up this increase:

Igitur beata Lucia salvo pudoris signaculo et consummato vitae curriculo gloriosum martirii triumphum meruit, dum mucrone confossa maluit purpureum sanguinem fundere quam pretiosam pudicitiam perdere.[33]

(Therefore the Blessed Lucia having preserved the seal of her chastity and having finished the course of her life, was found worthy of the glorious triumph of a martyr, since she preferred to spill out her crimson blood, having been pierced by the sword, rather than to lose her precious virginity.) (Lapidge and Herren, p. 109)

Lucy is pierced by the point of a sword ("mucrone confossa") : "mucro" has no especial sexual overtones—its semantic field centers primarily on sharpness. The color and quality of the blood she sheds ("purpureum sanguinem") is associated with battlefield violence. Although we might note the active voice ("maluit," "she preferred") to spill out or pour forth ("fundere") her blood, "fundere" can also connote giving birth. When Lucy reappears in verse, however, the change is striking, and worth examining closely:

Tunc igitur morbo mentis cruciatus acerbo
Non tulit opprobrium iudex a virgine factum
Candida sed rigido violavit viscera ferro:
Purpureus cruor extemplo de carne manavit.[34]

(Then, however, the prosecutor [i.e. Paschasius], who was troubled by a terrible disorder of the mind, could not bear the shame which had been done to him by the maiden, and he violated her fair inwards with a rigid sword, and dark red blood immediately flowed from her flesh.) (Lapidge and Rosier, p. 143)

In the poetic version her tormentor plays a more active role. Paschasius is seen as tortured ("cruciatus"), his troubled condition ("morbo mentis") connoting weakness, vice, and sexual perversion. He cannot bear ("tulit" also connoting pregnancy) the shame the virgin brings down on him, because of his failure, possibly sexual, to take this bride away from Christ (line 1817). Lucy's entrails ("viscera") are disembodied, radiant, white, shining ("candida") when violated by Paschasius, the verb "violare" clearly associated with sexual defilement and pollution. In such a context, it becomes difficult to avoid the sexual aspect of the rigid sword ("rigido ferro"). Lucy is reembodied in the next line when she sheds a different kind of blood, "cruor," the clotted blood associated with wounds and menstrual flow and an indication of her body as shamed. This criss-crossing of bodily signification at once transfers shame, sexuality, and defilement from the tortured body to the torturer, while retaining the body of the female saint as a site of signification and a public spectacle.

These brief examples culled from a much longer text raise the issue of excess. Aldhelm's text is excessively long, excessively violent, excessively rhetorical, excessively repetitious, and excessively difficult to read. In a contemporary classroom, the excess of sexualized violence spills over into the realm of the erotic, homoerotic, and/or pornographic; students find it shocking, "voyeuristic." As we attempt to follow the nuns' "gaze," questions of who is the voyeur and of whose body is on display begin to unravel contemporary theories of the field of vision. In the examples quoted above, how "visible" is the shorn Christina's beauty? How do we "see" the exposed bodies of Chionia, Irene, and Agape—through Dulcitius's "lustful eyes"? Does Aldhelm focus on Lucy or on her torturer, Paschasius? In the quotation from Aldhelm's account of Agnes's martyrdom that begins this chapter, do we gaze at her naked body in the brothel or do we gaze at her gazing outward upon angelic faces? Where, indeed, are the Barking nuns directed to look and where do they wish to look? Faced with this multiplicity of angles of vision, contemporary theories that simplify the dynamics of looking into that of a controlling subject producing a controlled object fail to address Aldhelm's particular brand of eroticism, homoeroticism, or scopophilia—if any of these categories indeed apply—and the complex process by which these bodies are both constructed and elided. Such theories identify sites of resistance and difference in the historical text; they do not allow us to follow the nuns as they read, to reconstruct a body through Aldhelm's dense layers of metaphor, through the continual metaphoric exchanges between outer and inner.

Other aspects of our own response as readers, however, might find more resonance with that of the nuns of Barking, specifically that of the difficulty of the reading process itself. Aldhelm can be spectacularly boring. His texts *are* repetitious, over and above the repetition occasioned by borrowing from and reworking classical and patristic sources. By the time the third or fourth or tenth virgin has been saved, burned, racked, rent, or horribly maimed, something happens to one's mode of reading. One begins to theorize to keep awake. Or perhaps in self defense. The overpowering use of repetition, the horror and terror that it dulls, the violence and repression that it elides, begin to resonate with another metaphor—Judith Butler's "citation" as the process of identity and gender formation, as the emergent citing of the self.[35] While there is no way to assess the nuns' aesthetic judgment of Aldhelm's text (we have only Aldhelm's word that they implored him to compose for them), we can still postulate the mental and possibly physical level of difficulty of reading. Aldhelm's didacticism here presupposes a specific volitional subject, or group of subjects, and the difficulty of his text, of its interpretation, can be placed in the context of a process of containment, direction, and control—in short as part of the Christian rhetorical disciplining of the educable subject.

Aldhelm's Christian rhetoric and Butler's cultural process of citation suggest how the text performs a female subject by producing, directing, and containing a female body, with the important distinction that Butler's cited body is reproduced without reference to religious belief systems. In identifying this embodied subject, however, we are faced with a contradiction between an overt denial of the female body in tension with an equally overt scrutiny of it. Aldhelm's rhetorical strategy does not quite succeed, as the examples of Lucy and Thecla graphically demonstrate. Such translation of the body into metaphor repeatedly poses the ironic problem of what to do with the historical, sealed body that is still female and sexual, and will not go away—the "real" woman. The body worries, haunts the text, in ways specific to late seventh-century England. The body that haunts Aldhelm's text is decidedly unsealed; it has sexual and material presence; it is rich, married at least once, well connected; it has social if not political authority; it may labor strenuously; it may possess its own athletic grace.[36] And it is not young. As the ostensible motivation for Aldhelm's "rhetorical pyrotechnics," this body is the site of literary invention and literate signification, but the presence of this old, rich, sexed body occasions its own absence. Aldhelm's text becomes another site of disappearance, similar to that of his riddles discussed in Chapter 2. The body's meaning and functions are contained, produced as textual effects that *depend* upon that body's absence in order to signify in the rhetorical system of the *De virginitate*—impossible as that may be to systematically characterize. But the difference between the rhetorical operations of the riddles and of the *De virginitate* is marked by the remarkable specificity of the latter; those specifics of motivation and reception that we may discover substantially increase the complexity of the performance of the subject and of the terms of its disappearance, bringing us once again to the edge of paradox when we raise the question of audience.

What *did* this bishop say to the abbess? We know a good deal, in relative terms, about the readers of the *De virginitate*, but trying to reconcile the input and output of this particular literary interaction raises more questions than it answers. What do these women get from this text is one question, and evokes those ever-present imponderables of aesthetics and interpretation and their intersection with belief, but *how* they might arrive at or internalize its meaning is far more puzzling. If we posit their presence, or the body, as a point of departure for the rhetorical neccessity for their absence on a theoretical level, what does that do for the practical analogue of the text as deferential/complimentary/edifying, presented by an intelligent (if somewhat verbose) cleric eager to please his aristocratic, discerning, female audience? Moreover, perhaps this is the most pointed moment to recall the possibility that his text was actively solicited by the nuns. At the end of the prose *De virginitate*, Aldhelm mentions his intention to write a poetic version, with the provision that the nuns solicit him as assiduously as they did for the prose one: "but that you deign to stimulate (me) with just as many repeated letters written as you were good enough to resolutely elicit the preceding text of this little book" (Lapidge and Herren, p. 131).

Returning to the concept of the rhetorical performance of a Christian subject, what this text produces is absence, a crushing and total absence in that it conjures a body metaphorized out of physical existence with the aid of the reading subject's effort, imagination and intellect. In one sense, then, Aldhelm's compliment is profoundly ironic, if not paradoxical; his text annihilates those selves which prompt/produce it, possibly actively request it. To say that surely those Barking women were smarter or at least more self-interested than that, that such cooptation of the heart and mind must be apparent at some level, and that coercion is surely experienced as such, is perhaps to underestimate the power of Christian rhetoric to perform its function and to create a subject. It is also an oversimplification, and contemporary wishful thinking. The text remains at a crossroads of intention and reception, and its peculiar dynamic of interdependent contradictions must complicate and enrich our reading of the female body with, at least, the attendant factors of class, age, and the masculinization of literacy—just a few of the specificities of historical difference it engages.

While Aldhelm's text can function as a means of asking questions about a particular group of women at a moment in time, and can elucidate the historicized instance of the embodied Christian subject, it may also participate in, even shape, a historical trajectory within the Anglo-Saxon period. Both versions of the *De virginitate* were much reproduced; Ehwald lists 21 codices for the prose, and 20 for the poetic text.[37] The immense popularity of the poetic *De virginitate*, its status as a "curriculum" text in England and on the Continent, and its repeated copying and circulation into the twelfth century are evidence of masculine clerical practice of endlessly glossing an arcane language which, by the end of the period, monastic women either could not read or could not access. One important complicating factor here, however, and an addendum to our earlier reminder of monastic women's complicity in the processes of their own disappearance within the symbolic, is the contribution of educated churchwomen who practiced their literary and literate skills often by imitation of patristic sources. As we noted in Chapter 1, the great monastic scriptoria were centers for the creation and reproduction of the cultural record of our period; churchwomen contributed, often ably and with artistry, to the production of the means of their own erasure. While Aldhelm praises the "extremely subtle sequence" (Lapidge and Herren, p. 59) of the writings of Abbess Hildelith, the principal devotee of the prose *De virginitate*, later female monastics would learn Latin verse technique by following the formulae laid down by Aldhelm. Fifty or so years later, Leoba, for example, reproduces such verse techniques, reproduced for her in turn by her teacher Edburga.[38] Thus one trajectory of disappearance, as it is suggested by Aldhelm's rhetorical mapping, is sustained in small part, and at an early stage, by monastic women themselves, but eventually wholly maintained by patristic literate modes.

The body may be already fully textualized when it is "read" (or perhaps even reproduced) by the Barking nuns, but the trajectory of the text within literate, disseminative modes suggests a deeper cultural textualization, where the body recedes ever further into the means of its representation, and its entry into the cultural symbolic is mediated by changing levels of containment. The female monastic body recedes within the cloister and within the literate trajectory of the text, such that the modes of its disappearance in the earlier text offer not only a recognizable continuity but also a graduated contrast to those in later texts. As we continue to examine the relation of representation to referentiality, the apparent paradox of smart old women accustomed to power (read the Barking nuns) countenancing their own containment, even becoming complicit in it, develops into the different complexities and exigencies of Christian rhetoric and its later hagiographic performance of the female subject. While we will look at some various metaphoric trajectories in the next chapter, here we continue to use the rhetorical coordinates of Aldhelm's extraordinary text to take us through to the latter part of the period.

Female Saints, Female Subjects?

They dragged then the maiden to the harlot's house, but she at once met there an angel of God shining, such that no man was able to look on her or touch her because of that mighty light, for that house all shone like the sun in day, and the more eagerly they gazed on her, the more their eyes were dazzled. (Agnes, Ælfric's *Lives of Saints*)

Aldhelm's considerable intellectual status in Anglo-Saxon England leads Orchard to comment that "no other figure was influential for so long," in an assessment of Aldhelm's impact on key figures within the English Church such as Boniface, Bede, Aediluulf, Frithegod, and Wulfstan of Winchester.[39] But the female body, which we argue is so much the elusive focus of his text in the seventh century, recedes within the monastic schools and within its apparatus of *grammatica*, especially glossing, in later West Saxon England, in marked contrast to the Barking women's earlier active role in production and reception. "The study of Aldhelm's prose . . . must have been reserved for the intellectual exercises of the more advanced students," points out Mechthild Gretsch in her analysis of the glossing traditions for this later period.[40] In these later centuries, however, evidence for religious women's learning and influence within and beyond the cloisters changes dramatically. The Benedictine Reform brings with it a tightening of monastic practices, both male and female, and a new emphasis on celibacy. The age of the double monastery is long gone. While some areas such as Winchester (where Æthelwold refounded Nunnaminster) retain their influence in areas of royal and ecclesiastical power, others are left unreformed or simply die out. By contrast, male monasticism and its partner—the ruling dynasty—increase their purchase on the Church and thereby on the social imaginary.[41] For these reasons, the tenth century is an important place to trace the historical trajectory of Christian rhetoric and its subjects. It is reasonable to ask, therefore, what happens to the performance of female sanctity and its relation to the constructions of Christian subjectivity in this later period.

The evidence will yield no easy answers, but raises important issues for future research. On the one hand, cult production, including that of the royal female cults, increases sharply. On the other, such production is maintained by the Church, centered on the Latin reforms at Winchester and other key sites of the Benedictine Reforms.[42] A document like the *Regularis concordia* witnesses the importance attached to the reform of female as well as male religious practices, and testifies to a royal division of authority, with the queen in titular charge of the nuns while the king assumes titular control of the monks.[43] The *Regularis concordia* thus provides a clear mandate for the queen's role in female monasticism, and strict separation of the sexes indeed characterizes Æthelwold's establishment or refounding of the great religious houses. How far queens were able to take up their mandate as outlined in the *Regularis Concordia*, however, is an open question. Like other royal women and men in the tenth and eleventh centuries, Queen Emma (wife of Æthelred and Cnut), is a generous patron of the Church, but Stafford points out that nunneries themselves "looked increasingly anomalous" in the reform and post-reform period.[44] Barking itself was refounded as a foundation for Benedictine nuns, but its history in these centuries, like that of Ely, hardly puts it in the forefront of reformist endeavor for female religious.[45]

According to the Latin *Life of Æthelwold*, Æthelwold refounds Ely as a monastery, ironically, in part because of his great love ("pro dilectione tantarum") of Æthelthryth and her saintly sisters, while his reestablishment of Nunnaminster, praised in the *Life*, supplants the earlier foundation by Ealhswith, Alfred's wife, on land she herself had owned.[46] In the conclusion to his account of Edgar's establishment of monasteries, Æthelwold targets abbesses in general, urging their loyalty and obedience to divine governance, and—a more pointed comment—warning them not to alienate the estates of the foundation.[47] Æthelwold here touches on one of the best-known aspects of the reform—its consolidation of monastic wealth for the Church and, because of the royal patronage of the reform, for the ruling families.

The *Life of Æthelwold* in fact makes much of Edgar's financial support for the refounding of Ely, for example, and Æthelwold himself is described as "lavishly" ("affluentissime") endowing it with land.[48] The male character of such corporate, officially inalienable, endowments and the prominence of the reformed monasteries as centers of intellectual and religious achievement is not in doubt, although the success of the reform in dispensing with family foundations (held responsible for the earlier decay of the monasteries) is limited. Despite the new rhetoric and the repeated injunctions against the alienation of monastic land, many foundations, including the great reformed houses, continue to be firmly associated with local and royal families.[49] Aristocratic women too are generous in their economic support of the reform (though the numbers of women so doing are relatively slender). In Chapter 3 we pointed to the pattern of aristocratic female gifts associated with reform establishments in the charter evidence, as well as Edgar's support for female religious. Later in the period, Queen Emma, whether on her own or with Cnut, is a conspicuous patron of religious foundations and of clerics and an avid collector of relics.[50] As in the case of the Barking women, then, wealth and class are prominent elements in any analysis of female monasticism, but this later evidence is differently complex. Against the obvious wealth flowing into, and retained by, the reformed houses (itself an important condition for their preeminence as centers for learning and the arts), we place this more diffuse pattern of female—largely aristocratic and secular—influence and patronage. Significantly, the parallel discourse about the moral importance of wealth, evidenced in Ælfric's work, for example, pays no attention to the ethical situation that rich women might pose for a Christian society; the rich, in Ælfric's writings, are implicitly male.[51] The contribution of women—rich, aristocratic, secular, or religious—to the English Benedictine reform is at best peripheral. Put another way, there is no *De virginitate* for the nunneries in this period.

Indeed, despite the evidence for Emma's enthusiastic patronage of ecclesiastical culture at the end of the period, there is scant evidence for any revival of female religious learning.[52] Yet the tenth century also sees the opening up of the new domain of vernacular literacy in both poetry and prose, clearly associated with the achievements of the reform. Poems such as *Elene* and *Judith* testify to a continued interest in female sanctity (and Elene is herself represented as a powerful, wealthy, and learned woman), although speculations about the audience for such works remain just that.[53] By contrast, the writing of Ælfric, masspriest and abbot, and the related anonymous vernacular homilists stand at a clearer intersection between the monastery and the secular Church, religious ideology and social practices (including patronage), vernacular literacy and Latin learning. As is well known, Ælfric is one of the few vernacular religious writers of this period for whom some parameters of audience can be fixed, however loosely.[54]

Ælfric's *Lives of Saints* (c. 998) may be read as the vernacular equivalent to Aldhelm's *De virginitate* despite the fact that his interest in sanctity is broader than Aldhelm's focus on virginity. Indeed, Aldhelm's direct influence on Ælfric is negligible.[55] Only in the vernacular prose of Wulfstan the homilist do we find a similar avoidance of the kinds of florid Latin style popularized by Aldhelm and revived by figures such as Wulfstan of Winchester and Byrhtferth in the tenth century.[56] Ælfric's major sources for his *Lives of Saints* are not Aldhelmian, but follow instead the traditions of Latin passionals, exemplified in his use of the Cotton-Corpus legendary.[57] Against Aldhelm's notoriously difficult Latin prose, then, stands Ælfric's English rhythmical prose, justly famed for its clarity; against Aldhelm's virtuoso display of classical and patristic reading stands Ælfric's careful, scholarly editing and translation of the Latin homiliaries and passionals of the Church fathers; and against Aldhelm's female patrons stand Ælfric's aristocratic lay patrons, Æthelweard and his son, Æthelmær, both closely associated with Ælfric's monasteries at Cerne Abbas and Eynsham.[58] The only firmly identifiable audience for this vernacular passional is masculine, upper-class, and lay.

Ælfric's Preface to the Lives of Saints, however, makes it plain that his intentions are not merely to satisfy the pious needs of his patrons. Rather, the collection makes the passions of the saints read in the monasteries available to a wider Christian audience outside the cloister. Ælfric's most explicit intention is to refortify a "failing faith" (Skeat, Ælfric's Lives of Saints, 1, p. 3). However limited the evidence for reception, it is premature to assume that, in dedicating the Lives of Saints to Æthelweard and Æthelmær, Ælfric's audience comprised only men.[59] Ælfric generally symbolizes his audience in terms of rank and state (lay or religious, chaste or married, for example). Gender functions as a marker within such categories, where the familiar hierarchy of the sexes—the female defined in relation to the male—prevails.[60] While we have no way of knowing whether individual women read the collection, the evidence suggests that women as a group were figured within Ælfric's conventional hierarchy of the sexes; "men" in this traditional patriarchal sense includes women as well. Crucial also to Ælfric's conception of his subjects is access to vernacular literacy. Writing in English, Ælfric aims his works at an audience larger than that for Latin works, but vernacularity remains heavily dominated in this period by the clergy and the upper ranks of lay society. As in the case of the De virginitate, class and literacy are dominant factors in our assessment of the construction of the Christian subject and of the role of gender in this period, here differently inflected by the use of English and by a late West Saxon audience. Ælfric's English style contests the kinds of domains (Latinate, explicitly ecclesiastical) that Aldhelm's characterizes throughout the period. Vernacularity thereby redefines the social imaginary of late Anglo-Saxon England.

Ælfric's conventional symbolization of his audience (which echos Aldhelm's structuring of the De virginitate in terms of first male and then female virgins) helps explain why Ælfric's Lives of Saints includes a substantial number of female saints (there are none in his earlier Catholic Homilies).[61] These female Lives offer a richly multivalent group, which can be read in terms of the traditional themes of Aldhelm's martyred virgins who resist marriage and devote their lives to God (Skeat I, VI–IX, Agnes, Agatha, Lucy), but who also practice chaste marriage (I, XX, Æthelthryth; II, XXXIV, Cecilia) and cross-dress (I, II, Eugenia). Other themes also emerge: the doubly married Æthelthryth, the only female English saint in the collection, is paired with the other male saint, Swithun (I, XXI), popularized at Winchester; Agnes, Constantia (I, VIIb), Agatha, and Lucy offer a conventional group dictated by the liturgy, which trace a history of female Christian relationships and influence; and the spiritual marriages of Cecilia and Æthelthryth find their echoes in the *Lives* of Julian and Basilissa (I, IV), and Chrysanthus and Daria (II, XXXV). The two anonymous *Lives* interpollated into the collection offer further dimensions— Mary of Eygpt (II, XXIIIb), discussed further in the next section, is the only old female body and redeemed fallen woman in the entire collection, while that of Euphrosyne (II, XXXIII) complements Eugenia in its emphasis on cross-dressing within same-sex monasteries.[62] These and other similar thematic patterns exploring many different routes to chastity suggest that identification across as well as within the sexes is encouraged. Despite Ælfric's dedication of the collection to his male patrons, and despite the fact that the *Life* of Æthelthryth concludes with an exemplum illustrating the value of spiritual marriage for men (I, XX, pp. 440–41), what appears to be at stake is not simply gender identification but the overarching dynamics of chastity, within which gendered roles are subjected and (re)performed.

In consequence, the close though conflicted relation between the sign of sanctity and its gendered referent evident, however complexly, in Aldhelm's *De virginitate* disappears. In its place is an increased emphasis on the iconic meaning of the saint's religious practices for a wider audience. For such an audience, what matters more than sex or gender—at least ostensibly—is the network of practices and ideologies centered on chastity. Ælfric's collection differs from Aldhelm's in its interest in narrative, speech, action, and relationships (Ælfric's female saints quite simply speak to others, both male and female, far more than Aldhelm's). Given Ælfric's interest in narrative, in the story of the saint, practices of reiteration and citation shift.[63] The familiar repetition of set scenes of torture, death, and attempted seduction are accompanied by set speeches of resistance and spiritual insight together with an increased narrative interest in devotional acts. Citation thereby produces the saint as an idealized subject whose will and whose faith, however much contested, remain resolutely uncontestable. Agnes (who resists the brothel scene that begins this section) stands amidst a burning fire, unharmed, her faith intact: "Ic bletsige ðe fæder bodigendlic god. þæt ic þurh fyr unforht to ðe faran mot. þæt þæt ic gelyfde þæt ic geseo. ðæt þæt ic gehihte. þæt ic hæbbe nu" ("I bless you, Father, proclaimed God, that I am able to pass through fire to you, without fear, that which I believed I see, that which I hoped for, I now have," Skeat I, VII, p. 182). This increased role played by the female voice and its direct relation to the tortured female body are another area for future research.[64] Such *Lives* are indeed intended to revive a failing faith. Fully idealized as icons, female saints have their referents in the abstracts of belief, which the individual saint renders visible by her acts, offering models of willing faith for the audience.[65] In this regard, the saint herself matters paradoxically less than her performance of sanctity.

Without the dense layers of metaphoric citing of the body found in Aldhelm (Ælfric's use of metaphors is notably restrained in general), the level of violence in these later female *Lives*, whether perpetrated on the saint or resisted by her, diminishes, perhaps sanitized for a wider, vernacular audience. Ælfric's narrative does not dwell on Lucy's death, for example. Describing Lucy wounded by a sword "þæt hire wand se innoð ut" ("so that her innards fell out," Skeat I, IX, p. 216), Ælfric resists the indulgences of the Aldhelmian accounts discussed above. Ælfric offers instead the spectacle of an immutable Lucy, bound hand and foot, who cannot be dragged to her brothel, "ac heo næs astyrod. ac stod swa swa munt" ("and she was not moved, but stood as firm as a mountain," p. 216). Similarly, the specter of sexual aggression that hovers so strongly over Aldhelm's saints is more firmly controlled. Agnes's own brothel scene lacks the "savagery of raging sexual desire" (Lapidge and Herren, p. 112), which Aldhelm emphasizes as much as the divine light that miraculously conceals her naked body, but concentrates more directly on the miracle itself, its resistance to visualization, and the reformation of the brothel that it prompts (Skeat I, VII, pp. 176–81). In another example where we might expect a higher degree of narrative interest in sexuality, Ælfric's account of Æthelthryth's remarkable chastity passes swiftly over Ecgfrith's attempted seduction in a couple of lines (I, XX, pp. 432–33) onto her freedom from "filth." Æthelthryth's cleanliness—her chastity—is literalized by accounts of her ordered life and body, her fasting, and her acts of washing, with their echo of the service of Christ memorialized on Maundy Thursday (pp. 434–35).

Such curtailment of violent and/or sexualized episodes in the Ælfrician corpus cannot be read simply as an index of his famed "abbreviated" style, but suggest instead an increased interest in controlling and defining the female subject and her body in relation to the unfailing will of the idealized Christian subject.[66] Ælfric's female saints still suffer, although the purpose of their suffering is more firmly and more often articulated. As icons of chastity, these saints remain resolutely female, however much they invite cross-gendered identification. Chastity remains tied to femininity, and the female body provides the vehicle for transcendence and transformation. For all Ælfric's innovations in the developing discourse of chastity, certain conventional emphases about female sanctity persist, as do the paradoxes they produce. Paramount among these is a certain nervousness about the power of the gaze and the knowledge it yields. We never see the tortured body of Lucy, and all the female *Lives* appear defended against the unregulated gaze: Agnes's nudity is miraculously concealed (I, VII, pp. 178–79); Agatha's breast, cut off by her torturers, is miraculously healed in a blaze of light that prevents any gaze on her new, spiritual, wholeness (I, VIII, pp. 202–5); and Mary of Eygpt, in an anonymous work that outperforms any of Ælfric's for its excessive interest in "unspeakable" vices of the fallen woman, engages in a delicate dance with Zosimus to avoid any sight of her naked, aged body (II, XXIIIb, pp. 14–17).

Such a high level of defense against the visible body necessarily invites its return. Mary's old, nude, and starved body haunts the text in much the same way that Eugenia's bodily chastity, "mannum uncuð" ("unknown to man," I, II, pp. 38–39) is in fact immediately made known to a man (her father) so as to prove her identity and chastity. We discuss the significance of Mary's body further in the next section, but more relevant here is the one body explicitly made available for viewing by both Bede and Ælfric—Æthelthryth's clean, chaste, and dead body. In the episode from Bede, Æthelthryth's explanation of the tumor on her neck follows the witnessing of the healed wound by her physician, Cynefrith, as the dead body is prepared for its translation into the church by Sexburg sixteen years after her death (*EH* 4. 19). Æthelthryth, we recall, interprets the tumor as divine punishment for vanity. The tumor is, in other words, exchanged for the gold and pearls she used to wear on her neck as a girl, and the miraculous translation of a material sign (the necklaces) for a divine one (the healed tumor) is revealed at another moment of translation— that of the body into the church. Metaphoric "translatio" and actual translation are simultaneous in Bede's narrative.[67] Ælfric, however, modifies Bede's account. Æthelthryth's explanation of her tumor and its lancing by Cynefrith is moved to before her death (Skeat I, XX, pp. 434–37), and the subsequent witnessing of the healed wound at her translation is accordingly much abbreviated (pp. 438–39). While Ælfric's reordering of the episode from Bede has a certain narrative logic, it lessens the powerful conflation of what amounts in Bede to two translations of Æthelthryth's body present in the same narrative instance. At the same time, however, what is at stake in both accounts and perhaps permits the viewing of this particular body is not any sexual valency, but the incorporation of material wealth, symbolized by the necklaces, into a spiritual economy, symbolized by the tumor and its healing. We recall here the many ways in which female aristocratic wealth and display were coopted for the Church in our discussion of Barking Abbey and Aldhelm's *De virginitate*, but note that Ælfric in this later era simply attaches less symbolic significance (or rather cultural capital) to the wealth of women in his moral discourses about wealth and power (discussed above).

However different the configurations of representation and referentiality between the Ældhelmian and Ælfrician corpus, the symbolic chaste body remains the firmly female site upon which cultural conflicts about the gaze are played out. Both groups of texts evoke imagined and unimaged violence on the female body, which is the occasion for a continual redirection and re-disciplining of the Christian will. Such complex relations between the female saint, her body, the conventions of the Christian subject with its disciplining of the will that are adduced from her narrative, and the dynamics of the regulated gaze merit further investigation. Indeed, they provide evidence for a subjectivity at the heart of Christianity, one that is realized in specific cultural circumstances.

Seeing Women: Mary of Egypt (Or, What *Did* Zosimus See?)

Eadige beoð þa clæn-heortan. forðan þe hi god geseoð (Skeat II, XXIIIB, p. 4, lines 40–41, cf. Matthew 5: 8)

(Blessed are the pure in heart, for they shall see God)

The Old English *Mary of Egypt* develops our conversation about the nature of Christian subjectivity, the female saintly body, the dynamics of the gaze, and the acquisition of Christian forms of knowing through dominant patterns of clerical reading explored more generally above. In its account of the conversion ("gehwyrfednysse," p. 1, line 1) of the penitent Mary and Zosimus's visionary apprehension of her, the Old English text subtly amplifies the relation of seeing to knowing, the visual to the visionary, beyond that of its Anglo-Latin source.[68] This relation, which is not immediately self-evident (at least not to Zosimus), posits that seeing—both physical sight and spiritual insight—and knowing are ultimately unified through the work of belief. Mary and Zosimus acquire apprehension and insight through spiritual labor, whether penitential (in the case of Mary) or ascetic (in the case of Zosimus). The spiritual work entailed by this vernacular *Life*—the struggle to understand the divine—recalls the sheer labor of comprehension of the Barking nuns demanded by Aldhelm's *De virginitate*. Of equal importance is that this labor is in fact an effort to understand the presence of one old, naked woman, Mary, by the monk, Zosimus. We analyze this text in detail, therefore, to ask just how the body functions in this particular work of belief.

To understand the connection between (literal) seeing and spiritual knowing is also to make sense of the twofold didactic message of the text.[69] Conversion of those who have devoted themselves, in their preconversion life, to the most parlous sins of the flesh can be achieved by penitence, the text argues, while those who are accomplished in their spiritual devotions have yet more to learn in the face of the ever-present danger of the sin of spiritual pride.[70] This dual theme is brought into explicit relation because Zosimus, who desires to learn something he did not know before (p. 4, lines 48–55, cf. p. 10, line 158), is led to Mary, who stands as the revealed object of—in the place of—Zosimus's desires and instructs him in the workings of the divine as exemplified by her life. Mary, the object of Zosimus's desiring sight, stands in place of, or for, another object—God. The Old English *Mary of Egypt* thus participates in a lengthy tradition in Western culture about the relation between seeing and knowing, where that which can be known is often mediated by a female figure, as we discuss in Chapter 5. It is, after all, Mary who knows how to pray with the eyes of her heart, "heortan eagan" (p. 28, line 425; p. 38, line 559),[71] in a reworking of the quotation from the Beatitude which prefaces this section, and who promises Zosimus, ambiguously, that he shall see her as God wills, "þu me þonne gesihst swa swa god wile" (p. 46, lines 708–9).[72]

This section, then, resituates the emphasis of recent criticism on the representation of Mary's gender and sexuality in the broader dynamics of her figurative meanings as a woman who stands in for God.[73] In so doing, we follow Mary, who as *meretrix* (prostitute) turned *mediatrix* (mediator) turns away from sexual knowledge, as she later does, literally, from Zosimus himself, toward spiritual knowing.[74] Turning, converting, and troping are closely associated in spiritual writing, of course, since both conversion and tropes involve the concept of a turn.[75] We also follow Zosimus, through whose eyes the text thematizes the problems of literal and visionary sight and the forms of knowing they yield. In turning to these themes, however, we do not leave behind the implications of sight and knowledge for our understanding of gender and sexuality. The relation between Zosimus and Mary is explicitly one of gender, represented asymmetrically (as discussed later); it is also one of sexuality, since the object that stands in the place of Zosimus's spiritual desires is an old, naked woman, whose genitalia are covered before her secret past is revealed.[76]

Two important guides to Mary's figurative meanings are Erich Auerbach and Colin Chase. Looking at medieval French representations of Mary, Auerbach (in his classic essay "Figura") first speculated that the legend derives its meaning from exegetical readings of Psalm 113 (114), "In exitu Israel de Egypto"—a remark later reiterated both by James W. Earl and Thomas D. Hill.[77] That this penitent whore journeys from Egypt to Jerusalem and hence into the desert to survive there for some 47 years on a handful of crumbs, levitate, and walk on water recalls not only the Egyptian whores of Ezekiel's prophecies (Ez. 23: 2–3), as Jane Stevenson points out,[78] but also the exodus of Israel from Egypt, the exile in the wilderness, Christ's temptation in the desert together with his own walking on water (cf. Matt. 4: 1–11; 14: 24–33, etc.). Mary is thus a figure of Israel, the chosen people, and hence, Ecclesia—the "prostituted" Church, liberated by the exodus, exiled and tested in the wilderness, and ultimately redeemed by Christ.[79] As a holy harlot, she is also of course a type of the Magdalen.[80] The typological implications of hagiography are in general well-established, though the critical interpretations of these implications in Old English prose works are paradoxically few.[81] Neither Earl nor Hill has pursued these implications systematically in the prose and, to the best of our knowledge, no one has yet explored the implications of Mary's figural meaning for a reading of any of the reflexes of the legend.

Colin Chase, in fact, offers no sense of such figurative meanings for Mary. As his title implies ("Source Study as a Trick with Mirrors: Annihilation of Meaning in the Old English 'Mary of Egypt'"), Chase argues instead for the essential unknowability of the text's meaning on the grounds of the indeterminacy of its sources—a point necessarily modified by more recent work on the Anglo-Latin sources for the Old English Life.[82] For Chase, *Mary of Egypt* poses the question of the perfectability of human life. This question, however, is never formally answered by the narrative; it remains, as Chase puts it, "unexpressed in the words in the text."[83] How to be perfect, a state that Mary has apparently already achieved in the desert, is a "residue," a symptom of the work's mystical interest in the *via negativa*.[84] Chase's emphasis on negativity of mystical knowledge and on the ways in which the meaning of Mary appears to be in excess of the literal words of the text, thus eluding specific definition, are worth pursuing. Mary is an excessive figure (few indeed are the penitent, old, nude whores in the Anglo-Saxon corpus), yet she is one whose figurative dimensions do not annihilate meaning, as Chase argues, so much as produce and multiply it.[85] Figurally, Mary's meaning is hard to pin down; whore and saint, she also images the Virgin and Christ, Israel and Ecclesia. The text's modes of representation for Mary are fundamentally allegorical and her meanings, in a Christian sense, are both immanent—latent in the text until apprehended by a reader or auditor—and ultimately mysterious. We fall short of acknowledging the rich multivalence of this figure when we contain her by contextual studies: Hugh Magennis's recent article on Mary is really one about Ælfric; the same can be said of Lees's remarks about her in the context of sexual representation in the Old English prose female lives of saints.[86]

Figuration as a hermeneutics comes into its own as a practice of reading. To read figuratively is to read retrospectively, meditatively, spiritually. Such a reading is necessarily dependent on the allegorical markers of the text. As already suggested, the Old English *Mary* is full of such markers. The symbolism of its places—Egypt, Jerusalem, the Jordan—and its visions of levitation and walking on water, its association of the Egyptian Mary with the Virgin, and its careful structuring of narrative time according to the liturgical season of Lent are ample evidence for the text's use of allegory.[87] Equally important is the fact that *Mary of Egypt* offers guides to a figurative reading in its account of the relation between Zosimus and Mary: this relation is explicitly one of seeing and knowing. These interrelated processes involve a realignment of physical sight and mental intellection in accordance with Christian forms of knowledge. How the body is seen and what such sight means—how it is read— are central. As in the case of the increasingly iconic figures of Ælfric's female saints, the body of Mary is represented within a cultural system of spiritual intellection. To read figurally is, counterintuitively, to learn how to see. Concomitantly, to learn how to see is to learn how to believe. *Mary of Egypt* is a text that addresses the continual processes of conversion; like Zosimus, the reader's belief is to be confirmed, or changed, in the process of spiritual reading. The coercive edge of this process of conversion and believing is in full force.

We are asked to make sense of Mary as a visionary figure—as a figure of sight and for insight—because Zosimus sees her in pursuit of spiritual knowledge. Knowledge is thereby structured as gendered and generational (the relation between an old man and an old woman), as well as clerical (monk and ascetic, priest and petitioner). It is also more fundamentally phenomenological and spiritual, that is, visual and visionary, literal and figurative. Mary is a figure for the workings of the spirit in this world rendered comprehensible in part because she can be seen—and hence perceived by the spiritual intellect. To underline the importance of spiritual interpretation, the text presents a series of hermeneutic conundrums or secrets, each of which offers insight into the paradoxical relation between the known and the unknown, the seen and the perceived. For Zosimus, for example, spiritual knowing is mistakenly synonymous with his desire for male spiritual guidance, whether from a monk (p. 4, lines 50–55) or a certain father, "sumne fæder" (p. 10, line 157). What is revealed to him, however, is a spiritual mother ("gastlice modor,"

p. 16, line 235), whose unknown identity is revealed post mortem and who is buried by a lion in a place where, the text emphasizes, no animals have been seen (p. 12, lines 180–4; p. 48, lines 772–76). The uncovering of secret knowledge is thus one of the main themes of *Mary of Egypt*.

The final revelation of Mary's identity and her burial is the culminating episode in the narrative sequence of other secrets and/or mysteries, some of which are not visualized by the narrative and hence remain out of sight. The monastery near Jordan to which Zosimus is sent by divine authority is so secret ("swa digle," p. 8, line 105) that even the inhabitants of that country are ignorant as to its location, "even unknown to the land-dwellers themselves" ("eac swilce uncuð þam land-leodum him sylfum," p. 8, lines 106–7);[88] the ascetic practices of its monks during Lent are, according to the rule of the monastery, solitary and secretive—unknown and unknowable—even to its other monks "such that none of them knew the ways or deeds of another" ("swa þæt heora nan nyste oþres wisan oþþe dæda," p. 10, lines 132–33); Mary commands Zosimus to keep her story from Abbot John until God asks him (p. 42, lines 635–36) while, in another register, her sins of the flesh, although not exactly secret, are so excessive as to be unspeakable and unrepresentable (cf. p. 26, lines 378–84).

Motivated by his desire for spiritual knowledge, instructed by a secret world resonant with scriptural allegory and, as we shall see, by the dynamics of sight and revelation, Zosimus renews his pact with the secrets of the divine. He guards the mysteries of God, but he is also granted partial revelation of them. As priest as well as monk, Zosimus performs the responsibilities of the priesthood (as Mary asks of him) when he first prays with her and then later ministers the Eucharist. Indeed, Mary reminds him of his sacerdotal duties at two crucial points in the narrative, after she has covered herself (p. 16, lines 227–31) and in their final meeting, "know that you are God's priest and have with you the divine mysteries" ("wite þæt þu eart godes sacerd. and þa godcundan geryne þe mid hæbbende," p. 46, lines 688–89). By never asking Mary her name (p. 48, lines 724–28), praying instead for knowledge of the hidden goldhoard ("gehydde goldhord," p. 48, lines 737–38) that Mary represents, her identity is finally revealed to him.[89] From the perspective of the reader, this final revelation is utterly banal. Mary's name and identity as penitent convert is evident from the opening lines of the prologue (p. 2, line 3). Mary is also explicitly named in the narrative itself before her death (p. 46, line 696). More interesting is the form this revelation of identity takes as a miraculous inscription in the earth, both seen and read, accompanying Mary's dead body: "there was revealed to him there a writing on the earth which said thus" ("þa wæs þær an gewrit on þære eorðan getacnod þus gecweden," p. 50, lines 748–49). By such means, the text protests its interest in secrets and revealed knowledge; yet, as Chase also stresses, the meaning of the knowledge so revealed is far from clear. Figuratively speaking, Mary symbolizes far more than she literally suggests; even her name, resonating with that of the Virgin, is richly ambiguous.[90]

These complex associations of secrets and knowledge, sight and miraculous revelation, are established early. The prologue to the text refers briefly and initially opaquely to Raphael's healing of Tobit's sight, "after the loss of his eyes and again after their glorious enlightenment" ("æfter þære eagena forlætnysse. and eft æfter þæra wulderfæstan onlihtnysse," p. 2, lines 7–8), and then paraphrases Tobit 12: 7: "truly it is very harmful when the secrets of mankind are revealed, and again it is very harmful to the soul when the work of the glorious God is concealed" ("soðlice hit is swiðe derigendlic þæt [man] mancynnes digle geopenige. and eft þære sawle is micel genyðrung. þæt mon þa wuldorfæstan godes weorc bediglige," p. 2, lines 9–12). Raphael's admonition in the Old English contrasts the secrets ("digle") of mankind, which must be concealed, with the works of God, which must be revealed for fear of harm to the soul. Raphael's original advice to Tobit, however, balances the secrets of the king—that is, we take it, of secular rulers—against the revelation of the works of the divine.[91] Whatever meaning this reference might accrue in the Latin version, apparently by Paul of Naples, is lost in the Old English (tempting though it is to speculate that *Mary* was perhaps interpollated into the *Lives of Saints* because that collection was dedicated to those who held secular though not regal authority—Æthelweard and Æthelmær).[92] Crucially, what Raphael's admonition does not demand, whether in the Scriptural source or in the Latin or English versions, is the revelation of God's secrets—merely his work ("godes weorc," p. 2, line 12).

Raphael's insight into the asymmetries of divine works and secular secrets was granted to Tobit only after he was blinded and then miraculously healed (as the Old English points out). Seeing is intimately related not only to insight and miracle, however, but also to spiritual labor. The Old English translator—and the text does not clearly distinguish between the voice of the Latin translation and its own here—protests his fidelity to Raphael's admonition to reveal the work of God by referring to the slothful servant of the parable of the talents, who hid his talent in the earth and received no increase from it for he did not use it (p. 2, lines 12–18, cf. Matt. 25: 14–30). For the translator, Matthew and Tobit sanction the revelatory account of Mary; these scriptural precedents command speech and revelation, the truth of a spiritual narrative, rather than secrets and silence: "nor be it fitting that I should falsify the holy narratives or that I should silence speech" ("ne gewurðe hit þæt ic on þam halgum grecednyssum wæge oþþe ic þa spræce forsuwige," p. 2, lines 17–18).[93]

Analogous to the translator, whose spiritual labor is communication and revelation of divine work, the visionary moment is the product of spiritual work—whether monastic or ascetic.[94] Both Mary and Zosimus are granted insight into the workings of the divine and, on every occasion, these insights take the form of visions that are the product of spiritual devotion. Mary's prayers for redemption and acts of penitential asceticism usher in her visions of the Virgin. Zosimus is granted his visions of Mary—the peak experience of his lengthy spiritual life—as a result of his monastic devotions and the disciplining of his humility by obedience. To make sense of the figurative dimensions of this text, then, we first have to learn how to see again, as does Tobit. So too does Zosimus, in spite of the fact that he has already attained considerable spiritual knowledge. We also have to learn to trust believing speech, the power of revelation, rather than silence, as the translator points out. Both factors come together later in the text when Zosimus sees the old, naked body of Mary and listens to her voice.

Learning how to see is closely related to learning how to break silence with speech, that is, the prologue reminds us, to communicate, read, and interpret. Raphael's admonition demands interpretation, as does the use of the parable of the talents in the context of the rest of the narrative. Seeing and speaking, in the sense of seeing and enunciating words on a page, M. B. Parkes reminds us, are stages in early medieval descriptions of the reading process, the goal of which is spiritual understanding—a spiritual knowing gained when the text is meditated upon.[95] Prayer and reading are closely associated. In medieval accounts, the text itself is often figured as a mirror for the eyes of the mind.[96] Mary prays silently (p. 18, lines 264–68), with the eyes of her heart (p. 38, line 559); she also has knowledge of the Scriptures in the desert without formal learning, "but the word of God is quick and sharp, teaching this human understanding within" ("ac godes word is cucu. and scearp innan lærende þis mennisce andgyt," p. 40, lines 595–96), and she is clothed in the words of God (p. 40, lines 583–85, cf. Isaiah 61: 10 and Zech. 3: 4). The miraculous inscription accompanying her dead body is similarly associated by Zosimus with her lack of formal learning (p. 50, lines 754–56). These examples signify that Mary has acquired spiritual knowledge as a direct consequence of her penitential conversion. Such forms of knowing, which Zosimus comes to appreciate during the course of the narrative, are held out as unattainable ideals, as miracles; yet appreciation of these ideals for both Zosimus and the reader is sharpened by the practice of spiritual interpretation.

The prologue thus initiates a thematic trajectory of secrets and insights, miracles and spiritual knowledge, writing and revelation, which is brought to fruition not in the final scene of Mary's burial, but with Zosimus's reaction to it. At the end of the text, Zosimus returns to the monastery, and reports to the monks the narrative of his encounter with Mary:

and naht ne *bediglode* ealra þæra þinga þe he *geseah* oððe *gehyrde.* þæt hi ealle godes mærða wurðodon and [mid ege and lufan and micclan geleafan] mærsodon. þære eadigan forð-fore dæg (p. 52, lines 798–801, emphasis added)

(and concealed none of those things which he had seen or heard so that they all honored God's wonders and glorified the day of her blessed passing-on with awe and love and great faith)

Zosimus fulfills Raphael's admonition to Tobit by concealing nothing of the works of God, nothing of what he saw or heard.[97] Note, however, that he does not explain or comment upon these workings of the divine (the secrets of God remain intact), but instead praises both God and the saintly Mary. In one sense, the text has come full circle, since its opening lines speak of Mary's praiseworthy conversion ("herigendlicestan gehwyrfednysse," p. 2, line 1)[98] and since the prologue commands the communication of revelation. In another, the reader has been instructed in the nature and goals of figural reading; spiritual understanding leads to a deepened sense of worship and compels reiteration—the retelling of Mary's story. Zosimus, who by the end of the text has been instructed in the spiritual relation between sight and insight in order to better understand the praiseworthy nature of the divine, is therefore our best guide to the narrative's instruction of the reader.

Zosimus's privileged relation to insight and the knowledge that comes from spiritual discipline is the first thing we learn about him. So well has he perfected the life of the spirit, subjecting the flesh to the spirit, practicing utter obedience to the rule, and perfecting his knowledge of Scripture and worship (p. 4, lines 25–36), that he has already been granted divine revelation:

he wære gefremed wyrðe beon þære godcundan onlihtnysse þurh æteowednyss fram gode þære gastlican gesihþe (p. 4, lines 37–39)

(he was made worthy of the divine enlightenment through a revelation from God of a ghostly vision)

Zosimus's attainment of divine illumination is further underscored by a quotation from the Beatitudes that prefaces this section of our chapter, "Blessed are the pure in heart for they shall see God" ("Eadige beoð þa clæn-heortan. forðan þe hi god geseoð," p. 4, lines 40–41, cf. Matt. 5: 8). Purifying the heart, the Beatitude reminds us, carries the promise of seeing the divine. The positioning of this quotation so early in the narrative, however, is both ironic and prophetic. Zosimus's insight has yet to be tested, indeed for most of the narrative he is conspicuously lacking in knowledge of that which he sees. He does not know who Mary is until the final scene of her burial. Zosimus's lack of knowledge, his lack of insight, is directly related to his inability to see and hence to know the woman later to be called Mary. The Beatitude poses the question of how moral purity is related to sight and, accordingly, Zosimus's journey—both literal and spiritual—stages perfection as a process of spiritual labor (imaged as monastic obedience) toward greater insight. While Zosimus does not actually see God, he does see Mary as God wills, just as she promised him (p. 46, lines 708–9)—a point we will return to later.

By contrast, in his first encounter with Mary during his solitary devotions for Lent, Zosimus does not know that which he sees at all. His desire to be "strengthened in some thing which he himself did not know before" ("on sumum þingum getimbrede þæs ðe he sylf ær ne cuðe," p. 10, line 158) is a quest for a father ("sumne fæder," p. 10, line 157) or some man ("sumum menn," p. 12, line 160). This desire for masculine guidance is understandable, given Zosimus's earlier wish for a monk who might teach him something new (p. 4, lines 51–52), and given that his own angelic visitor had instructed him to find a monastery in the first place (p. 6, lines 58–60). What *did* Zosimus see, then? What he sees, on his right side, at noon that day during prayer after looking to the heavens—all reminders of the world of scriptural allegory in which he is placed—is both unclear and unknowable. At least to him. The considerable emphasis on the same verbs of seeing in the Old English, however, alerts the reader to the significance of Zosimus's confused sight:[99]

and mid *þære geornfullan behealdnysse* up locode. and *þone heofon beheold. þa geseah* he him on þa swiðran healfe þær he on gebedum stod. swa swa he on mennisce gelicnysse on lichaman. hine æteowan. and þa wæs he ærest swiþe afyrht. forþan þe he wende þæt hit wære sumes gastes scin-hyw. *þæt he þær geseah*. (p. 12, lines 165–70, emphasis added)

(and with eager regard he looked up and beheld the heavens, and then he himself saw on the right side as he stood in prayer as if someone showed himself bodily in human likeness, and he was straightaway very fearful because he thought that it was some phantasm of a spirit that he saw there)

Zosimus can neither clearly see nor conceptualize the person running from him. Is it a figure, a human image in bodily form ("on mennisce gelicnysse on lichaman," p. 12, line 168), or a spirit ("sumes gastes," p. 12, line 170)? Concluding his prayer with the sign of the cross, Zosimus turns his eyes and sees a person, who is in fact a woman:

he þa *his eagan bewende.* and þær *soðlice man geseah* westweardes on þæt westen efstan. and witodlice *þæt wæs wifman. þæt þær wæs gesewen.* swiðe sweartes *lichaman* heo wæs for þære sunnan hæto. and þa loccas hire heafdes wæron swa hwit swa wull. and þa na siddran þonne oþ þone swuran (p. 12, lines 173–77, emphasis added)

(he then turned his eyes, and there saw in truth a person hastening westwards into the desert and indeed it was a woman who was visible there. She was very black of body because of the sun's heat, and the hair on her head was as white as wool, and no longer than to her neck)

However the reader interprets this cannily alliterative,[100] astonishingly condensed (that is, scripturally overdetermined) figure—an image from the Song of Songs, her shorn hair a sign of a woman without or beyond shame, a devilish temptress in the wasteland, an orientalist vision, Israel and hence Ecclesia—two things are clear.[101] First, Zosimus's perceptual skills are apparently so disoriented in the desert that he classifies women with images (likenesses), spirits, the flesh, and the animal world. Clarity of sight here does not deepen spiritual knowledge; for Zosimus, the woman is either a vision ("gesihðe," p. 12, line 179) or a wild animal ("wildeora," p. 12, line 183) in a place where he had previously seen no such animals (p. 12, lines 180–83). Second, it is precisely Zosimus's confused and conflicting accounts of that which he sees that demand interpretation from the reader. Even the narrative is at pains to keep Mary's meaning ambiguous; as Zosimus draws closer to her, it is a body ("se lichama," p. 14, line 203) that speaks. These ambiguities of perception and classification signal the need for a spiritual interpretation of the narrative. Seeing through Zosimus's misperceptions, we learn to read.

Seeing a body rather than the "fæder" he had wished to find, Zosimus does not know what or who it represents, whether literally (a woman or animal) or figurally (a spirit). Mary, by contrast, who is not actually looking at Zosimus, already knows who he is, addressing him by name, and is quite precise about who she is and what she wants. Mary represents herself in this first encounter as she does consistently throughout the text—as a woman and sinner ("wifhades mann," p. 14, lines 206–7; "synful wif," p. 14, line 222), with feminine frailty ("wiflican tyddernysse," p. 14, line 211). What she wants are Zosimus's prayers and clothing. It is only at this point in the narrative that the reader (like Zosimus, perhaps) becomes aware of her nudity. As a literal, material, phenomenon of this world, Mary is also represented simultaneously by the narrative as a figure, embedded in scriptural history and endowed with the power of revelation (of spiritual knowing), exemplified in this instance by her prior knowledge of Zosimus. Her miraculous insight, which Zosimus recognizes (p. 14, lines 215–16), contrasts powerfully with Zosimus's failure to interpret that which he sees—that is, to perceive Mary as both literal and figural. The distance between Mary's perception and Zosimus's misperception measures the weakness of his spiritual intellect. This failure of Zosimus's understanding ushers in the spiritual disciplining of his sight through his repeated visions of Mary. Sight, perception, and spiritual interpretation are intimately related.

Given the considerable emphasis in the Old English text on verbs of seeing in this initial meeting between Zosimus and Mary, it is worth pausing to consider also what is removed from the field of vision. Zosimus glimpses the fleeing Mary only fleetingly until she reaches the other side of the burn that is visible ("þe þær gesewen wæs," p. 14, line 200). Here Mary calls out to Zosimus, announcing her identity as a woman unable to show herself because:

ic eom wif-hades mann. and eallunga lichamlicum wæfelsum bereafod. *swa swa þu sylf gesihst,* and þa sceame mines lichaman hæbbende unoferwrigene (p. 14, lines 206–9, emphasis added)

(I am a woman and all bereft of bodily clothing, as you yourself can see, and having the shame of my uncovered body)

Drawing attention to Zosimus's sight of her naked body, Mary immediately requests that he throw her his cloak to cover her womanly weakness ("wyflican tyddernysse," p. 14, line 211) so that she can turn toward him and accept his prayers. The first stage in the disciplining of Zosimus's spiritual understanding is the clothing of Mary. Her nudity, specifically her genitalia that the text does not explicitly and characteristically name, has to be concealed to be understood:

And gegyreded hire be þam dæle þe heo mæste mihte. and mæste neod wæs to beheligenne (p. 14, lines 219–20)

(And girded herself about the part of which she most needful to and had most need to conceal)

Echoing yet modifying Raphael's admonition to Tobit, in this text the secret parts of the female body (as the Old English elegantly emphasizes) will be covered before the works of God are revealed.[102] Zosimus's gaze here is frustrated—directed by Mary away from, not toward, what is assumed to be at least one object of his sight. What can be seen and hence understood thus turns on an object of sight (a naked female body), which is also a secret (her genitalia) that is rendered invisible.[103] This moment is crucial to the rest of the narrative. Only after her genitalia are covered in a symbolic gesture of her public shame does Mary narrate to Zosimus just what she did with them in her past.[104] Mary's sexual knowledge will be converted through penitential speech into spiritual knowledge, while this episode ensures for Zosimus that her sexuality will remain an issue relevant to her past.[105] Only after Mary's necessary part is covered does Zosimus address her as a spiritual mother ("gastlice modor," p. 16, line 235). Quite literally, then, the transformation of the sign of the sinner into the figural sign of the saint turns on the latter clothing, concealing the former. What is achieved here is the literal distancing of the female body as it is transformed into a spiritual figure. We might measure, in this gap between the physical female body and the spiritual sign, the many other bodies of female saints submitted to similar processes of figuration in late Anglo-Saxon England (discussed above).

The success of the gradual purification of Zosimus's heart toward greater insight is evident in another gap—that between his first encounter with Mary, where his initial confusion of the field of vision is reoriented into spiritual seeing, and the final burial scene, where his clarity of visionary sight is paramount and uncontested. This final scene deliberately parallels that of their first encounter. Again after prayer, this time for further revelation of "that hidden goldhoard which you yourself once deigned to reveal to me" ("þæt gehydde goldhord. þe þu me sylfum ær gemedemodest æteowan," p. 48, lines 737–38), Zosimus returns to the burn where they first spoke. He sees first an image of a shining sun ("swa swa scinende sunne," p. 48, line 741) with Mary's dead body. After performing the burial service, he next reads the miraculous inscription pointed out to him ("getacnod," p. 50, line 749) that reveals Mary's identity, and finally sees ("þa he hine beseah þa geseah he," p. 50, line 772) the lion who buries her.[106] Women as figures are indeed classified with the spirit, the flesh, and the animals, though it is only the spiritual intellect that can make sense of this taxonomy. Zosimus sees Mary spiritually just as she had promised him, her flesh transfigured by the presence of the divine, symbolized by the illuminating light of sun and the lion who retreats into the desert like a lamb (an image borrowed from Jerome's *Vita Pauli*).[107] Zosimus reads the inscription in the same way, as a spiritual revelation of Mary's saintly identity and death. Yet, as discussed earlier, the figural implications of this remarkable scene remain implicit and uninterpreted by the text. Through seeing and reading, Mary's identity is revealed to Zosimus, and he goes on to fulfill Raphael's admonition by relating all that he has seen and heard of God's works to his community. These final lines thus conclude the process of devotional reading encoded in the text; figural insight remains implicit until activated by the eyes of the pure, imaged here by the purity—that is, clarity—of Zosimus's visionary sight.

Mary is ahead of Zosimus in acquiring visionary sight and spiritual understanding; through her he fulfills his wish to learn from someone who is before him in his works ("þe me on his dædum beforan sy," p. 4, lines 54–55)[108] and something he had not known before ("ær," p. 10, line 158).[109] Mary never looks anywhere save at the heavens in the desert; she perceives with the eyes of her heart and miraculously has knowledge of God and the Scriptures without knowing how to read. Moreover, her own story of the translation of her unrepresentable (that is, unseen) desires of the flesh to those of the spirit also turns on an episode of seeing. Mary's wish to see the Holy Cross in Jerusalem is initially and repeatedly refused (symbolized by the closed doors of the temple, cf. p. 28, lines 403–24).[110] Penitential remorse, however, leads her to meditation. Mary's knowledge of salvation is perceived inwardly through the mind's spiritual sight, "and the understanding of salvation touched in truth my mind and the eyes of my heart" ("þa onhran soðlice min mod and þa eagan minre heortan hælo andgit," p. 28, lines 424–25),[111] and she sees ("geseah ic," p. 28, line 429) an image ("anlicnysse," p. 30, line 430) of the Virgin Mary.[112] In her prayers to this "anlicnysse," she humbly acknowledges the polluted looks ("besmitenum gesihþum," p. 30, lines 435–36) of her sinning life, pledging purification and renunciation of the world if permitted sight ("gesihðe") of the Cross (p. 30, lines 443–44).[113] The turning point of her conversion is thus achieved when the visual realm (the sight of the Cross) is conditioned by the visionary (the image of the Virgin, who later guides her through her arduous life in the desert, cf. p. 34, lines 507–9). Indeed, once inside the temple, Mary sees the mysteries of the divine ("I saw there the mysteries of Holy God," "ic þær geseah þa halgan godes gerynu," p. 32, line 467)[114], and fulfills the promise of the Beatitude: "I saw the glory which we sinners through our merits never see"("ic geseah þæt wuldor þe we synfulle mid gewyrhtum ne [geseoð. sy]," p. 32, lines 474–75).[115] It is therefore entirely consonant with the allegory of the text that Mary has attained both purity of heart and clarity of spiritual insight. By the time she meets Zosimus, and in contrast to him, her eyes are firmly set on the heavens.

In their different relation to time, Mary is before Zosimus, literally and figuratively. Small wonder he is always running after her, trying to catch sight of her.[116] As a condensed figure of Ecclesia in this world, Mary speaks in history (human time) of God's eternity, where knowing and place are synonymous, ungrounded in this world. Hence the difficulty of seeing her in place, exemplified by the episode when Zosimus sees her levitate (pp. 18–20, lines 264–90). Here, too, Zosimus mistrusts his perception, wondering whether he is in the presence of some spirit ("gast," cf. p. 18, lines 280–81). Mary rebukes him firmly:

Ac wite þu man þæt ic eom synful wif. Swa-þeah-hwædere utan ymbseald mid þam halgan fulluhte. and ic nan gast ne eom ac æmerge and axe and eall flæsc and nan gæstlice (p. 20, lines 284–87)

(But know oh man that I am a sinful woman, however much enclosed on the outside with holy baptism, and I am no spirit but embers and ashes and all flesh and not spiritual)

Mary gives voice to the spiritual paradox that she represents as a woman of ashes and embers, wholly flesh, who rises above the world in prayer. As in the scene of their initial meeting, Mary is here represented figurally (in God's eternity) and literally (in historic time), with the narrative giving equal weight to both levels. Zosimus, who has to learn the commensurability of spiritual knowledge and time that Mary both achieves and represents, is her belated witness. He is beneath her in spatial terms, and behind her in temporal terms; her levitation and his pursuit of her are both symbolic and literal acts. A figural reading of Mary reveals, therefore, how she—as a figure—condenses and transforms both time and place.

Aware of such dynamics of figuration, the reader is rightly concerned when Zosimus literally turns his back on Mary ("on bæclincg gewend," p. 14, line 218) when he first meets her. On the literal level, Mary cannot turn toward Zosimus until clothed because of her nudity and the shame it signifies (p. 14, lines 204–12). As already discussed, Zosimus turns from Mary in order to unclothe himself and throw her his cloak. On the figural level, however, discrepancies appear between the meanings of these apparently complementary actions. Firm in her promise to the Virgin (p. 30, lines 451–53), Mary has already turned from the world that Zosimus represents by running from him; she turns back (p. 14, line 221) only when clothed in and by that world, but the meaning of her action has already been framed by her conversion. In other words, Mary is consistent, unifying the spirit and the letter. Zosimus, by contrast, is inconsistent, severing the letter from the spirit. He initially turns his back on the world of the spirit, which Mary represents and of which he desires further knowledge, because he cannot clearly see or apprehend Mary's figural significance; in so doing, he is caught instead by the literal dilemma of her nudity. Hence the didactic importance of Mary's speech, after she turns toward him clothed in his cloak:

Hwi wæs þe la abbod Zosimus swa micel neod. me synful wif to geseonne. oððe hwæs wilnast þu fram me to hæbbene. oþþe to witenne þæt þu me slawedest swa micel geswinc to gefremmanne for minum þingum; (p. 14, lines 221–24)[117]

(Why oh Abbot Zosimus do you have so great a need to see me a sinful woman, or what will you have from me or know of me that you have not slowed to perform so great a labor for me?)

Challenging the nature of Zosimus's desiring sight, Mary's speech covers all the main themes of the text; why, indeed, has Zosimus so great a desire to see this sinful woman that he has worked so hard to attain it? The question goes formally unanswered (a textual strategy that Chase first pointed out) and the speech silences them both for several hours as they pray, prostrate, each requesting the blessing of the other. This is a profoundly uncanny moment in the text, whose power is registered in three ways. First, by the fact that Mary's question echoes that posed by Abbot John at the beginning of his spiritual education (cf. p. 6, lines 68–70), where Zosimus makes explicit his desire for spiritual knowledge (p. 6, lines 70–72). Second, by the lengthy silence and prayer that follows Mary's question. And third, by this episode's almost parodic charting of the relations between an old partly clothed woman, who has neither been seen nor seen anyone for many years, and an old partly unclothed monk in search of spiritual knowledge who has to learn how to see.

The text's formal strategies in charting this uncanny moment of stasis and prayer between Mary and Zosimus are self-evident. The exchange of clothing equalizes the distance between them. Mary is brought down to Zosimus's level, and both lie prostrate in prayer (pp. 14–16, lines 225–26).[118] Mary (as woman and Ecclesia) needs Zosimus (as priest and monk) as much as Zosimus needs Mary on both levels, gaining spiritual knowledge from her transfigured life from prostitute to reformed saint (from Israel to Ecclesia). At the same time, however, incommensurabilities between Zosimus and Mary persist, measured by the obvious (and hilarious) gender dissonances on the literal level. Mary needs that which represents her sexual shame covered, and Zosimus is the one to cover her. Sins of the flesh are almost too easily assimilated to the feminine here (indeed Zosimus appears to associate the flesh with women almost as soon as he sees her). By contrast, Zosimus does not so much represent the masculine as the priestly, as Mary herself points out by reminding him of his sacerdotal powers immediately after this moment of prostrate prayer (p. 16, lines 226–31).

The disparity or asymmetry between genders on the literal level—where feminine signifies the sexualized flesh and masculine the priestly—lies at the heart of the allegory in the Old English.[119] Its entire figural thematics of sight and insight turns on the moment when one object is removed from sight. It is no accident that the object is Mary's unnamed genitalia or that both Mary and Zosimus are old—sexual knowledge (firmly associated with youth in this text) has been replaced by spiritual knowledge. In case the reader does not grasp this crucial point, the narrative returns to it in the burial scene. Preparing Mary's body for burial, Zosimus is careful only to wash her feet with his tears: "indeed he did not dare to touch any other part of the body" ("ne geþrystlæhte he soðlice nan oþer þæs lichaman oðhrinan," p. 48, lines 744–45).[120] Mary will be buried naked just as he first met her, save for the clothing he threw to her (p. 52, lines 791–94). In a move more familiar from later medieval texts and parodied in the Miller's Tale, revelation of divine works is made possible by literally concealing the secrets of woman.[121] Once her body is covered, Mary's secret past is revealed, but the account now works to promote spiritual understanding of that past. Woman's unmentionable body parts remain a secret and are rendered invisible, but so too are God's own mysteries. Only the workings of the divine are revealed.

As a woman who stands in for God, Mary figures belief itself, however incredible her behavior might be. Both the Anglo-Latin and the Old English texts insist on the credibility, the veracity, of her life of the spirit within history, as they also insist on the labor of spiritual interpretation in understanding her figuration. This veracity—we might term it the insistent reality of the figural mode within spiritual discourse—turns out to be the Life's main lesson for Zosimus and for all subsequent readers who follow its conversionary dynamics.[122] One such reader was almost certainly the Old English translator, judging from the subtle amplification of the relation of sight to spiritual knowledge in this Old English Life contrasted with its Anglo-Latin source.

To read this text figurally is to learn how sight and knowledge are clarified by the insights of belief. As our analysis demonstrates, the Old English *Mary of Egypt* is a work of considerable intellectual sophistication; it is also much more coherent and unified in its goal of rhetorical persuasion than Aldhelm's *De virginitate*, in spite of that work's rhetorical display. While both engage their readers in the work of belief, Aldhelm's, we have suggested, is far from coherent about either the nature of the female body or the implications of looking at that body. *Mary of Egypt*, by contrast, though certainly the lesser known work, enacts a thorough and ongoing process of spiritual interpellation. We might resist this process by concentrating on the humorous dimension of the text, as does Orchard, but such a reading minimizes the figuration of Mary's body by spiritual interpretation and thus the force of its tropes.[123] Mary is, in fact, systematically and seamlessly aligned with the most sophisticated and deepest level of patristic explication. In consequence, her body is much more overtly contained, or rather suppressed, by exegesis than either of those saintly bodies written up by Aldhelm and Ælfric.

The kind of subjectivity we have been describing in this chapter, and the religious and historical circumstances of its formation, can only be ignored by later critics at the cost of arguing that Christianity has no dominant role in the formation of precisely those cultural relations that persist long after the Anglo-Saxon period. Contemporary theories of subjectivity as a performative function of culture can provide, in our view, a more viable and flexible critical tool if the performative power of the rhetoric of belief is included in the paradigm. Our example here has been the rhetoric of Christian belief in the Anglo-Saxon period, but this example also argues for a reorientation of paradigms of culture more generally so as to include formations of belief, both past and present. By taking Butler's theories of gendered subjectivity to the remote period of the Anglo-Saxon with its specific instance of Christian formations of belief, we complicate and enrich both Anglo-Saxon studies and contemporary studies of gender. Theories of the gaze and notions of citation, both of which are central to contemporary gender studies, are radically modified by history. Such theories are the beginnings—though not the endings—of a historical study that takes difference (whether of gender, the body, or belief) as its object.

As we complement, and complicate, the binary dynamic of the gaze with the metaphorical and historical vision of the seventh-century spectator, so we also argue that the religious and secular dimensions of subjectivity should be examined in tandem; mutually reinforcing, the religious and the secular are inseparable strands of Anglo-Saxon culture. The same point holds true for later periods, although the particular relation between the religious and the secular will be necessarily different according to the historical moment.

In the case of Anglo-Saxon England, Christian rhetoric must engage the secular, temporal self even as it performs its didactic function as indicated by our study of *Mary of Egypt*; as such, it can serve as a lens through which to observe an apparent contradiction between the secular and the spiritual as a locus of intersection and the text as a site of its performance. Aldhelm's catalogue of virginal bodies, with its indulgence in metaphoric display, might be read as an early and excessive case of a hermeneutics of violence found more often in later medieval accounts of female religious. The *De virginitate*, however, is situated at the crossroads of political, ecclesiastical, and cultural conditions specific to seventh-century England. The rich, old, intelligent, and often married women who form at least one element of his audience are also enclosed, subject to ecclesiastical and political masculine authority, and enjoined to engage on an extremely complex, peculiarly gendered metaphorics of spiritual devotion. The Barking nuns are encouraged to think of themselves as sometimes embodied and gendered—sometimes male, other times female. They contemplate the pure will or intellect via images of tortured sanctity that witness the resistance of the saintly to that same torture. Sometimes we see the saint, sometimes we do not. At all times, however, the reader of the *De virginitate* is subject to the continuing discipline of Christianity. One might also connect Aldhelm's rhetorical violence—the violence of denial *and* avowal—to the violence inherent in seventh-century society outside the cloister (which is, for example, only thinly veiled in Bede's *History*).[124] The assumption that ascetic Christian practices are predicated on a denial of the body that must be seen to be understood, and thereby denied, only takes force when related to specific sociocultural factors.

Ælfric's hagiographical body is similarly though differently multivalent. It is a product of the Benedictine Reform's purchase on secular life outside the monastery and a measure of the success with which the idea of a Christian subject as a disciplinary practice is embedded in this culture's imaginary. It is also a *female* body, a product of the separation of the sexes in both clerical and secular spheres. The ideology at work here is worth pausing on: "real" religious women disappear from the cultural record at precisely the moment when the female saint triumphs in her chastity. "Woman" in the tenth century is a figure or icon within an emergent discourse of chastity, as *Mary of Egypt* makes clear.[125] As icon, the female saint secures a cultural ideal of a Christian, universalized subject, whose referent—as is so often the case—is most often male. The mechanisms of control over the female body's multivalence extend both to its representation (the dynamics of the gaze), and to the violence it endures.

Unlike later medieval hagiography (Margaret comes to mind), or earlier (Aldhelm), Ælfric's tortured women are represented much less graphically. It is in the early years of the so-called "golden age" of Anglo-Saxon women that we find Aldhelm's excessive violence, not in these later years of an apparent decline in women's status. Where we have firm evidence, historically, for the participation of real women in the dynamics of chastity and the performance of belief, the degree of metaphorical violence sharpens upward; where it is harder to locate the woman, the degree of narrative violence goes down— female bodies become static icons. Only further research will cast light on the historical implications of this proportionate correlation between presence and absence, between rhetorical practices for the embodiment of the chaste female body and its simultaneous denial. At the least, such evidence demands caution in our use of developmental models for gender roles in the medieval period, and argues for a more nuanced emphasis on continuity as well as change.

Indeed, the *De virginitate* and the *Lives of Saints* are only two products of a much larger web of connections and intersections that produce culturally specific formations of the Christian subject and its body in Anglo-Saxon England. Such a web includes the ritual practices and discourses associated with chastity in monastic and clerical milieu: those that accompany, for example, the passage of the translated and perfected saintly body voided of its marks of violence and rank into the church and into history (for example, Æthelthryth's healed scar where once she hung jeweled necklaces). It also includes, in its manipulations of metaphors of the body, notions of *translatio* (or metaphoric exchange) within written cultural discourses that are themselves translations, as is so often the case with hagiography in Anglo-Saxon England. When the body is simultaneously the site and referent of such practices *and* the source of metaphors in clerical discourse within a culture that is famously ambivalent about the body, questions of the continuing historical relation between subjectivity and sanctity offer fruitful avenues of research to the cultural historian.

The conventions of rhetoric and the historical instance are profoundly related. Clerical metaphors perform vital ideological work in structuring the relations between the sexes and their significance. That ideological work can only be recovered by a testing of the continuities of clerical discourse (Agnes is as well known to Bede and Aldhelm as to Ælfric and later clerics) against the specific historical instances of a text's production and reception. Theoretical positions worked out on the basis of later, post-Conquest evidence are often strained beyond recognition when applied to this earlier history. The seventh century is quite simply not the same as the tenth or twelfth (or any other century).

What emerges from such a methodology is the critical importance of the body's, especially the female body's, symbolism and materiality, which complicates and contradicts generally held assumptions about the diminished role the body plays in early medieval England (that is, that there is no body in Anglo-Saxon England, no sex, and little gender). Indeed, attention to the complex, historicized production of the body not only is evidence for the making of the difference of gender, but also helps make evident the difference of Anglo-Saxon England itself.

Chapter Five
Pressing Hard on the "Breasts" of Scripture: Metaphor and the Symbolic

From Hild as spiritual mother to Mary of Egypt as both holy har-lot and mother church, we have paid attention to the operations of gendered metaphor in specific texts, both in Latin and English and from early, middle, and late periods of Anglo-Saxon England. In this chapter, we engage more directly with the general process of metaphorization and its gendering, as well as with some particular metaphors as these might be culturally enacted as well as textually traced. Our purpose here is to explore at the levels of metaphoric and cultural process the liaison between reference and representation evident in the cultural record that we considered in detail in Chapter 4, and that we hold central to any investigation of the Anglo-Saxon female agent. In so doing, we put to use more concretely and systematically than elsewhere in this book the methodology of a feminist patristics (first outlined in our Introduc-tion). We trace the relation between patristic rhetoric (with its intellectual and ethical traditions) and the "real," that of the sociocultural world of the Anglo-Saxons as it engages women and their bodies, whether dead or alive.

We examine, for example, how Wisdom's femininity is put to use and strained beyond recognition in clerical thought as evidenced by Pseudo-Bede's image of her nurturing and generous lactation in the *Collectanea*. We also ask what it might mean to discover that Lady Philosophy has changed sex, name, and even in part function in Alfred's version of Boethius's *Consolation of Philosophy*.[1] We chose these Latin works deliberately. Boethius's *Consolation*, first rendered into English by Alfred, remains a core text throughout the Middle Ages, drawn on by both clerical and secular culture.[2] A consolatory work engaged with the nature, limits, and extent of human forms of knowing, the *Consolation* offers insights into the relation between cognition and meta-phor that Alfred's version modifies in terms of his own cultural understanding of a Christian patristic wisdom. Pseudo-Bede's *Collectanea* is, by contrast, a much lesser known (indeed, only recently fully edited) work, which is not so much firmly identified with English as it is with Insular (probably Irish) and continental clerical culture. In this handbook of odd clerical jottings—bits and pieces of knowledge, as it were—we find a structural organization and a mode of knowing that clearly resonate with other kinds of instructional and informational genres used in Anglo-Saxon England (*florilegia*, wisdom texts, riddles, for example).[3] The *Collectanea* and the *Consolation* thus provide examples of the forms of cultural cognition available in Anglo-Saxon England as well as in the wider early medieval Christian context that appeal especially to clerics. That both the *Consolation* and the *Collectanea* are in Latin is entirely to our point. Most of the genres we have chosen to work with in this book (charters, riddles, saints' lives, etc.) have Latin and English reflexes. While we have demonstrated the need to respect the different aims and interests of vernacular and Latin cultural contexts, we do not underestimate the overlap between the two; this overlap is particularly evident where clerical culture is concerned. Indeed, it is only by examining both Latin and vernacular contexts that we can begin to reconstruct the ways in which the traditional forms of knowing encoded by patristic rhetoric are modified by place, time, and language.

Central to the examples of Lady Philosophy and Wisdom, not to mention other similar examples that we discuss here, is the issue of the relation of the "real" woman—however difficult she may be to access—to the personified, metaphorical feminine so common in the patristic symbolic. In examining this relation, we see just how deeply embedded in the cultural imaginary is the dynamic of female absence and presence that we have been tracing throughout this book. While metaphorical realignments between the female and the symbolically feminine (or indeed, the male and the symbolically masculine) may point to aspects of a masculine hegemonic purchase on literacy, they also call attention to the process of making meaning itself, to the purchase of rhetoric on acts of understanding and on the cognitive process. Metaphors are means to ways of knowing, even as they structure that knowing. We recall here the performative power of Christian didactic rhetoric in both Latin and English (discussed in Chapter 4) and its aim, overt or otherwise, to create, educate, and control its subject. In such a context, what is the cultural performative currency, secular or religious, of an image like that of the generously lactating feminine Wisdom in the *Collectanea*, or of Alfred's reconstructed masculine figure of Wisdom? The connections between grammatical gender and clerical output, between the technicalities of rhetoric (or, indeed, its tools) and the patristic enterprise as it receives literate expression in the Anglo-Saxon period overall are obviously considerations with which to begin this chapter. Equally important is the related issue of how rhetorical images evolve in relation to and in terms of bodily containment and disappearances in the real. What guarantees the symbolic assertion of gendered cognition? Who controls how we know? How does gender feature in this knowing, and by what means are bodies included and excluded in the process of signification? These are questions we take up in this chapter. We consider what it means when a metaphor is alive and thriving, and the body it signifies is long dead: how do these disembodied sites of signification register within the cultural symbolic or (to make the point more emphatically) over her dead body? And so, by way of brief conclusion, we return to the project with which we began this book: what are the connections between female agency, rhetorical process, and historical change?

When Is a Woman Not a Woman?

The mothers, stepmothers, companions, handmaids, and maids of Roman rhetoric had a most extensive progeny in the Middle Ages. (E. R. Curtius)

Metaphors live and die, and die hard, throughout the Anglo-Saxon period. They also change sex. E. R. Curtius's list of women attendant at the site of metaphoric signification[4] are sometimes barely present, or their absence is a condition *for* signification, a rhetorical necessity, and their "progeny" are birthed by a set of masculine literate procedures in much the same way that images of birth are used by Bede in his account of Hild (detailed in Chapter 1). These rhetorical procedures reveal much about clerical use of, fear of, ambivalence toward, and containment of women and their bodies. Put another way, they enable us to explore when a woman is not a woman, when "she" is a rhetorical figure.

　　If these remarks seem little more than a series of counterintuitive statements about metaphors, signification, and the referential process in the early Middle Ages, let us start with a few basics. Grammatical personification is a major method of signification in both classical and medieval Latin rhetoric. According to Cicero, all arts and sciences are "companions and handmaids" of the orator ("comites et ministrae").[5] Curtius similarly reminds us that the "personal metaphor," as he puts it, exemplified by those "mothers, stepmothers, companions, handmaids, and maids of Roman rhetoric," has "a most extensive progeny in the Middle Ages." The use of the "personal metaphor" is equally prolific in that other main vehicle of knowledge in this period, the Bible.[6] Small wonder that medieval patristic writers are so fond of grammatical personification—the feminine personification both of the vices and the virtues in the Latin *Psychomachia* tradition is well known, for example.[7]

The passage of the "extensive" and extensively female progeny of the "personal metaphor" and its referents in medieval Latin and vernacular works merits further study. In so doing, we need to go beyond Curtius's identification of the topos and its enumeration to consider its operation and impact in clerical discourse. Metaphors are ways of making meaning, of structuring knowledge, as we have already pointed out. To study the "personal metaphor" in Anglo-Saxon culture, then, is to study the purchase of the rhetorical on acts of understanding, and hence on deep-set and long-lasting patterns of cultural cognition. Patristic rhetoric, especially in its use of metaphor, is central to the process whereby didacticism in this period creates a Christian subject, as we explored both in our Introduction and in Chapter 4. Given that "personal metaphors" are generally feminine because Latin abstract nouns are mostly grammatically feminine, there is space here to consider the role of gender in both the signifying and the referential processes of making meanings and performing Christian subjects, especially in the Latin tradition.

In Chapter 1, we explored how metaphors of birthing are appropriated by masculine clerical culture and, as it were, sterilized for use in Bede's account of Hild in the *Ecclesiastical History*. This "mother" produces both clerical and secular masculine culture—Whitby is famous for the vernacular poet, Cædmon, as well as the five bishops trained there. The elision of Hild's own mother and the absence of maternity elsewhere in this text are conditions for the resignification of "birthing" as masculine: the presence of this spiritual maternity is a rhetorical condition of the masculinization of literate procedures. A similar case might be made for the grammatically feminine personification of Continence (*continentia*), the chaste mother whose lap is filled with her Christian offspring beckoning to Augustine at one of the most crucial moments in Book VIII of his *Confessions*:

and while I stood trembling at the barrier, on the other side I could see the chaste beauty of Continence in all her serene, unsullied joy, as she modestly beckoned me to cross over and to hesitate no more. She stretched out loving hands to welcome and embrace me, holding up a host of good examples to my sight. With her were countless boys and girls, great numbers of the young and people of all ages, staid widows and women still virgins in old age. And in their midst was Continence herself, not barren but a fruitful mother of children, of joys born of you, O Lord, her Spouse.[8]

Augustine's personification (itself so familiar a technique in classical rhetoric) here neatly replaces the "real" mother in the text, Monica, with Continentia in a conceptual system dominated by the paradox of a maternal, fruitful chastity. Monica's fertility is subject to this paradox, no less than Augustine in his own struggle for chastity. Both examples make sense finally in the *Confessions* by means of a signifying system that uses grammatical personification to deny fertility itself. Indeed Monica's maternity meets Augustine's paternity only to be resignified in this image of Continentia. Monica had two other children besides Augustine, while Augustine's own child is Adeodatus. In the *Confessions*, however, filial relations, the ties of family and blood—whether of Augustine with Monica or of Augustine with Adeodatus—are subsumed by spiritual relations, which are instead dictated by the logic of continence, chastity, and rhetoric.

We also discussed in Chapter 3 how the nuns of Barking Abbey are described by Aldhelm in his seventh-century prose *De virginitate* as "adoptive daughters of regenerative grace brought forth from the fecund womb of ecclesiastical conception." These "adoptive daughters" are encouraged by Aldhelm to think of their minds as male, and to think of the acquisition of scriptural learning as a wrestling routine. Tracing the connections between Aldhelm's metaphorics, the rhetorical articulation of making meaning, and the apparent references of such meanings to the Barking nuns is no simple matter, we note. But it is a matter upon which the nuns are invited to meditate as they read the text. The nuns are taught to think of their learning, hence their spirituality and their agency, as a complex series of symbolic negotiations between female and male signifiers in which the women themselves and preeminently their bodies are in continual danger of elision and omission. The "daughters of regenerative grace" are—equally symbolically—male athletes. If metaphors change sex, as the instances of clerical birthing and mothering from Bede and Aldhelm similarly suggest, so too and metaphorically do the subjects they perform—the Barking nuns.

The nun who mothers clerical sons, the mother who produces chastity, and the sex-changed female religious of Barking Abbey are all examples of clerical exploitation of and ambivalence about the meanings of the female and female bodily processes in the service of devotional behavior and patristic learning. In these examples, religious knowledge is symbolized by a metaphoric process that uses the gendered other for a source of its meanings. The exuberant baroque quality of such "personal," carnal, and femininized metaphors is a commonplace of patristic exegesis. Bede, to continue with the best-known exegete of the Anglo-Saxon period, offers this analogy for sacred study: "We press hard on the breasts [of Scripture] when we measure the words of sacred eloquence with a subtle mind."[9] Boethius describes Philosophy as the prisoner's former nurse, nourished on the "milk" of her "learning" (Book I. ii); later she is the "mother of all virtues" (Book II. iv). Such metaphors invite us to consider how and to what extent the feminine is implicated, contained, or expelled in this process of making clerical meanings and also—crucially—of making Christian subjects.

In the context of the gendered modes of clerical learning (and their interest in the breasts as a site of learning, virtue and wisdom), the opening item from Pseudo-Bede's *Collectanea* becomes both highly suggestive and less alien to early medieval clerical culture than its editors would have us believe: "Tell me, please, who is the woman who offers her breasts to innumerable sons, and who pours forth as much as she is sucked? This woman is wisdom."[10] To say that the grammatical gender of *sapientia* is the sole cause and explanation of this spectacularly feminine image of wisdom is simply inadequate. We are by no means the first feminist critics to call attention to liaisons between grammatical and so-called "natural" gender, though this subject has barely attracted attention among Anglo-Saxonists.[11] We note, too, how yet again a critical discourse insensitive to gender issues selectively naturalizes its subject and sets the body beyond critical purview. To us, however, the *Collectanea*'s image of wisdom inevitably evokes the female body. In fact, the site of wisdom's signification here is a complexly overdetermined image of the female body—maternal, nurturing, sexed, and intellectual. (Time and again as we have reviewed the material for this book, we have wondered what did our writers think they were writing.) And yet our response to this image of plenitude is that this wisdom is no woman. Further, she is no woman in much the same way that Bede's scriptural breasts do not intend a referent to the female body in the real. As Bede's metaphor and Boethius's personification of Philosophy suggest, the *Collectanea*'s image is a variant on a relatively common association between woman and wisdom in the patristic tradition, which is itself a subset of a wider series of associations between abstract virtues and the feminine. Indeed, Wisdom's fertile plenitude here is an apt counterpart to Augustine's image of the chaste but nurturing Continence in his *Confessions*: the female body is either perfectly chaste or spectacularly maternal (as ever?). These images from Bede, Boethius, Augustine, and the *Collectanea* indicate how the patristic imaginary disciplines and crafts for symbolic use a female body evidently perceived to be otherwise indiscriminate and out of control.

Furthermore, as we consider the relation between signification and reference in the *Collectanea*'s image of Wisdom, note that it is those "innumerable sons" who suck the milk from her breasts. We are only too aware that few women have access to the kind of clerical training in rhetoric and knowledge in the early medieval period that the *Collectanea* appears to represent. The *Collectanea* would seem to agree, or at least it expresses the kind of default misogyny and compensatory idealization of women common in the clerical tradition throughout the Middle Ages. Other items in the collection include remarks like "Constant sight of women softens the mind and dulls the judgement and does not allow for a man to be wise" (item 203). But the collection also finds room for this formally unanswered question: "Who can find a wise woman?" (item 204), and swiftly admonishes that "The wise man shuns every woman, the fool desires her and is wretchedly deceived by her" (item 206).[12]

If woman cannot be wise, then what of wisdom's femininity? Wisdom in the *Collectanea* is elsewhere imaged as a wellspring and nurse (item 144), in an echo of that overdetermined and indiscriminate mother with her many sons of the first item; as a key (item 26); as better than gold (item 63); and as a golden fountain (item 64), with its own echoes of idealized fluidity. Woman as referent, as opposed to personified metaphor, appears variously in questions about the first holy woman and the first prophetess (respectively Mary, sister of Abraham, item 7, and Dina, daughter of Jacob, item 8). But she is also the womb that is never satisfied (item 38)—not all forms of plenitude are as desirable as wisdom, clearly—and the source of domestic evil and temptation.[13] "What is worse than a house where woman has control over man?," muses one item (item 193), while another advises "Pay no heed to a woman's appearance, lest her face tempts you to evil" (item 214).[14] The juxtaposition between two other items (or "factoids" as we might now call them), which appear sequentially in the text, is particularly satisfying when we consider the disjunction between woman-as-referent and woman-as-metaphor evident in our other examples: "Remember always that it was a woman who expelled the first inhabitant of paradise from his inheritance," admonishes item 247, but then enumerates that "There are three daughters of the mind: faith, hope, and charity" (item 248).[15] The question here is what levels of the real are pointed to in both these examples? Not only do we see clerical ambivalence toward woman in full operation in this text, we also see just how indiscriminate—if not outright confused—is the compilation's own wavering between referential and symbolic modes, between the categories of woman and of the feminine. This wavering is a good analogy for the kinds of confusion (or rather, mess) that concepts of grammatical and "natural" gender create in assessing Old English (is it grammatical? is it "natural"?), but it is also an analogy for another kind of confusion, that of modern distinctions between "sex" and "gender."[16]

Most of the items about women or the feminine in the *Collectanea* are commonplaces, either from Scripture, the Church Fathers, or clerical (espe-cially insular) learning. Many have parallels with the kinds of knowledge about women codified in later medieval praise or blame traditions, though this compilation certainly does not belong to that tradition.[17] The items which either idealize or denigrate women that we have quoted above and that Alcuin Blamires terms pro- and antifeminine do not appear in a single block.[18] Nor are they necessarily related one to another, or indeed to other items in the *Collec-tanea*. The *Collectanea* comprises some 304 items, with a subsequent "appen-dix" of a further 84 items. There is, in other words, compelling evidence that it was compiled in at least two stages and over a period of time.[19] In consequence, the *Collectanea* does not have a center and therefore none of its items, whether pro- or antifeminine or not, are incidental to it. Its structure is best described instead as a clerical anthology of wisdom literature, heavily influenced by the genre of the patristic florilegium (so popular between the eighth and tenth centuries in early medieval Europe), and combined with a healthy dash of the "joca" tradition (clerical question and answer texts, which are equally popular in this period, and which so often feature riddles—a genre we have returned to many times in this book). Hence its editorial title, the *Collectanea*. Although its circumstances and origins are at best vexed (as all its commentators would agree), critical consensus argues for a probable Insular origin (that is, produced by an English or Irish cleric, either in the British Isles or in continental circles known to have British connections), and dated variously between the late eighth and tenth centuries.[20] The resistance of the *Collectanea* to dating and provenance, however, is a useful indication of the traditionality of the knowl-edge it encodes, and is therefore entirely consonant with our general investiga-tion of the role of gendered metaphors in the clerical tradition.

Indeed, wisdom literature, patristic florilegia, and question and answer texts such as the *Collectanea* are central to Latin and English traditions of knowing that order knowledge-as-commonplace in the early medieval pe-riod.[21] Traditionality is a powerful social process in the early Middle Ages, yet its specificities (its structures, its use of commonplaces, and its rhetorical modes) are barely understood.[22] What the *Collectanea* elegantly exemplifies is how knowledge about women and gender (no less than other forms of know-ing) in the early medieval period is structured according to dominant, conven-tional, and rhetorical modes. Such modes are specific to period, culture, and social formation—that is, they are thoroughly historical, and so too must be our methods of analysis. Further, the *Collectanea* reminds us that modes of knowing do not necessarily take the relation between gender and knowledge as their ordering principle. Wisdom is no woman, for example. In the *Collec-*

tanea, women can be subjects for knowing and objects of knowing (as in the cases of Dina, Mary, and Eve discussed above) while at the same time women are also obstacles to knowledge ("The wise man shuns every woman," item 206) *and* vehicles for knowledge (woman-as-wisdom, woman-as-womb). Above all and unlike men in this text, women never generate, never create knowledge. Recall the man impeded by the sight of a woman in his pursuit of wisdom already mentioned (item 203), or consider this item, "The wise man does not think he will die, but pass over; not leave his friends, but change them" (item 142). Insofar as they are explicitly gendered, men in the *Collectanea* are embedded into moral discourses of learning and ignorance: "The mouth of a just man is a vein of life" argues one item (item 230), while another suggests that "it is not enough to be indifferent to evil men if you are neutral to good men" (item 213). Given such gender asymmetries in the relation of subjects to knowledge, the pro- and antifeminine items in the *Collectanea* invite meditation more generally on the complex relations between woman as subject and object, as metaphor and referent, in discursive formations. These are relations of rhetoric, knowledge, and power that cut across the ad hoc structure of this particular text.

Read alongside our examples from Bede, Boethius, Augustine, and Aldhelm, the *Collectanea* provides strong evidence that Latin grammatical gender is profoundly coterminous with the gendering of knowledge itself in early medieval clerical culture. Although (as we have already mentioned) it is more conventional to argue that grammatical gender somehow "explains" such metaphors, it is clear that grammatical gender in fact lacks sufficient power to explain the ways in which the "personal metaphor" draws on cultural, clerical attitudes toward the feminine and the female body. Indeed, the complex ways in which the female body is *present* at such sites of signification are dependent, paradoxically, on the *absence* of that body as the point of reference.

There is some evidence that grammatical personification, especially feminine personification of abstract nouns (vices and virtues, for example), had less currency in vernacular Old English than in the Latin tradition. Though the influence and circulation of the *Psychomachia* material in Anglo-Latin culture is profound, Prudentius's use of female personification is not regularly picked up by vernacular authors (though it is there for all to see in the illuminations to the manuscripts, many of which have an Anglo-Saxon provenance).[23] Indeed, the Old English poems *Solomon and Saturn I and II*, which are at least partially influenced by Prudentius's *Psychomachia*, are thoroughly masculine allegories—agonistic struggles between forms of knowing.[24] Similarly, female personification is at best cursory and occasional in the *conflictus* tradition of the vices and virtues.[25] In the context of our discussion, then, what does it mean to discover that Philosophy has changed sex, name, and function in Alfred's radically modified English version of Boethius's *Consolation of Philosophy*?

The first thing to note is that Alfred eliminates from his version two of the best known female personifications in medieval literature—Fortune (*Fortuna*) and Philosophy (*Philosophia*)—both of which are endowed with the material trappings of "real" women as misogynistically understood in patristic and later clerical cultures. In Boethius, Philosophy is not merely the spectacular allegory presented in the opening sentences of the work (Book I, i)—towering high over the Prisoner to be lost in the clouds, awe-inspiring, dressed in ornately curious but dusty robes—she is also the nurturing mother of learning discussed above, chastizing her errant child, and thus recognizable in later medieval personifications such as Holy Church in *Piers Plowman*.[26] In much the same way, the Fortune of Book II is that familiarly mutable, capricious, not to mention callous though seductive woman who inspires at least in part such well-known figures as Chaucer's Criseyde. A Boethius without Fortune or Philosophy would seem to be unthinkable, but in restructuring Boethius's ethical system by making "Mod" ("mind") speak for and as the Prisoner, by redistributing the role of Fortune between "Wyrd" ("fate," "fatum") and Wisdom ("se Wisdom"), and by remodeling Philosophy as a grammatically divine wisdom ("se Wisdom," "sapientia Dei"), this is exactly what Alfred does.[27] The grammatically feminine faculty of reason ("gesceadwisness")—the faculty of discrimination—is a much more shadowy figure; barely personified, reason is an aspect of mind ("Mod") and wisdom ("Wisdom"). As both the distributor and origin of the good, Wisdom, not Philosophy, is the driving force behind Alfred's *Consolation* and Wisdom, following Old English grammatical gender, is masculine.

It is not implausible, however, that a grammatical personification based on the Latin might have given rise to a female figure in the vernacular. After all, "sapientia" is grammatically feminine, and there are sufficient other examples in Latin texts of the tradition of wisdom-as-woman (Bede, Pseudo-Bede, to name but two discussed here) to suggest that this topos might have held sway even across the language divide of Old English: the later medieval period managed to exploit woman-as-wisdom with considerable ease as evidenced by the example of Langland. By demonstrating the availability of choice, we underline Alfred's conscious decision to move from feminine to masculine figuration. This is part and parcel of a more sweeping series of changes that radically alters Boethius's philosophy, but it is also in part a response to an early vernacular cultural environment that barely uses female personification for abstract virtues.[28] And Alfred's Wisdom is in many ways a more abstract figure than Boethius's Philosophy or Fortune. On the one hand, Lerer notes that Alfred's approach to the idea of discovering wisdom frames itself anew in a vocabulary of hunting. A masculine Wisdom is now pursued, by men, with all the tropical attendance of the hunt (as opposed to those attendant "mothers, stepmothers, companions, and handmaids" of Latin rhetoric discussed earlier). Lerer's analysis of Alfred's metaphorical reworking of Boethius's text thus asserts the masculine, literate, and authoritarian project that we examined in Chapter 2.[29] On the other hand, Wisdom is hardly materially or sensibly present in Alfred's text in the way that both Philosophy and Fortune are in the Boethian text; in fact, Alfred's work becomes in many ways an interior dialogue between mind and wisdom, with the exterior apparatus of the Prisoner gradually minimized.[30] Indeed, Elaine Scarry reads the personifications of both Philosophy and Wisdom in Boethius as deliberate evocations of the sensible apprehension of knowledge, as "knowledge as material particular."[31] This is a compelling argument. The personification of Philosophy is not simply a default contribution to a long-lasting classical tradition of the "personal metaphor"; she is the materialization of philosophy accessible to the senses. At the same time, she also embodies the other levels of knowledge crucial to Boethius's system—Philosophy thus personifies knowledge sensitive to its material, imaginative, and rational aspects.[32] As a result, Boethius has breathed new life into that old classical association between women and matter, although his Philosophy (as matter) is no more a material woman than is the Wisdom of the *Collectanea*.[33]

Scarry's reading, however, flies in the face of many Anglo-Saxonists, who see Boethius's text as more abstract and less material than Alfred's or who confuse Alfred's fondness for the "concrete" metaphor or image (as opposed to Boethius's nominal personifications) with a thorough and ongoing apprehension of knowledge in all its aspects.[34] This is not to say that Alfred necessarily misunderstood Boethius. To the contrary, Alfred is certainly aware of the material world, applying his Christian insights into the material importance of freedom and kingship, as is well known. But it is to argue that in choosing not to develop "Se Wisdom" into a full-blown masculine personification allegory (the counterpart to Boethius's feminine personification of Philosophy), Alfred is redirecting Boethius's own apprehension of knowledge. What has occurred in the process of Alfred's modifications is crucial; woman-as-wisdom (and matter) is eliminated. Philosophy is dematerialized only to rematerialize as a masculine *abstraction*. Here, then, we glimpse a possible explanation for the relative infrequency of female personification in the vernacular during our period. Knowledge, as popularized by Alfred in his English version of Boethius (intended at least in part for an upper-class secular audience), is modeled as both universal (abstract) and male (recall the vocabulary of the hunt); the feminine, however misogynistically construed as the material embodiment of knowing in the classical text, has virtually no role to play in the vernacular text.

Philosophy's sex change into Wisdom, in sum, is no more simple than the metaphorical sex changes enjoined on the gendered subjects of the Barking Nuns. Alfred's replacement of the lady with (the grammatically masculine) "Wisdom"—an apparent reversal of the maternal wisdom of the first item in the *Collectanea*—may not fully eradicate or suppress the female body, however. For one thing, and especially for a clerical, learned audience, the Latin Boethius (with his lady Philosophia and his fickle Fortune) continues to circulate alongside Alfred's text.[35] For another, components of desire, longing, and revelation haunt the display and pursuit of Wisdom in the now homosocial world of Alfred's rhetoric. The psychosexual dynamics of seeing and knowing (also familiar to us from the life of *Mary of Egypt* in Chapter 4) are further complicated elsewhere in Alfred's rhetorical figurings. In his version of the *Soliloquies*, for example, desire for wisdom and hence spiritual knowing (in the image of the ungloved hand) is developed by Alfred into a metaphor that is explicitly sexual, erotic, and complexly masculine and feminine.[36] In the *Soliloquies*, as in the other examples of cognition and knowledge discussed here, we note how the process of knowing takes place against and over the female body as a site (variously construed as both absent and present, material and immaterial) for the representation of knowledge, but not as a place where woman can be represented as a seeker of that knowledge (whether of wisdom or philosophy). To demonstrate how this hegemony of knowing is enacted time and again in other cultural genres and practices, we turn next to the penitentials.

Cognition and Containment

If the *Collectanea* and Alfred's translations reveal clerical as well as regal modes of cognition, then one other place to examine issues of interiority and cognition, and of psychic and physical control in our period is in the penitentials, a group of Irish and Anglo-Saxon texts that has recently received careful and illuminating scholarly attention. These texts are an important early landmark in the formation of a patristic symbolic.[37] In their cataloging of sins and penances, nondiscriminate targeting of personal, social and religious behaviors, and highly discriminating categorization (in terms of class, church, and secular differentations), the penitential texts make plain a directive to control the difference they assign, to contain the body, and indeed the psyche. Allen J. Frantzen suggests that the focus of the penitentials on sin and intention anticipates a concept of "interiority" that has been reserved as a twelfth-century psychological innovation—once again calling attention to the alienating presence of a historical master paradigm that constructs the difference of our period.[38] Katherine O'Brien O'Keeffe examines the idea of self through the legal enactment of punishment upon the body, which can be "read" as a disclosed self and cultural document, and which affords an opportunity "to speculate on the ways in which the subject is formed through such discourse."[39] Her argument also takes issue with the notion of a sudden twelfth-century genesis of forms of interiority that may be recognised as modern. While the mutilated punished body may "speak" itself and its crimes or history in a manner different from later forms of medieval confession, O'Brien O'Keeffe asserts that "other it may be, but opposite it is not."[40]

While the didactic purpose of the penitentials is overt and unchallenged as such, there is some range of opinion as to how far these texts permeated and influenced Anglo-Saxon society, both monastic and lay. Although he argues that Theodore's penitential "unquestionably enlarged the role of penitential practice in church government and invited closer interaction between the church and secular authority," Frantzen also concludes that such practice was "part of the religious life of the few."[41] Alan Thacker's assessment of the impact of Theodore's self-consciously disciplinary penitential, for example, raises issues of detection and enforcement; the relative absence of personal privacy in living conditions suggests that "Theodore may well have expected his rulings to be effective."[42] Thacker also wryly observes that the penitential program was so severe that "it is difficult to believe they can ever have expected to achieve all this without the use of force."[43]

The woman entering a church during her "time of impurity" might be policed by a whistleblowing public, as might the penitent "who pollutes himself through the violence of his imagination,"[44] but whether menstruation or masturbation might be more or less easy to detect, or whether "he who amuses himself with libidinous imagination" might be detectable at all,[45] the construction of accountability as external and communal as well as individual and psychic adds the important dimension of publication of bodily process, as well as its containment, to the force of these texts. Thacker, however, cannot rationalize the widespread adoption of such a rigorously monastic program for behavior in the context of Anglo-Saxon secular social development.[46] Stephanie Hollis takes a somewhat different view of the social significance of Theodore's rulings, especially as these aim to control marriage; the elements of compromise to be found in regional variations of the penitential canons, however guarded or reluctant, suggest a degree of accommodation to existing (i.e., pre-Christian) Anglo-Saxon cultural practice and some doctrinal flexibility.[47] This in turn might result in greater social viability and currency for a text that addresses the secular and religious condition of the married body. Whether or not one adopts a specific view of their significance, it is worth emphasizing that these texts lay an important claim to the making of meaning—indeed, the identification of sin and its consequences—and as such they function as guarantors of the symbolic.

It may not be possible to gauge the religious and cultural effect of the penitentials beyond an assessment of the intent, direction of containment, and historically detectable trajectory of individual directives. The demarcation of categories and assignments of difference in Theodore's penitential, however, provide in themselves a working glimpse of the operation of the symbolic. In a ruling concerning penance for perjury, for example, we discover the status of oaths in a transitional stage of embodiment. An oath sworn upon the hand of an ordained deacon (here on a par with the bishop or priest) has the same status as one sworn on "an altar or a consecrated cross."[48] In this case the physical body of the deacon (or at least, one part of it, his hand) can signify in much the same way as the overt symbolic structures of the altar and the cross, and indeed the covert relic within the altar, and be symbolically identified with other sacerdotal signifying bodies. But rank interrupts the transition, and the deacon's body does not signify in other circumstances. (Indeed, at the top of the scale, priests lose out too—only a bishop can absolve from a vow.[49]) Giving penance to the laity and saying mass are the privileged functions reserved for the body, priestly and episcopal, which has wholly entered the symbolic and may participate in cultural as well as eucharistic transsubstantiation, "Deacons can baptize, and they can bless food and drink; they cannot give the bread."[50] The hierarchy of rank (the seven grades of the clergy) is also a hierarchy of sacerdotal mystery, which serves to register degrees of embodiment within the symbolic as well as the processes and means by which the symbolic is guaranteed. Of course, this relates to our discussion of the priestly body in Chapter 3.

As sacerdotal male bodies enter the symbolic, and then stand as its guarantors, in strict gradation, lay men and women register within it in equally strict terms of containment—whether such containment is seen in terms of secular rank or gender. The penitential assignment of difference develops according to ecclesiastical priorities; whereas Ethelbert's laws a century or so earlier make a distinction between wergild for a murdered slave and a freeman, Theodore marks the penitential difference in terms of clergy and lay victims.[51] Sites of containment can also be assessed via the sheer variety of possibilities for sin—that is, the more possibilities there are, the more means of containment are needed. Frantzen points out that there are more "new" sins, and especially sins for women, in Theodore's penitential in comparison with the Irish texts,[52] although there are places where it is hard to know whether the reference to the masculine is inclusive of the feminine.[53] And so we return to the issues of grammatical gender and the difficulties posed by adopting developmental models of women's history. But whether sins and their penances are gender specific or not, one can follow lines of demarcation in Theodore's text and ask how this overt, that is, recorded containment, which marks the body's entry into the symbolic, can at the same time make it disappear—albeit with a trace. We note that this same dialectic operates in sacramental, elegiac and riddling discourses, as explored in Chapter 3.

The ranks in the penitentials literally close against religious women ("the handmaidens of Christ") in Theodore's specific directives concerning women's ministry: "Women shall not cover the altar with the corporal nor place on the altar the offerings, nor the cup, nor stand among ordained men in the church, nor sit at a feast among priests," although they may perform ministries tangential to the altar.[54] This ruling has the dual effect of imaging women *and* their exclusion, evoking presence to specify absence, and demarcating religious women's lack of physical incorporation into the symbolic and the ranks of its ecclesiastical guarantors. Such documented absence parallels the theoretical conundrum of Æbba's situation discussed in Chapter 2, where lack of structural incorporation is more clearly at issue. Recall that Æbba (whose tenure as abbess of Minster-in-Thanet roughly coincides with the compilation of Theodore's rulings) appears within the documentary record, but may not act as cultural guarantor and stand witness to it. Exclusion at the most abstract or most mundane levels of the symbolic, sacred and secular, reveals the same dynamic and trajectory of containment, which in turn filters through culture at those same abstract and mundane levels. These are the quotidian domains of the double agent, and the catch, as ever, is that it is only through understanding exclusion and containment that we see the agent herself.

As we have also argued, sites of containment leave traces, even enact the historical and textual detail of the process of containment, and, moreover, define and create trajectories of absence. This is to suggest that when Alfred makes his foray into rhetoric, looks about for a metaphor several centuries later than Theodore's penitential, and seeks to image the processes of under-standing and interpretation that will create and apprehend the symbolic, it should come as no surprise that he does not, cannot, "see" a woman.

We have also argued that, as our period comes to its critically legislated close, the sites of containment of the female body are culturally detectable at the most abstract of representational levels; female bodies become static icons and the icon secures a cultural ideal of a Christian, universalized subject that is most often male. Women's absence is continually reconfigured in such shifting liaisons between representational and referential practices, and Alfred's meta-phorical sex change for Philosophy is thus more clearly understood in terms of continuity than of rhetorical rupture. But neither does Alfred move us directly from point A to point B. The trajectory of disappearance suggested by Theodore's lines of demarcation has no consistent coordinates; moreover, some metaphors die hard, and in doing so undergo transformation.

Relics: Dead Bodies, Living Metaphors

Where the living or "real" female body is suppressed or eradicated within the cultural symbolic, the dead one retains a remarkably vital rhetorical currency. The line we will follow here is the convoluted passage of female body into static icon—how the body becomes the relic, and the ambiguities and para-doxes of that passage. To ask questions like when is a relic a metaphor, when is it a thing, and when is it a body is to ask how the dead (female) body "matters" within culture, and is to encapsulate the issues of representation and referen-tiality that we consider so central to our rereading of clerical culture and its modes of knowing.

Whether burial may be seen as a final "containment" of the female body is one issue raised by monastic burial practices and the extent to which sex-segregated cemeteries were adopted or required. Hollis discusses instances where gender may or may not be a deciding factor in the chosen or assigned burial places of monastic women; while men and women were often buried together in double monasteries, changes in this practice paralleled the slow but steady influence of Theodore's overall disapproval of the double monas-teries themselves.[55] Thacker points out that Theodore is not much concerned with actual burial practice, and that who got buried where, of either sex, lay or secular, was often a matter of ecclesiastical and secular alignments of the regional *monasteria*, and of whether one was either very holy or very rich.[56] As dead bodies become sanctified, however, and turn into relics, issues of class and gender raised by burial practice become far more politically charged. The cult of the saints, which gathers continuous momentum throughout the period, becomes an important place to look for women's (dead and alive) entry into and containment within the symbolic. Leoba's body, as we will see, exemplifies much of the ambivalence and complexity surrounding the dead, female, saintly body and its transition into relic, but first it will be interesting to note a few earlier cases of clerical ambivalence where the dead and living are in uneasy rhetorical cohabitation.

Theodore maintains a clear position on the dead sanctified body: "the relics of saints are to be venerated."[57] And when the relics are those of a dead heretic, the church's mandate is equally clear: these must be destroyed by fire, suggesting both the power of the idea of the relic, the potential for its abuse, and the need to legislate its representation.[58] Such potential for abuse is somewhat nervously imagined in Stephen of Ripon's Life of Bishop Wilfrid, as he remarks upon the outragious behavior of Queen Jurmenburg.[59] After the unfortunate Wilfrid has been thrown into prison by her husband Ecgfrith (himself no respector of papal or episcopal pomp as we saw in Chapter 2), the queen adds insult to injury:

His queen, moreover, whom we have mentioned before, took away the reliquary of the man of God which was full of holy relics and (I tremble to say it) she wore it is as an ornament both in her chamber at home and when riding abroad in her chariot.[60]

In the highly politicized world of early eighth-century Northumbrian politics, to which this episode belongs, Hollis argues persuasively for the demonization of Jurmenburh along party lines, as one possible result of the threat she may pose—and the ecclesiastical discomfort she may cause—in her role as female royal advisor and confidant.[61] But whatever the actual source of Stephen's disapprobation, more to the present point is his manner of expressing it, his fearful, almost unspeakable imagining of the dead body in concert with the practices—all too physical—of the living one. The intimations of physical aversion to this coupling are spelled out more clearly in Alcuin's later comments concerning the abuse of relics among the English:

The amulets which many people there are accustomed to carry, wishing to have sacred things round their necks, not in the heart, and with these holy words of God or the relics of the saints go to their filthy acts and even do their duty by their wives; this is a sin.[62]

Religious and sexual zeal rhetorically cohabit rather less easily here than they do in Bede's *History*, when, for example, the pope enlists Æthelburg to join the effort to convert her resistant husband, King Edwin. The papal request and its suggested tactics hold out the future enjoyment of "undefiled union" (clearly emphasizing her current state of defilement), once she has managed to "inflame his cold heart" with desire for conversion (*EH*, 2. 11). There is some rhetorical overlap in Bede's account, in contrast to the clearly delineated bifurcation of desire imaged by Alcuin and Stephen. And perhaps the polarization is strengthened, even motivated by the dis-ease caused by metaphorical corporeal overlap. The metaphor for the dead body (the relic) haunts the living body, even as the idea of a corporeal (female?) presence worries the dead in return, and interrupts the smooth operation of the symbolic, even threatens its power *as* metaphor.

Of course, relics could also be a liability, and a popularizing, potentially demystifying force in themselves. Control over their dissemination and representation is an ongoing challenge to both ecclesiastical and secular formations of the symbolic throughout the period. Witness the entanglement of politics, power, and body parts, in the story of Edburga's relics discussed in Chapter 1, to name but one saint whose dead body remained the source of lively dispute. Here the symbolic value and force of the relic are juggled alongside the demands of the living communities, vying with one another in their claims for control of its representation.[63] This is to acknowledge that the relic (the dead body) can coexist in some dynamic relation to the living, or current, symbolic—that it may have plenty of metaphoric shelf life remaining, and that we would do well to allow it to continually complicate our understanding of the operation of metaphor within the symbolic.

Finally, in the middle of our period, an evocation of one dead body remarkable for its multivalence—a study in dying hard. Leoba (d. 780) is relatively well recorded within and without our period, and it is our intention not to rehearse her life story, but rather to focus attention on the odd peregrination of her dead body. Hollis has provided us with a thorough and convincing analysis of the literate means by which her story is both revealed and concealed in her discussion of three hagiographical sources, Rudolph of Fulda's *Life of Leoba*, Willibald's *Life of Boniface*, and the *Life of Sturm* by Eigil.[64] Moreover, Leoba's career as an English-trained missionary abbess to the continent in the mid-eighth century is of key significance in tracing a specific trajectory for the demise of the prominent churchwomen of the late seventh and early eighth centuries, as Hollis details a progression from missionary leadership to passive enclosure, and the movement from active teaching to becoming an *exemplum* to one's pupils.[65] Although Leoba's wisdom, her function as educator, and the power of her words resonate with those of Hild or Ælfflaed, her English antecedents, an accurate assessment of her contribution to, or degree of erasure within the cultural record, depends upon the same examination of what Hollis terms "orthodox censorship" and its ecclesiastical motivations. And nowhere is such censorship more obvious than in the matter of what to do with Leoba's dead body.

In Rudolph's *Life*, Boniface makes a clear if unusual request that he and Leoba be buried together, a request that Hollis finds wholly credible: "Rudolph cannot have invented Boniface's instruction that Leoba was to be buried in his tomb; it is so entirely at odds with his own rigidly orthodox position on monastic separation."[66] His request is nowhere mentioned in other sources, which also effectively erase the impact of Leoba's leadership, but, curiously, Rudolph's *Life*, the only evidence we have for the extent of Leoba's influence and the details of her career in the Church, let alone Boniface's burial wishes, is occasioned by the presence of her relics at the monastery at Fulda. While the fact that we have Rudolph's documentation of Leoba's impact at all is "a salutary reminder of the limitations of the surviving documentation of the early church," it is also a function of the dead body's intrusion into the living symbolic.[67] The literate account of her life is motivated by the ecclesiastical need, apparently ongoing, to rationalize the presence of the dead female body, which rests far from peacefully.

Leoba's remains are "translated" three times. She dies some twenty-five years after Boniface, and is initially buried close to her friend and mentor, at an altar he had dedicated, but not with him, as requested. Hollis explains this compromise in terms of monastic embarassment and Rudolph's admitted reluctance to open a tomb of such a revered figure.[68] But her bones still rest uneasily, and during a rebuilding phase at Fulda she is later removed to a more remote and "least hallowed" precinct of the church. Eventually, as monastic separation of the sexes is enforced, she experiences a final, but still ambiguous "translation" (ca. 837 or 838) to a prominent church built by Hrabanus Maurus. The church may have been prominent, but her bones are "consigned to a reliquary in the crypt, placed behind an altar dedicated to the Mother of God and the female virgins of Christ."

There are many symbolic lines both drawn and traceable in such an itinerary. Hollis finds it "graphically emblematic" of profound cultural shifts in perception, the "correlative of a developing conception of monastic women as inalienably and dangerously other."[69] What we emphasize here is that such deep divisions, such cultural othering and assignment of difference, are processes writ in bodies, both living and dead. The rhetorical passages of bodily containment point again and again to the vital necessity of the body, metaphorical and "real," dead or alive, as a site of signification. The body does not effectively disappear within the symbolic. In other words, we could say that the metaphor, especially as it engages the female body, always dies hard.

Over Her Dead Body: Rhetoric, Agency, and History

As we come to the end of this book, we remember the women whose lives drew us into rethinking their relation to their culture in the first place. Some have come into clearer focus; others remain anonymous and obscure. Hild in some respects was an exemplary double agent: she offered us a clear track to follow across the reticences of the cultural record and a glimpse of the "real." Others prompt more questions than answers, such as the enigmatic queen mother, Osburh, who gave her sons a taste for their own culture, or the Hereford mother who would not give a penny to hers. These women stay with us and remind us that the writing of their histories is an ongoing project. Our questions about women and agency in the Anglo-Saxon period, however, beg more general questions, and we offer some of them here as one way to continue this project.

In insisting on the possibility of agency (however mediated) and its recovery, we might be described as working between two theoretical domains at the same time: the structural (not structuralist) view of history, which centers on institutional formations of the social and cultural symbolic, and the realm of the subject, the possibilities of describing the self that emerges from and in relation to those formations. For us, however, the difference of the Anglo-Saxon period is a way to understand how these theoretical domains are mediated in this instance by our formulation of the Christian subject. With this model, we acknowledge the importance of rigorous historicization of institutional forms of the symbolic as well as the interaction of these forms with the domain of the subject. Just as there are many ways to think about and describe institutional formations, there are many ways to think about the Anglo-Saxon Christian self. How gender and class complicate and enrich these models has been our predominant concern in this book—we are talking here about elision, absence, and suppression as well as factors that enable agency. We have sought a means of discussing agency, but also of recovering it working against these obscuring veils of clerical discourse.

Agency and the historical forces that interact with or suppress it are part of a larger debate about persecution in the Middle Ages. We are profoundly indebted to R. I. Moore, who asked far-reaching questions about the persecution of minorities using the later medieval evidence of Jews, heretics, and lepers.[70] Moore established a sociostructural model for extreme forms of the suppression of individual agency and demonstrated how violence becomes culturally normative. The idea that violence becomes so naturalized that it is habitual and quotidian resonates deeply with us because of its analogies with instances of structural suppression of women's agency in the Anglo-Saxon period.[71] We cannot emphasize too strongly here that we are not claiming a level of persecution of women in any way comparable to that of later medieval minorities. Nor do we claim by any stretch of the imagination that the Anglo-Saxon period is synonymous with the later "formation of a persecuting society."[72] What we take from Moore is his uncompromising insistence on the nature of persecution as structural, institutional, habitual, and therefore very powerful. To us, the denial, silencing, and elision of women's agency in the Anglo-Saxon cultural record at this structural level is so pervasive as to seem utterly naturalized. In short, there is a point where "over her dead body" carries a more straightforward literal message that is no longer veiled by the operations of patristic metaphor.

The problem with the structural view of the suppression of women's agency in the Anglo-Saxon period is, of course, the problem of any structural model that does not mediate the domain of the individual and her possibilities for local interaction and negotiation with broader institutional and social structures. As we have said before and indeed exemplified in this book, there are lots of women—upper class women especially—living their lives productively in both social and cultural spheres. The more apparent the forms of naturalization of suppression, the clearer the rationale for further research into its multiple processes. Such research needs to continue to work in and across the domains of both self and society. The areas we are particularly concerned with here are the categories of self, pysche, body, and the possibilities for the Christian subject; the massively complex relation between the feminine, orality, and literacy that we have only begun to uncover; and the labor (which we suspect will be lifelong for us) to demystify the naturalizing forces of patristic rhetoric and its power to structure cognition.

Abbreviations

ASE	*Anglo-Saxon England*
ASPR	George Philip Krapp and Elliott Van Kirk Dobbie, eds., *Anglo-Saxon Poetic Records*. New York: Columbia University Press, 1932–53
B	W. G. de Birch, ed. *Cartularium Saxonicum*. 3 vols. London: Whiting and Co., 1885–89.
CCSL	*Corpus Christianorum Series Latina*. Turnhout: Brepols, 1953–.
EH	*Bede's Ecclesiastical History of the English People*. Ed. and trans. Bertram Colgrave and R. A. B. Mynors. Oxford: Clarendon Press, 1969.
EETS	*Early English Text Society*. London: Trübner (et al.), 1864–.
JMEMS	*Journal of Medieval and Early Modern Studies*
MS	*Medieval Studies*
MGH	*Monumenta Germaniae Historica*. Hanover: Impensis Bibliopolii Hahniani (et al.), 1826–.
PL	J.-P. Migne, ed. *Patrologia cursus completus . . . series Latina*. Paris: Garnier Fratres and J.-P. Migne, 1844–.
PMLA	*Proceedings of the Modern Language Association*
S	P. H. Sawyer, ed. *Anglo-Saxon Charters: An Annotated List and Bibliography*. London: Royal Historical Society, 1968.
W	Dorothy Whitelock, ed. *English Historical Documents c. 500–1042*. Vol. 1. London: Eyre and Spottiswoode, 1955.

Notes

Introduction

1. Exemplified by Martha C. Howell, *Women, Production, and Patriarchy in Late Medieval Cities* (Chicago: University of Chicago Press, 1986); and Judith M. Bennett, *Women in the Medieval English Countryside* (Oxford: Oxford University Press, 1987) and *Ale, Beer, and Brewsters in England: Women's Work in a Changing World, 1300–1600* (Oxford: Oxford University Press, 1996). See also the increased emphasis on historicism in studies of fourteenth-century England by David Aers and Lynn Staley, *The Powers of the Holy: Religion, Politics, and Gender in Late Medieval English Culture* (University Park: Pennsylvania State University Press, 1996); Sarah Beckwith, *Christ's Body: Identity, Culture, and Society in Late Medieval Writings* (New York: Routledge, 1993); Steven Justice, *Writing and Rebellion: England in 1381* (Berkeley: University of California Press, 1994); and Lee Patterson, *Chaucer and the Subject of History* (Madison: University of Wisconsin Press, 1991).

2. Allen J. Frantzen compellingly elucidates the role of origins and beginnings in Anglo-Saxon studies in *Desire for Origins: New Language, Old English, and Teaching the Tradition* (New Brunswick, N.J.: Rutgers University Press, 1990), pp. 23–24.

3. Lee Patterson's comment on subjectivity is characteristic: "To write the history of the medieval subject is in effect to write the history of medieval culture." See "On the Margin: Postmodernism, Ironic History, and Medieval Studies," *The New Philology*, ed. Stephen G. Nichols, *Speculum* 65 (1990): 100. Patterson's work on this subject, however, makes no room for the early medieval subject or the culture of Anglo-Saxon England, although he does make a plea for a "return" to Anglo-Saxon studies in "The Return to Philology," *The Past and Future of Medieval Studies*, ed. John Van Engen (Notre Dame, Ind.: University of Notre Dame Press, 1994), p. 242. For similar elisions on work on the body, see Caroline Walker Bynum, *Fragmentation and Redemption: Essays on Gender and the Human Body in Medieval Religion* (New York: Zone Books, 1992) and *The Resurrection of the Body in Western Christianity, 200–1336* (New York: Columbia University Press, 1995); Sarah Kay and Miri Rubin, eds., *Framing Medieval Bodies* (Manchester: Manchester University Press, 1994); Linda Lomperis and Sarah Stanbury, eds., *Feminist Approaches to the Body in Medieval Literature* (Philadelphia: University of Pennsylvania Press, 1993). Contrast Allen J. Frantzen, "When Women Aren't Enough," *Speculum* 68 (1993): 445–71, repr. in *Studying Medieval Women: Sex, Gender, Feminism*, ed. Nancy F. Partner (Cambridge, Mass.: Medieval Academy of America, 1993), pp. 143–69; "Between the Lines: Queer Theory, the History of Homosexuality, and Anglo-Saxon Penitentials," *JMEMS* 26,2 (1996): 255–96; "The Fragmentation of Cultural Studies and the Fragments of Anglo-Saxon England," *Anglia* 114

(1996): 310–39; and Carol Braun Pasternack, "Post-Structuralist Theories: The Subject and the Text," *Reading Old English Texts*, ed. Katherine O'Brien O'Keeffe (Cambridge: Cambridge University Press, 1997), pp. 170–91.

4. For the role of origins and oppositions in constructing Anglo-Saxon England, see Frantzen, *Desire for Origins*, pp. 18–22. Notions of the so-called "golden age" of Anglo-Saxon women are heavily influenced by Christine Fell, with Cecily Clark and Elizabeth Williams, *Women in Anglo-Saxon England* (Oxford: Blackwell, 1984); for a survey of gender studies in Old English literature, see Clare A. Lees, "Engendering Religious Desire: Sex, Knowledge, and Christian Identity in Anglo-Saxon England," *JMEMS* 27,1 (1997): 17–45. The common phrase, "no sex please, we're British," activates much thinking about the period; see Hugh Magennis, "'No Sex Please, We're Anglo-Saxons'? Attitudes to Sexuality in Old English Prose and Poetry," *Leeds Studies in English* n.s. 26 (1995): 1–27, and Clare A. Lees, "At a Crossroads: Old English and Feminist Criticism," *Reading Old English Texts*, ed. O'Brien O'Keeffe, pp. 146–69.

5. For further discussion see Lees, "At a Crossroads."

6. See such studies as Jane Chance, *Woman as Hero in Old English Literature* (Syracuse, N.Y.: Syracuse University Press, 1986); Fell, *Women in Anglo-Saxon England*; Helen Damico and Alexandra Hennessey Olsen, eds., *New Readings on Women in Old English Literature* (Bloomington: Indiana University Press, 1990).

7. *Anglo-Saxon Women and the Church: Sharing a Common Fate* (Woodbridge: Boydell, 1992). Other studies we have found particularly helpful are Pauline Stafford, "Women and the Norman Conquest," *Transactions of the Royal Historical Society* 6th ser., 4 (1994): 221–49, and *Queen Emma and Queen Edith: Queenship and Women's Power in Eleventh-Century England* (Oxford: Blackwell, 1997).

8. Fell, *Women in Anglo-Saxon England*, remains the only full-length study of women in Anglo-Saxon England; there is no such analysis of gender more generally.

9. An exception here is Henrietta Leyser, *Medieval Women: A Social History of Women in England 450–1500* (London: Orion Books, 1995).

10. The absence of formations of belief from the study of culture, both modern and medieval, is further discussed by Lees in the Introduction to *Tradition and Belief: Religious Writing in Late Anglo-Saxon England* (Minneapolis: University of Minnesota Press, 1999), pp. 12–18.

11. See Patterson, "On the Margin," and David Aers, "A Whisper in the Ear of Early Modernists; or, Reflections on Literary Critics Writing the 'History of the Subject,'" in *Culture and History, 1350–1600*, ed. Aers (Detroit: Wayne State University Press, 1992), pp. 177–202, and "Preface," *Historical Inquiries/Psychoanalytic Criticism/Gender Studies*, *JMEMS* 26,2 (1996): 200–208. For a longer study of the Christian subject, see Lees, *Tradition and Belief*, pp. 106–32.

12. Bynum's important study on the resurrected body (*The Resurrection of the Body*), which explicitly excludes the Anglo-Saxon period, is characteristic in this regard.

13. As Bynum (*Fragmentation and Redemption* and *The Resurrection of the Body*), and Aers and Staley demonstrate (*The Powers of the Holy*), although this work tends to concentrate on the later medieval period.

14. Michel Foucault, *The History of Sexuality*, vol. 1, *An Introduction*, trans. Robert Hurley (New York: Random House, 1978). Public as well as private confession

characterizes late Anglo-Saxon England, as Frantzen demonstrates in *The Literature of Penance in Anglo-Saxon England* (New Brunswick, N.J.: Rutgers University Press, 1983). For a critique of Foucault's influence on recent work in sexuality and subjectivity in medieval studies, see Karma Lochrie, "Desiring Foucault," *JMEMS* 27,1 (1997): 3–16.

15. Toril Moi, *What Is a Woman? and Other Essays* (Oxford: Oxford University Press, 1999), esp. pp. 3–250.

16. *EH* 1. 27. See also Lees, "Engendering Religious Desire."

17. See our discussion of Hild in Chapter 1, and of Æthelthryth in Chapter 4.

18. See Jane Tibbetts Schulenberg, "The Heroics of Virginity" in *Women in the Middle Ages and the Renaissance: Literary and Historical Perspectives*, ed. Mary Beth Rose (Syracuse, N.Y.: Syracuse University Press, 1986), pp. 29–72, for a discussion of the possible genesis of the epigram "to cut off your nose to spite your face."

19. See, for example, the work of Elisabeth Schüssler Fiorenza, especially *But She Said: Feminist Practices of Biblical Interpretation* (Boston: Beacon Press, 1992); and Andrew Kadel, *Matrology: A Bibliography of Writings by Christian Women from the First to the Fifteenth Centuries* (New York: Continuum Press, 1995).

20. For an introduction to Aldhelm, see Michael Lapidge and Michael Herren, trans. *Aldhelm: The Prose Works* (Cambridge: D.S. Brewer, 1979), pp. 1–19, and Andy Orchard, *The Poetic Art of Aldhelm* (Cambridge: Cambridge University Press, 1994), pp. 1–18. All references to Aldhelm's *De virginitate* are to the prose version, translated by Lapidge and Herren, unless otherwise indicated, and will be cited in the text by parenthetical page reference (i.e., Lapidge and Herren and page number, or page number alone where context is clear). For Ælfric, see Jonathan Wilcox, ed., *Ælfric's Prefaces* (Durham: Durham Medieval Texts, 1994), pp. 1–15, and Peter Clemoes, "Ælfric," *Continuations and Beginnings: Studies in Old English Literature*, ed. Eric Gerald Stanley (London: Nelson, 1966), pp. 176–209; his *Lives of Saints* are edited by W. W. Skeat, *Ælfric's Lives of Saints*, vol. 1, *EETS* 76, 82 (1881, 1885, repr. as one vol., Oxford: Oxford University Press, 1966), vol. 2, *EETS* 94, 114 (1890, 1900, repr. as one vol. 1966), and will be cited in the text by parenthetical reference. All translations from Ælfric are authorial.

21. For a critique of the "change" model for women's history in the later medieval period, see Judith M. Bennett, "Medieval Women, Modern Women: Across the Great Divide," in *Culture and History, 1350–1600*, ed. Aers, pp. 147–75; and more generally "Women's History: A Study in Continuity and Change," *Women's History Review* 2,2 (1993): 173–84; and *Ale, Beer, and Brewsters in England*.

Chapter 1

1. Frank M. Stenton, "The Historical Bearing of Place-Name Studies: The Place of Women in Anglo-Saxon Society," in *New Readings on Women in Old English Literature*, ed. Damico and Olsen, pp. 79–88 (at p. 79); see also Peter Hunter Blair, *An Introduction to Anglo-Saxon England* (Cambridge: Cambridge University Press, 1959), p. 25; Patrick Sims-Williams, *Religion and Literature in Western England, 600–800* (Cambridge: Cambridge University Press, 1990), p. 102.

2. Frantzen, *Desire for Origins*, p. 142.

3. Frantzen, *Desire for Origins*, pp. 18–20.

4. Kevin S. Kiernan, "Reading Cædmon's 'Hymn' with Someone Else's Glosses," *Representations* 32 (1990): 157–74; Martin Irvine, "Medieval Textuality and the Archaeology of Textual Culture," in *Speaking Two Languages: Traditional Disciplines and Contemporary Theory in Medieval Studies*, ed. Allen J. Frantzen (Albany, N.Y.: SUNY Press, 1991), pp. 181–210 (at pp. 197–99); Seth Lerer, *Literacy and Power in Anglo-Saxon Literature* (Lincoln: University of Nebraska Press, 1991), pp. 30–60. Arguing that he is realigning "the study of Cædmon by situating it in the narrative trajectory of Book 4" (p. 33), Lerer relates Bede's narrative of Cædmon to his account of Imma (*EH* 4. 22), thus eliding the chapter on Hild altogether. Lerer's account of Bede's interest in the signifying power of Christian letters as opposed to the dead letters of the Imma narrative is indeed important, but Bede's Book 4 is also arguably the book of female abbesses, as we suggest below, note 47.

5. Christine Fell, "Hild, Abbess of Streonæshalch," in *Hagiography and Medieval Literature: A Symposium*, ed. Hans Bekker-Nielsen, Peter Foote, Jorgen Hojgaard Jorgensen, and Tore Nyberg (Odense: Odense University Press, 1981), pp. 76–99. See also Chance, *Woman as Hero in Old English Literature*, pp. 53–64; Joan Nicholson, "*Feminae gloriosae*: Women in the Age of Bede," in *Medieval Women*, ed. Derek Baker, Studies in Church History, Subsidia 1 (Oxford: Basil Blackwell, 1978), pp. 15–29; Jo Ann McNamara and Suzanne Wemple, "The Power of Women Through the Family in Medieval Europe, 500–1100," *Feminist Studies* 1 (1973): 126–41; and Suzanne F. Wemple, "Sanctity and Power: The Dual Pursuit of Medieval Women," in *Becoming Visible: Women in European History*, ed. Renate Bridenthal and Claudia Koonz (Boston: Houghton Mifflin, 1977), pp. 90–118.

6. A notable exception in this regard is Stephanie Hollis's reading of this episode in *Anglo-Saxon Women and the Church*, pp. 246–58.

7. Britton J. Harwood, "The Plot of *Piers Plowman* and the Contradictions of Feudalism," in *Speaking Two Languages*, ed. Frantzen, pp. 91–114 (note 21).

8. For a major study of the meanings of "culture" in this materialist sense, see Raymond Williams, *Culture* (London: Fontana, 1981). For an analysis of the relation between cultural studies, cultural materialism, and Anglo-Saxon studies, see Lees, *Tradition and Belief*, pp. 12–18.

9. Our thesis complements but does not replicate Lerer's in *Literacy and Power*, which does not address the question of female engagement in the production of literacy or examine female access to the social structures and institutions empowered by literacy. While there is as yet no detailed study of this phenomenon in the Anglo-Saxon period, see the summaries of basic information by: Sims-Williams, *Religion and Literature*, pp. 184–242; Fell, *Women in Anglo-Saxon England*, pp. 109–28, and "Some Implications of the Boniface Correspondence," in *New Readings on Women in Old English Literature*, ed. Damico and Olsen, pp. 29–43; Patrizia Lendinara, "The World of Anglo-Saxon Learning," in *The Cambridge Companion to Old English Literature*, ed. Malcolm Godden and Michael Lapidge (Cambridge: Cambridge University Press, 1991), pp. 264–81 (at pp. 270–71); and Janet Nelson, "Women and the Word in the Early Middle Ages," in *Women in the Church*, ed. W. J. Sheils and Diana Wood, Studies in Church History 27 (Oxford: Blackwell for Ecclesiastical History Society, 1990), pp. 53–78. For a useful survey of female literacy in the Carolingian period that emphasizes

the possibility that women acted as a conduit for education within the aristocratic family, see Rosamond McKitterick, *The Carolingians and the Written Word* (Cambridge: Cambridge University Press, 1989), pp. 223–27. We continue to explore female literacy and orality in Chapters 2 and 3.

10. Kiernan, "Reading Cædmon's 'Hymn' with Someone Else's Glosses," and Frantzen, *Desire for Origins*, p. 142.

11. Dorothy Whitelock, "The Old English Bede," *Proceedings of the British Academy* 48 (1962): 57–90 (at pp. 58–78), but see also Janet M. Bately, "Old English Prose Before and During the Reign of Alfred," *ASE* 17 (1988): 93–138 (at pp. 103–4).

12. Katherine O'Brien O'Keeffe, "Orality and the Developing Text of Cædmon's *Hymn*," *Speculum* 62 (1987): 1–20; and *Visible Song: Transitional Literacy in Old English Verse* (Cambridge: Cambridge University Press, 1990), pp. 23–46.

13. Frantzen, *Desire for Origins*, p. 144.

14. Thomas Miller, ed. *The Old English Version of Bede's Ecclesiastical History of the English People*, Part I, 2. EETS 96 (1891; repr. Oxford: Oxford University Press, 1959), pp. 342–48.

15. Sims-Williams, *Religion and Literature*, p. 185, discusses the slender evidence for the sixth, Tatfrith, who died before he could be consecrated bishop.

16. Hild is never referred to as a virgin by Bede, and her more usual designation is by institution, Abbess: for a speculative discussion of Bede's reasons, see Fell, "Hild, Abbess of Streonæshalch," pp. 78–81. Fell also calls attention to Bede's "untypical compliment that all who knew her called her mother" (p. 86), which is echoed by Eddius Stephanus in his *Life of Wilfrid*: "matre piissima" (Stephen of Ripon, *The Life of Bishop Wilfrid by Eddius Stephanus* ed. and trans., Bertram Colgrave [1927; repr. Cambridge: Cambridge University Press, 1985], p. 20). For the reattribution of this life to Stephen of Ripon, see Chapter 2, note 39. This detail is not found in the account of Hild's *Life* in the *Old English Martyrology*, which also omits discussion of her educational role at Whitby; see J. E. Cross, "A Lost Life of Hilda of Whitby: The Evidence of the *Old English Martyrology*," *Early Middle Ages, Acta* 6 (1979): 21–43. Although "mother" is a conventional appellation for an abbess, Bede's accounts of other female abbesses, such as Æthelburg (*EH* 4. 7–11), have a different resonance; see note 64.

17. For a convenient translation of this *Life*, see C. H. Talbot, trans., *The Anglo-Saxon Missionaries in Germany* (New York: Sheed and Ward, 1954), pp. 205–26. For the account of Leoba's mother's dream, see pp. 210–11.

18. Peter Hunter Blair, "Whitby as a Centre of Learning in the Seventh Century," in *Learning and Literature in Anglo-Saxon England: Studies Presented to Peter Clemoes on the Occasion of his Sixty-Fifth Birthday*, ed. Michael Lapidge and Helmut Gneuss (Cambridge: Cambridge University Press, 1985), pp. 3–32.

19. For the important relationship between place, text, and self, see Gillian R. Overing and Marijane Osborn, *Landscape of Desire: Partial Stories of the Medieval Scandinavian World* (Minneapolis: University of Minnesota Press, 1994).

20. Miller, *Old English Version of Bede*, p. 322.

21. Quoted from Frantzen, *Desire for Origins*, p. 142.

22. Blair, "Whitby as a Centre of Learning in the Seventh Century," at pp. 3, 25.

23. For further analysis of Ælfflæd's own problematic prominence, see Chapter 2.

24. For references to Fell, Chance, and Nicholson, see note 6 above.

25. Colgrave, *The Life of Bishop Wilfrid*, pp. 20–21.

26. See Hollis, *Anglo-Saxon Women and the Church*, pp. 253–70, for a more detailed analysis of such "omissions."

27. Fell, "Hild, Abbess of Streonæshalch," pp. 87–88. The identification of Hild with one Hildeburh (possibly the full form of Hild's name according to Fell, p. 78) in the litany of saints in London, British Library, Cotton Galba A. xiv, ed. Michael Lapidge in *Anglo-Saxon Litanies of the Saints*, Henry Bradshaw Society 106 (London: Boydell, 1991), p. 168, is mere speculation.

28. Cross, "A Lost Life of Hilda of Whitby."

29. The post-Conquest evidence is surveyed by Fell, "Hild, Abbess of Streonæshalch," pp. 88–94, to which should be added the seventeenth-century *Life*, apparently translated from the *Nova Angliae Legendum* into English by Thomas Astley; see C. Horstmann, ed. *The Lives of Women Saints of Our Contrie of England, also some other Liues of Holie Women Written by Some of the Auncient Fathers*, EETS 86 (1886), pp. 56–58.

30. The frequently rehearsed evidence for Latin learning at Whitby—the earliest *Life of Gregory*, Ælfflæd's Letter to an unknown abbess of Pfalzel, and the archaeological presence of styli and book-clasps—is conveniently summarized by Sims-Williams, *Religion and Literature*, pp. 185–86, in his account of the scholarly Oftfor, who left Whitby to join Theodore's school at Canterbury. See also, more generally, Carol Neuman de Vegvar, "Saints and Companions to Saints: Anglo-Saxon Royal Women Monastics in Context," in *Holy Men and Holy Women: Old English Prose Saints' Lives and Their Contexts*, ed. Paul E. Szarmach (Albany, N.Y.: SUNY Press, 1996), pp. 50–93 (at pp. 62–65).

31. Frantzen, *Desire for Origins*, p. 142.

32. See Jane Tibbetts Schulenburg, "Female Sanctity: Public and Private Roles, ca. 500–1100," in *Women and Power in the Middle Ages*, ed. Mary Erler and Maryanne Kowaleski (Athens: University of Georgia Press, 1988), pp. 102–25 (at p. 110). See also more generally her essays in *"Forgetful of Their Sex": Female Sanctity and Societies, ca. 500–1600* (Chicago: University of Chicago Press, 1998).

33. Blair, *An Introduction to Anglo-Saxon England*, p. 148; Fell, "Hild, Abbess of Streonæshalch," p. 85. While the evidence for Hild's acquisition of land for Whitby is ambiguous (*EH* 3. 24), it is perhaps worthy of note that the Old English translation states that she "gebohte tyn hida lond hire in æhte in þære stówe" (Miller, *Old English Version of Bede*, p. 236, lines 31–32). Many early monasteries were founded by royal grants of land: for examples, see Sims-Williams, *Religion and Literature*, pp. 92–97, 103–4.

34. The extent of female governance of these early foundations is difficult to establish since, for one thing, the practice of following a particular rule was not firmly instituted in England until the tenth-century Benedictine Reform: Whitby, for example, stipulated the commonality of all possessions (*EH* 4. 23), which does not appear to have been the case at Much Wenlock (Sims-Williams, *Religion and Literature*, pp. 117–18). Although the *Regularis Concordia*, ed. Dom Thomas Symons (London: Thomas Nelson, 1953), one of the principal policy documents of the tenth-century reforms, is written for both monks and nuns, it is notoriously vague on provisions for female religious life, as is indicated by the revisions that replace "abbot" with "abbess" in the

fragment in Ms. Cambridge, Corpus Christi College 201. Post-Conquest evidence is more suggestive. Heloise, for example, notes that the Rule of Benedict can only be fully observed by men and accordingly requests that Abelard provide a rule for the nuns at the Paraclete; see J. T. Muckle, "The Letter of Heloise on Religious Life and Abelard's First Reply," *MS* 17 (1955): 240–81, at p. 242. Abelard's reply, while insisting on the authority of the abbess in her community (and suggesting that it is the role of the chantress to copy books, or make suitable arrangements for copying), is equally insistent that ultimate authority rests not with the abbess but with her male superiors, the abbot and male ecclesiasts; see T. P. McLaughlin, "Abelard's Rule for Religious Women," *MS* 18 (1956): 241–92.

35. Anglo-Saxon evidence for female teachers and scribes is also hard to interpret. Hild is certainly praised as an instructor, but it remains unclear who actually educated Cædmon. Evidence from the "Boniface" correspondence, discussed below, is relevant here; it is edited by Michael Tangl, *Die Briefe des heiligen Bonifatius und Lullus, MGH, Epistolae Selectae* 1 (Berlin: Weidmannsche Buchhandlung, 1916), and translated by E. Kylie, *The English Correspondence of Saint Boniface* (London, 1911). Boniface's letter to Eadburg (epistle 35)—possibly Abbess of Wimborne or Thanet, according to Sims-Williams, "An Unpublished Seventh- or Eighth-Century Anglo-Latin Letter in Boulogne-sur-Mer MS 74," *Medium Ævum* 48 (1979): 1–22—asks her to copy Peter's Epistles in letters of gold and thanks her for other gifts of books and vestments, but does not illuminate us as to who did the copying. It is perhaps significant that we have no named female scribes—in contrast to the continental evidence cited by Bernhard Bischoff, "Die Kölner Nonnenhandschriften und das Skriptorium von Chelles," *Mittelalterlichen Studien* 1 (Stuttgart, 1966): 16–34, now supplemented and revised by McKitterick, "Nuns' Scriptoria in England and Francia in the Eighth Century," *Francia: Forschungen zur westeurpäischen Geschichte* 19 (1992): 1–35. See also McKitterick, *Carolingians and the Written Word*, p. 257, and the relevant bibliography on female literacy including that by McKitterick in Chapter 2, note 5. Evidence such as Aldhelm's *De virginitate* for the nuns at Barking (discussed in Chapter 4), or the provisions made by Jerome in his Letter to Laeta, a popular text for female education in the early Middle Ages according to M. L. W. Laistner (*Thought and Letters in Western Europe, A.D. 500–900* [1931; repr. Ithaca, N.Y.: Cornell University Press, 1957], pp. 47–48), suggests at least the notion of a separate curriculum for women. We are on firmer ground with the examples of female ownership of books (for example, Cuthswith's ownership of Jerome's commentary on Ecclesiastes, discussed by Sims-Williams, *Religion and Literature*, pp. 190–91): readers (particularly in the cases of early prayer books—the Harley Fragment and the Book of Nunnaminster); and correspondence, as in the "Boniface" letters discussed below—though even here we might ponder the significance of the male postscript by a certain Ealdbeorht to epistle 13 (he is also known from epistle 129), which may indicate that he was the scribe of both these female-authored letters (Sims-Williams, ibid., pp. 224–25).

36. "Women's Monastic Communities, 500–1100: Patterns of Expansion and Decline," *Signs* 14 (1988–89): 261–92 (at pp. 291–92).

37. The terms "public" and "private" are at best vexed for the Anglo-Saxon period; see Lees, "At a Crossroads," p. 155. We retain the term "private" here in order to bear in mind distinctions in social theory that, while not necessarily accurate for the

period, are nevertheless suggestive of long-term historical developments worth bearing in mind. Schulenburg also raises the interesting and as yet largely unresearched issue of women's relation to rural/urban and peacetime/wartime economies ("Women's Monastic Communities," p. 290).

38. Recent studies develop Engels' evolutionary perspective on the decline of women's rights and the parallel emergence of social hierarchies; Friedrich Engels, *The Origin of the Family, Private Property, and the State* (New York: International Publishers, 1972). For examples, see Rayna R. Reiter, ed., *Toward an Anthropology of Women* (New York: Monthly Review Press, 1975); Sherry B. Ortner and Harriet Whitehead, eds. *Sexual Meanings: The Cultural Construction of Gender and Sexuality* (Cambridge: Cambridge University Press, 1981); and Stephanie Coontz and Peta Henderson, "Property Forms, Political Power, and Female Labour in the Origins of Class and State Societies," *Women's Work, Men's Property*, ed. Coontz and Henderson (London: Verso, 1986), pp. 108–55.

39. See Schulenburg, "Female Sanctity: Public and Private Roles, ca. 500–1100," and "Strict Active Enclosure and its Effects on the Female Monastic Experience," in *Medieval Religious Women*, vol. 1. *Distant Echoes*. ed. John A. Nichols and Lillian Thomas Shank (Kalamazoo, Mich.: Cistercian Publications, 1984), pp. 51–86.

40. Male priests, of course, were essential to these communities since only they could perform the necessary sacerdotal duties. Consider also the evidence for relationships between bishops and female religious: for example, Ælfflæd, who benefitted from the advice of Bishop Trumwine, is also closely associated with Bishop Wilfrid (as is Eanflæd, her mother, and Æthelthryth; see Colgrave, *The Life of Bishop Wilfrid*, pp. 6–9, 40–47); Hild herself is at least initially guided by Bishop Aídán (*EH* 4. 23). The account of Wimborne in the *Life of Leoba* by Rudolf of Fulda stresses the extraordinary lengths that the first abbess, Cuthburh, went to exclude even bishops; see G. Waitz, ed., *MGH SS* 15.1, 1887, pp. 118–31, and the translation by C. H. Talbot, *The Anglo-Saxon Missionaries in Germany*. For a survey of the degrees of strain in the relationship between the early Abbesses and the bishops, see Sims-Williams, *Religion and Literature*, pp. 138–43. While Archbishop Theodore of Canterbury rules in favor of dual monasteries since they are the established practice in England, there is a touch of reluctance in the wording of his decision; see Arthur West Haddan and William Stubbs, eds. *Councils and Ecclesiastical Documents Relating to Great Britain and Ireland*, vol. 3 (1871; repr., Oxford: Oxford University Press, 1964), p. 195. Outside the ecclesiastical sphere, it is important to stress that these women appear to have been dependent, at least in part, on royal grants to found their monasteries in the first place. Ælfflæd, for example, is dedicated to God by her father, Oswiu, together with 12 grants of land for foundations in Deira and Bernicia (*EH* 3. 24); see also note 33 above. If we add this tentative evidence to the evident patriarchal slant of the cultural record, it is hard indeed to consider these women as anything other than instrumental in promoting their patriarchal religion.

41. For further discussion, see Coontz and Henderson, "Property Forms, Political Power," pp. 150–53. Many early "family" monasteries enjoyed ecclesiastical tax immunities that clearly defined the status of the house relative to royal and episcopal obligations. The advantages of such immunities were mixed since other obligations were

expected in return; see Sims-Williams, *Religion and Literature*, pp. 134–37, for an introductory summary.

42. Roberta Gilchrist, "The Spatial Archaeology of Gender Domains: A Case Study of Medieval English Nunneries," *Archeological Review from Cambridge* 7,1 (1988): 21–28 (at p. 22). See also more generally her *Gender and Material Culture: The Archaeology of Religious Women* (London: Routledge, 1994).

43. Gilchrist, "Spatial Archaeology," p. 26.

44. Gilchrist, "Spatial Archaeology," p. 27. For alternative views, see Marilynn Desmond, "The Voice of Exile: Feminist Literary History and the Anonymous Anglo-Saxon Elegy," *Critical Inquiry* 16 (1990): 572–90; Janemarie Leucke, "The Unique Experience of Anglo-Saxon Nuns," *Medieval Religious Women*, vol. 2. *Peaceweavers*, ed. Lillian Thomas Shank and John A. Nichols (Kalamazoo, Mich.: Cistercian Publications, 1987), pp. 55–65; Nicholson, "*Feminae gloriosae*: Women in the Age of Bede"; McNamara and Wemple, "The Power of Women Through the Family in Medieval Europe, 500–1100," and Wemple, "Sanctity and Power: The Dual Pursuit of Early Medieval Women."

45. Gilchrist, "Spatial Archaeology," p. 25.

46. Schulenburg, "Female Sanctity: Public and Private Roles, ca. 500–1100," pp. 115, 104.

47. Schulenburg, "Female Sanctity: Public and Private Roles, ca. 500–1100," p. 105.

48. Coontz and Henderson, "Property Forms, Political Power," p. 151.

49. Stafford stresses the importance of analyzing the historical categories of "woman" and other related terms for the later Anglo-Saxon period in *Queen Emma and Queen Edith*, pp. 65–96.

50. Coontz and Henderson, "Property Forms, Political Power," p. 42.

51. For a recent study of the role of kinship in the conversion, see Joseph H. Lynch, *Christianizing Kinship: Ritual Sponsorship in Anglo-Saxon England* (Ithaca, N.Y.: Cornell University Press, 1998).

52. See D. W. Rollason, *The Mildrith Legend: A Study in Early Medieval Hagiography in England* (Leicester: Leicester University Press, 1982), pp. 9–14. The Mildrith legend is taken up further in Chapter 2.

53. Quoted from McNamara and Wemple's title, "The Power of Women Through the Family in Medieval Europe, 500–1100."

54. As argued by Rollason, *Saints and Relics in Anglo-Saxon England* (Oxford: Blackwell, 1989), p. 115.

55. Quoted from Coontz and Henderson, p. 42. In this connection, consider the example of the Mildrith legend, painstakingly reconstructed by Rollason, *The Mildrith Legend*. Æthelberht I and Bertha of Kent are the parents of a royal dynasty well known for its superabundance of saints, many of whom are women. In this network, we detect the political strategies of an aggressively ambitious family, actively forging links with the kingdoms of Northumbria and the Mercians as well as the East Anglians. Indeed, as Rollason points out (p. 41), the peculiarly genealogical character of the Mildrith legend, particularly in its pre-eleventh century phase, serves the interests of the dynasty above and beyond the saintly royal women (many of whom were mothers) who

distinguish its line. Hollis stresses the changing historical importance of the Mildrith legend, which initially served to bolster the female line in "The Minster-in-Thanet Foundation Story," *ASE* 27 (1998): 41–64. Similar strategies are also at work in the later royal cults of the West-Saxon royal families investigated by Susan J. Ridyard, *The Royal Saints of Anglo-Saxon England: A Study of West Saxon and East Anglian Cults* (Cambridge: Cambridge University Press, 1988). The cults of Edburg, Edith of Wilton, and the revival of the cult of Æthelthryth of Ely (which also celebrates Seaxburg and Eormenhild) owe more to the complex interests of the royal families and the Church, than to their importance as sacred royal women (ibid., pp. 96–97, 169, 179–96). It is intriguing to note that the *Lives* of these royal women (many of which survive in post-Conquest recensions—a fact that may be more significant than Ridyard is inclined to suggest) appear to play down their aristocratic connections (see, for example, pp. 82–92).

56. The "Boniface" correspondence is edited by Michael Tangl, and translated by E. Kylie, (see note 35 above). The debate between Peter Dronke, *Women Writers of the Middle Ages: A Critical Study of Texts from Perpetua to Marguerite Porete* (Cambridge: Cambridge University Press, 1984), pp. 30–35, and Fell, "Some Implications of the Boniface Correspondence," pp. 29–43, centers on the extent to which these letters may be read as personal, private, and emotional, or formal, public, and rhetorical. Further research, however, is required to establish just how conventional is their language and to what extent this rhetoric can be said to be gendered. For example, how formulaic is the Saxon nun Huneberc's extreme self-deprecation as she sets out to arrogate a "masculine prerogative" and write the life of a saint, as documented by Schulenburg, "Saints' Lives as a Source for the History of Women, 500–1100," in *Medieval Women and the Sources of Medieval History*, ed. Joel T. Rosenthal (Athens: University of Georgia Press, 1990), pp. 285–320 (at p. 295). For a recent assessment of the Latinity of one of the letters, Ep. 13, by Ecgburg, in comparison with that of Burginda, see Sims-Williams, *Religion and Literature*, pp. 211–42, who describes both as "beginner's essays" (p. 242).

57. The burden of the loss of kin is not exclusive to the female letters of the Boniface mission: the letter written by Lull, Denehard, and Burghard to Abbess Cyneburg (Ep. 49) offers the deaths of mother, father, and other kin as a reason for joining the mission. The most dramatic example of rhetorical and affective "play" with kinship ties is surely that of Heloise: "Domino suo immo patri, coniugi suo immo fratri, ancilla suo immo filia, ipsius uxor immo soror, Abaelardo, Heloisa" (ed. J. T. Muckle, "The Personal Letters Between Abelard and Heloise," *MS* 15 [1953]: 47–94, at p. 68): "To her lord, or better, her father; to her husband, or better, her brother; his handmaid, or better, his daughter; his wife, or better, his sister—to Abelard, Heloise," translated by Peter Dronke, *Women Writers*, p. 112.

58. For discussion, see Dronke, *Women Writers*, pp. 30–32.

59. The stylistic connections between Berhtgyth's letters and the expression of exile and isolation in the so-called Old English Elegies are noted by Dronke, *Women Writers*, p. 31, and Fell, "Some Implications of the Boniface Correspondence," p. 40, but would merit further investigation.

60. In addition to Leoba, who claims kinship with Boniface on her mother's side,

we might add Tecla, Abbess of Kitzingen, also related to Leoba; see Wilhelm Levison, *England and the Continent in the Eighth Century* (1946; Repr., Oxford: Clarendon, 1966), pp. 76–77. Fell, "Some Implications of the Boniface Correspondence," p. 39, points out that Boniface refers to Leoba, Tecla, and Cynehild as "daughters," suggesting that this indicates their youth relative to Boniface; we note in addition that the term replaces the evident close relations between Leoba and Tecla. Cynehild does not seem to be related to either of these women, but she is the maternal aunt of Lull, whose daughter is Berhtgyth of the Berhtgyth/Baldhard correspondence.

61. Aristocratic women often sought spiritual instruction abroad in the seventh century. Bede explains that there were few English monasteries at the time (*EH* 3. 8), and cites the examples of Sæthryth, stepdaughter of Anna of East Anglia and Æthelburg his daughter, both of whom become abbesses of Faremoutiers-en-Brie. Æthelburg's niece, Eorcengota, was also a nun at Faremoutiers. In the same account, Bede also mentions Chelles (founded by the English wife of Clovis II, Balthild), where Mildrith is said to have studied as well as Hild's sister, Hereswith (Rollason, *The Mildrith Legend*, p. 11), and Andelys-sur-Seine. The traffic may not have been all in one direction, however, since the later *Life* of Bertila, first abbess of Chelles, describes how she sent men, women, and books to England in response to a request from the Saxon kings for assistance in founding monasteries. It is possible that Liobsynde, the apparently Frankish named first abbess of Much Wenlock, was one of Bertila's mission; see James Campbell, "The First Century of Christianity in England," repr. in *Essays in Anglo-Saxon History* (London and Ronceverte: Hambledon Press, 1986), pp. 49–67 (at p. 58). As is well known, the English practice of double monasteries is closely related to that of similar houses in Gaul upon which it may be modeled; early examples may also appear in Spain (Campbell, p. 61).

62. For the continental evidence, see Patrick Wormald, "The Uses of Literacy in Anglo-Saxon England and Its Neighbours," *Transactions of the Royal Historical Society* 5th ser., 27 (1977): pp. 95–114 (at pp. 98 and 105).

63. See William Henry Stevenson, ed., *Asser's Life of King Alfred* (1904; Repr., Oxford: Clarendon Press, 1959), p. 20.

64. In addition to the brief notices of the deaths of Eorcongota and Æthelburg of Faremoutiers-en-Brie (*EH* 3. 8), Bede gives only three full female Lives in *EH*: Hild, Æthelburg, and Æthelthryth, all in Book 4, which is arguably the book of the abbesses. Each narrative is governed by similar generic constraints to that of Hild, as we might expect, and each focuses on their deaths rather than their lives—arguably to an even greater extent than the male *Lives*. All three women are abbesses of dual foundations (Whitby, Ely, Barking), although Bede does not stress this dimension of monastic life in the early period: indeed, it is possible that the majority of monasteries in England at this time were dual. The fullest discussion remains Mary Bateson, "Origin and Early History of Double Monasteries," *Transactions of the Royal Historical Society* 13 (1899): 137–98. Æthelburg of Barking, like Hild, is known as "mother" but delimited as "instructress of women" (her convent was founded by her brother, Bishop Eorconwald, also founder of the monastery of Chertsey, *EH* 4. 6). Æthelthryth of Ely, distinguished by her miraculous virginity through two marriages at the expense of her royal connections (a point that Ælfric subsequently also emphasizes in his version of her

Life, Skeat, *Ælfric's Lives of Saints*, p. 435, lines 37–41), is said to have conducted her community in motherly fashion (*EH* 4. 19). Like Hild, then, the trope of mothering is deployed in such a way as to favor product over process; Bede and Ælfric in the case of Æthelthryth are notoriously vague about the force and practice of such maternal instruction. Bede's accounts of Hild and Cædmon are directly followed by an example of the antithesis of the well-run foundation in his narrative of the burning of the monastery at Coldingham, which is also governed by an Abbess, Ebba (*EH* 4. 25). The contrast with the foundations of Barking, Ely, and Whitby could not be clearer, with Bede stressing the moral lesson of Coldingham, where the nuns in particular are singled out for their immodest and inappropriate behavior and where a monk, Adam-nan, is instrumental in trying to remedy the situation. But what really sets Bede's strategies into relief, perhaps, is a comparison with the continental *Life of Leoba*, written by Rudolf of Fulda (ed. Waitz, trans. Talbot). Though largely a pastiche of earlier hagiographic motifs, most often associated with male saints (and perhaps this is the point), Rudolf paints a picture of a woman instrumental in providing instruction for other women and teachers in the province of her own foundation and, even more importantly, so distinguished by her learning she corrected the nuns who were reading to her in her sleep. It is Leoba too, who writes to Boniface asking for advice about her compositional skills, and encloses a short Latin poem for comment; see Ep. 29.

65. Ridyard, *Royal Saints of Anglo-Saxon England*, pp. 91, 142–44.

66. Julia Kristeva, "Stabat Mater," *Tales of Love*, trans. Leon S. Roudiez (New York: Columbia University Press, 1987), pp. 234–63; Karma Lochrie,"The Language of Transgression: Body, Flesh, and Word in Mystical Discourse," in *Speaking Two Languages*, ed. Frantzen, pp. 115–40. Ann Marie Rasmussen takes on modern theories of maternity (offering a good bibliographical overview) and their applicability to medieval representations of mothering in *Mothers and Daughters in Medieval German Literature* (Syracuse, N.Y.: Syracuse University Press, 1997), see esp. pp. 14–18, although the whole book is essential for understanding the historical specificity of motherhood in the medieval period. More narrowly focused on the Anglo-Saxon period is Mary Dockray-Miller, *Motherhood and Mothering in Anglo-Saxon England* (New York: St. Martin's Press, 2000).

67. *Vita Edburge*, cited by Ridyard, *Royal Saints of Anglo-Saxon England*, p. 19.

68. Ridyard, *Royal Saints of Anglo-Saxon England*, p. 130.

69. For Asser, see Lerer, *Literacy and Power*, pp. 86–88, who discusses the concept of the "absent" author in the creation of Alfred as a writer. Alfred's use of the conceit of the poet paradoxically erased and written by his poetry is explored by James W. Earl, "King Alfred's Talking Poems," *Pacific Coast Philology* 24 (1989): 49–61. Ælfric presents a slightly different authorial *persona*: see, for example, the first Prefaces to the Catholic Homilies, where Ælfric is subordinate both to the Fathers whom he "translates" and his ecclesiastical and lay patrons while providing a series of prescriptions for the correct use of the homilies; *Ælfric's Catholic Homilies: The First Series Text*, ed. Peter Clemoes, *EETS* ss 17 (Oxford: Oxford University Press, 1997), pp. 173–77.

70. O'Brien O'Keeffe, *Visible Song*, p. 52.

71. O'Brien O'Keeffe, *Visible Song*, p. 54.

Chapter 2

1. O'Brien O'Keefe, *Visible Song*, p. 4.

2. See Ward Parks,"The Textualization of Orality in Literary Criticism," in *Vox Intexta: Orality and Textuality in the Middle Ages*, ed. A. N. Doane and Carol Braun Pasternack (Madison: University of Wisconsin Press, 1991), pp. 46–61, for a discussion of some of the ways in which we impose the literate upon the oral.

3. For a discussion of women's connection to oral modes, see Deborah Cameron, *Feminism and Linguistics* (London: Macmillan, 1985) and *Women and Their Speech Communities*, ed. Deborah Cameron (London and New York: Longman, 1989). For a discussion of coexisting though segregated male and female oral traditions in African cultures and their connections to medieval orality, see Elisabeth van Houts, *Memory and Gender in Medieval Europe, 900–1200* (Toronto: Toronto University Press, 1999), pp. 11–13.

4. For an overview of scholarship on oral-formulaic theory, see John Miles Foley, *Oral-Formulaic Theory and Research: An Introduction and Annotated Bibliography* (New York: Garland, 1985), and *The Theory of Oral Composition: History and Methodology* (Bloomington: Indiana University Press, 1988); for examples of discussions that engage the oral and the textual and/or literate, see also Foley, "Orality, Textuality, and Interpretation," in *Vox Intexta*, pp. 34–45; Ursula Schaefer, "Hearing from Books: The Rise of Fictionality in Old English Poetry," also in *Vox Intexta*, pp. 117–36; and O'Brien O'Keeffe, *Visible Song*. O'Brien O'Keeffe's introduction (pp. 1–22) provides a useful outline of the scope and nature of the questions raised by the intersecting modes of orality and literacy in the Anglo-Saxon period.

5. *The Uses of Literacy in Early Mediaeval Europe*, ed. Rosamond McKitterick (Cambridge: Cambridge University Press, 1990), p. 2. She refers to Brian Stock, *The Implications of Literacy: Written Language and Models of Interpretation in the Eleventh and Twelfth Centuries* (Princeton, N.J.: Princeton University Press, 1983).

6. Benedicta Ward, " 'To My Dearest Sister': Bede and the Educated Woman," in *Women, the Book, and the Godly: Selected Proceedings of the St. Hilda's Conference, 1993*, vol 1, ed. Lesley Smith and Jane H. M. Taylor (Cambridge: D.S. Brewer, 1995), pp. 105–11.

7. *Women, the Book, and the Godly: Selected Proceedings of the St. Hilda's Conference, 1993*, vol. 2. ed. Smith and Taylor (Cambridge: D.S. Brewer, 1995).

8. Alan Thacker makes this subject present, at least, by asking questions about lay audiences and pastoral care practices within and attached to monasteries. See "Monks, Preaching and Pastoral Care in Early Anglo-Saxon England," in *Pastoral Care Before the Parish*, ed. John Blair and Richard Sharpe (Leicester: Leicester University Press, 1992), pp. 137–70.

9. See McKitterick, "Introduction," *Uses of Literacy*, pp. 1–10.

10. For more specific and various discussions of this general development, see, for example: Miri Rubin, "The Eucharist and the Construction of Medieval Identities," in *Culture and History, 1350–1600: Essays on English Communities, Identities, and Writing*, ed. David Aers (Detroit: Wayne State University Press, 1992) pp. 43–63; Kathleen

Biddick, "Genders, Bodies, Borders: Technologies of the Visible," *Speculum* 68 (1993): 389–418, esp. pp. 409–15.

11. Biddick, "Gender, Bodies, Borders," p. 410, note 46.

12. Biddick, "Gender, Bodies, Borders," p. 410.

13. Biddick, "Gender, Bodies, Borders," p. 412.

14. The historical debate about pros and cons of the advent of literacy, its alienating functions, and its alliance with western hegemonic discourses, and the theoretical debate about the relative primacy of speech versus writing, largely fueled by critics such as Walter Ong (*Orality and Literacy: The Technologizing of the Written Word* [London: Methuen, 1982]), and Jacques Derrida (*Of Grammatology*, trans. Gayatri C. Spivak [Baltimore: Johns Hopkins University Press, 1976]) respectively, continue to provoke critical responses. See for example Ward Parks's critique of Derrida's prioritization of writing as "the very precondition" of speech ("The Textualization of Orality in Literary Criticism," *Vox Intexta*, p. 48); and Allen J. Frantzen, *Desire for Origins*, pp. 103–4.

15. Ch. 23, p. 75. Chapter references are from *Asser's Life of Alfred*, ed. W. H. Stevenson (1904; Repr., Oxford: Clarendon Press, 1959), and page references are to Simon Keynes and Michael Lapidge, eds. and trans., *Alfred the Great Asser's Life of King Arthur and Other Contemporary Sources* (Harmondsworth: Penguin, 1983). Both will henceforth be cited in parenthesis in the text.

16. Seth Lerer, *Literacy and Power*, p. 91.

17. Lerer, *Literacy and Power*, p. 63.

18. Lerer, *Literacy and Power*, p. 91.

19. Lerer, *Literacy and Power*, p. 91.

20. Lerer, *Literacy and Power*, p. 92. For an overview of the plentiful scholarship in praise of Alfred, see Allen J. Frantzen, *King Alfred* (Boston: Twayne, 1986), pp. 1–3. A recent collection of essays continues to honor Alfred, with a slight change of emphasis from Alfred the Great to *Alfred the Wise: Studies in Honour of Janet Bately on the Occasion of her 65th Birthday*, ed. Jane Roberts, Janet L. Nelson, and Malcolm Godden (Cambridge: D.S. Brewer, 1997). See also Nelson, "Reconstructing a Royal Family: Reflections on Alfred, from Asser, chapter 2," in *People and Places in Northern Europe, 500–1100: Essays in Honour of Peter Hayes Sawyer*, ed. Ian Wood and Neils Lund (Woodbridge: Boydell Press, 1991), pp. 47–66, for a detailed study of his family history and genealogy.

21. "Royal Government and Written Word in Late Anglo-Saxon England," in *The Uses of Literacy in Early Mediaeval Europe*, ed. Mckitterick (Cambridge: Cambridge University Press, 1990), pp. 226–57, p. 243.

22. This recalls Pauline Stafford's argument in "Women and the Norman Conquest," pp. 221–49, concerning the amorphous term "women" as an entirely problematic category of historical analysis; even such distinctions as "high-status" can be misleading. Women's "status" is difficult to define and ascertain, given the commutable intersections of both critical criteria and historical circumstance. See esp. pp. 229–30.

23. Lerer, *Literacy and Power*, p. 91.

24. Stephanie Hollis raises this intriguing point in her discussion of "The Minster-in-Thanet Foundation Story."

25. Karen Louise Jolly examines the often dichotomised worlds of the "popular" (which includes the oral) and the "formal" (which includes the literate) in *Popular Religion in Late Anglo-Saxon England* (Chapel Hill and London: University of North Carolina Press, 1996). While she emphasizes throughout the connectivity and "shared culture" (p. 21) of the two worlds, thus attenuating some of the same binaries that concern us, gender is seldom included as a working variable in the dynamic of connection. When women's specific roles are discussed, it is largely in tandem with speech: with their power as wielders of words and as "evil wisewomen" as this is found in charms (pp. 146, 149, 157), and with their contribution to the conversion process. Taking the Christian queen Bertha and her attempts to convert her recalcitrant pagan husband Edwin of Northumbria as a model, Jolly extrapolates that "similar processes undoubtedly occurred in the homes of the less socially prominent" (p. 45). While it is true that such "processes of acculturation at the domestic level" are "virtually impossible to document" (p. 45), such assumptions rely to a large extent on the association of women with oral modes, whether speech is used for benign conversionary purposes, or otherwise.

26. Asser may have have exaggerated the beauty of the manuscript, according to Lerer, as his description "fails to match what we know of English bookmaking at the time of Alfred's boyhood" *Literacy and Power*, p. 66.

27. "Wealth and Wisdom: The Politics of Alfred the Great," *Kings and Kingship*, *Acta* 11 (1986 for 1984), ed. Joel T. Rosenthal, pp. 31–52, p. 44.

28. "Reconstructing a Royal Family," pp. 47–66.

29. Nelson, "Reconstructing a Royal Family," p. 50.

30. Pauline Stafford argues that lack of queenly status for the king's wife was normative in ninth-century Wessex ("The King's Wife in Wessex, 800–1066," *Past and Present* 91 (1981): 3–27; repr. in *New Readings on Women*, ed. Damico and Olsen, pp. 56–78), and that Judith's coronation serves by contrast to bring this pattern into clear relief. Nelson localizes Osburh's demotion, however, and the contrast bears its own pointed purpose: "in the period before Alfred's own reign, Osburh is the only West Saxon king's wife whose lack of a queenly title is clear. If Æthelwulf did plan to repudiate and replace her in 855/6, it could have suited him very well to emphasize to the Franks her lowliness and their glory through the honorable status reserved, by contrast, for the Carolingian king's daughter" (p. 55).

31. Nelson's suggestion departs from a received assumption that Osburh died before her husband married again; the reasons for such an assumption, Nelson cogently argues, have much to do with critical views of Æthelwulf's benign and pious nature, an emphasis on Osburh's role as mother not queen, and a nineteenth-century reluctance to view "Judith as stepmother" as an educating force. See her note 39, p. 54. The chronology leaves much open to conjecture: Alfred, born in 849, travels to Rome at the age of four and again two years later "with his recently widowed father" (Keynes and Lapidge, p. 14); on their return journey Æthelwulf marries Judith at the French court of her father, Charles the Bald. The second marriage lasted from 856 to 858, when his father died. Alfred's status as child prodigy becomes the issue, then, if we believe he is learning (memorizing) English poetry and reciting it sometime before the age of six, a learning process punctuated by long journeys apparently undertaken without his mother. In chapter 22, immediately preceding the book scene, Asser reports the

"shameful negligence of his parents and tutors," which results in Alfred being "igno-rant of letters until his twelfth year, or even longer"(Keynes and Lapidge, p. 75). Whatever the degree or nature of the king's literacy (see Keynes and Lapidge, p. 239, note 46), or the idiosyncracy of Asser's ordering of events, Nelson accurately asserts that there is ample room for speculation about Osburh's marital and ancestral status.

32. See Nelson, "Reconstructing a Royal Family," pp. 55–56.

33. Nelson, "Reconstructing a Royal Family," p. 54.

34. Nelson, "Reconstructing a Royal Family," p. 66. See also pp. 63–66, for a detailed discussion of the various interests at stake in the question of Alfred's succes-sion, and a discussion of why Alfred's wife Ealhswith receives so little specific docu-mented attention.

35. *Handbook for William: A Carolingian Woman's Counsel for her Son by Dhuoda*, trans. C. Neel (Lincoln and London: University of Nebraska Press, 1991). In her discus-sion of women as "commemorators," Elisabeth van Houts calls attention to an inter-esting intersection of oral and literate modes and the aristocratic woman's use of them: in Book Ten of her handbook, Dhuoda records the names of eight of her son's paternal ancestors; this encouragement to her son to "remember" also functions as a literate record of his land claims and rights (*Memory and Gender in Medieval Europe, 900–1200*, p. 66).

36. *Carolingians and the Written Word*, pp. 225–26; see also Chapter 1, note 35. In this context, consider too Theodoric's daughter, Amalasuntha, and her plans to edu-cate her son Alaric.

37. Rudolph of Fulda's *Life of Leoba* (ed. Waitz, trans. Talbot, *The Anglo-Saxon Missionaries in Germany*, pp. 205–26) is dated 837 or 838 (Hollis, *Anglo-Saxon Women and the Church*, p. 271), although Leoba died circa 780.

38. Hollis, *Anglo-Saxon Women and the Church*, p. 163.

39. Authorship of the *Life of Wilfrid* has been previously attributed, albeit tenta-tively, to Eddius Stephanus (*The Life of Bishop Wilfrid by Eddius Stephanus*, text, translation and notes by Bertram Colgrave (1927; Repr. Cambridge: Cambridge Uni-versity Press, 1985); we follow Walter Goffart in his assessment of the evidence of Stephen as the more likely author. For a discussion of the history and the details of this debate, see Goffart, *The Narrators of Barbarian History (A.D. 550–800)* (Princeton, N.J.: Princeton University Press, 1988), pp. 274, 281–83.

40. Both are found in *Two Lives of Saint Cuthbert*, ed. and trans. Bertram Col-grave (Westport, Conn.: Greenwood Press, 1969).

41. See Hollis, *Anglo-Saxon Women and the Church*, chapters five and six, pp. 151–207. All these texts appeared in the first quarter of the eighth century (Cuthbert died in 687, Wilfrid in 710, Ælfflaed in 715). For a discussion of questions of dating and authorship, see David Rollason, "Hagiography and Politics in Early Northumbria," in *Holy Men and Holy Women*, ed. Paul Szarmach (Albany: SUNY Press: 1996), pp. 95–96, and throughout. For a discussion of the larger context of Bede's *Life of Cuthbert*, see also Walter Goffart, *Narrators of Barbarian History*, pp. 281–90.

42. Colgrave, *The Life of Bishop Wilfrid*, ch. 60.

43. Hollis, *Anglo-Saxon Women and the Church*, p. 207.

44. Hollis, *Anglo-Saxon Women and the Church*, p. 207.

45. Colgrave, *Life of Wilfrid*, ch. 59.

46. Colgrave, *Life of Wilfrid*, ch. 43.

47. Colgrave, *Life of Wilfrid*, ch. 24.

48. Colgrave, *Life of Wilfrid*, ch. 34.

49. Colgrave, *Life of Wilfrid*, ch. 57.

50. *Alcuin: The Bishops, Kings, and Saints of York*, ed. and trans. Peter Godman (Oxford: Clarendon Press, 1982). See Godman, pp. xxxix–xlvii, for a discussion of questions of dating the text.

51. Alcuin's and Bede's works are vastly different in scope and design, and we do not propose to compare apples with oranges here but to point out a pattern of redaction that erases women's names from this later version of the ecclesiastic record. One such instance is Alcuin's rendering of the story of the nun of Watton; in Bede's *History*, Bishop John visits the monastery of Abbess Hereburh, whose own daughter ("filia ipsius carnalis") Cwenburh is sick; she is subsequently healed by the bishop's ministrations and prayers (*EH*, 5. 3). In Alcuin's account the abbess disappears completely in name and function, replaced by a "community of holy nuns" ("sanctarum . . . famularum," *Bishops, Kings, and Saints of York*, line 1122), and her daughter becomes a nameless virgin. See the discussion of charter evidence later in this chapter for a parallel development, in that formal names and titles for women become less frequent in these documents, especially notes 108 and 112. It is also interesting to consider here, as we will in our discussions of Aldhelm, the role of poetic form in this process of obliteration from or abbreviation within the written record; that the women's names might not comply with metrical exigencies is offset by (albeit rare) instances where Alcuin does incorporate them: for example, Queen Osthryth of Mercia, recorded via her uncle, the "sainted king Oswald" (line 357); and, not surprisingly, Æthelthryth, who is named not only once, but twice (lines 753, 764).

52. Godman, *Bishops, Kings, and Saints of York*, pp. cx, xlvii.

53. Alcuin's letters indicate that he was on familiar terms with both noble and religious women in England, but the tone of these communications is far more concerned with women's spiritual welfare and the importance of chastity than with learning (ed. Dümmler; trans. Stephen Allott, *Alcuin of York, c. A.D. 732–804: His Life and Letters* [York: William Sessions Limited, 1974]). See, for example, his letter to the nun Hundrud, where he enjoins her to teach by means of her moral example and behavior (Ep. 36), or his letter to the priests of Ireland advocating modesty, humility and chastity for nuns (Ep. 34). Elsewhere, however, he appears entirely sensible of noblewomen's political influence and of religious women's continuing roles as royal confidants; he asks the same Hundrud to greet Queen Cynethrith of Mercia in his name. He writes in sympathy to Ethelburga, Abbess of Fladbury, when her sister Ethelfleda's husband, Ethelred of Northumbria, is assassinated, and while he urges her to persuade her widowed sister to join a convent, he also encloses a present from Liutgard, wife of Charlemagne, whose "friendship is honourable and useful to you" (Ep. 42).

54. *The Riddles of the Exeter Book*, ed. Frederick Tupper Jr. (Boston: Ginn, 1910), p. lxxxvi. Also quoted in John W. Tanke, " 'Wonfeax wale': Ideology and Figuration in the Sexual Riddles of the Exeter Book," in *Class and Gender in Early English Literature: Intersections* ed. Britton J. Harwood and Gillian R. Overing (Bloomington: Indiana University Press, 1994), p. 22; see also Tanke, pp. 21–27, for a good overview of criticism on the riddles.

55. Tanke, " 'Wonfeax wale,' " pp. 23–27, and throughout.

56. Lerer, *Literacy and Power*, p. 198.

57. Lerer, *Literacy and Power*, p. 25.

58. Howe, "Aldhelm's *Enigmata* and Isidorian Etymology," *ASE* 14 (1985): 37–59.

59. See the general discussion of Aldhelm's works and influence in *Aldhelm: The Poetic Works*, trans. Michael Lapidge and James L. Rosier (Cambridge: D. S. Brewer, 1985), pp. 1–24; see also Orchard, *Poetic Art of Aldhelm*, pp. 1–18.

60. See Michael Lapidge, "Aldhelm's Latin Poetry and Old English Verse," *Comparative Literature* 31 (1979): 209–31.

61. Orchard, *Poetic Art of Aldhelm*, p. 72.

62. *Aldhelm: The Poetic Works*, p. 64.

63. According to Ernst Robert Curtius, this image is Aldhelm's own (*European Literature and the Latin Middle Ages*, trans. Willard R. Trask [London: Routledge and Kegan Paul, 1953], p. 137); as an image for rebirth within the church, the "vulva" appears three times, and only in the prose version of the *De virginitate* (*Aldhelmi Opera* ed. R. Ehwald, *MGH* 15, 1919, pp. 260, 277, 295). While Curtius draws attention to Aldhelm's unusual use of "vulva," Lapidge and Herren deemphasize the image by translating it in these three instances as "womb." Aldhelm may have intended a specificity overlooked by his translators, however; elsewhere in the prose *De virginitate* he choses other terms for womb: for example, "matrix" (pp. 247, 253), and "utero" (p. 230).

64. See Orchard, *Poetic Art of Aldhelm*, p. 68, for an elaboration of this point. See Chapter 4 for further discussion.

65. Nos decem et septem genitae sine voce sorores
Sex alias nothas non dicimus annumerandas.
Nascimur ex ferro rursus ferro moribundae
Necnon et volucris penna volitantis ad aethram;
Terni nos fratres incerta matre crearunt.
Qui cupit instanter sitiens audire docentes
Tum cito prompta damus rogitanti verba silenter.
(Ehwald, *Aldhelmi Opera*, p. 110)

Trans. Lapidge and Rosier, *Aldhelm: The Poetic Works*, p. 76. For the riddles in general, we also refer to Nancy Porter Stork's edition, *Through a Gloss Darkly: Aldhelm's Riddles in the British Library ms. Royal 12 C.xxiii* (Toronto: Pontifical Institute of Mediaeval Studies, 1990), and to Ehwald's edition where we refer directly to the Latin, or when we comment on the translation.

66. Nunc mea divinis complentur viscera verbis
Totaque sacratos gestant praecordia biblos;
At tamen ex isdem nequeo cognoscere quicquam:
Infelix fato fraudabor munere tali,
Dum tollunt dirae librorum lumina Parcae,
(Ehwald, *Aldhelmi Opera*, p. 138)

67. O'Brien O'Keefe, *Visible Song*, pp. 53–54.

68. O'Brien O'Keefe, *Visible Song*, p. 54.

69. The "bastards" ("nothas") are the letters h, k, q, x, y, and z (Lapidge and Rosier, *Aldhelm: The Poetic Works*, p. 250, note 27). The primary connotation of

"nothus" is illegitimacy; Stork chooses the less physical term "counterfeits" (*Through a Gloss Darkly*, pp. 134–35) in her translation, thus neutralizing the connection to birth.

70. Lapidge and Rosier, *Aldhelm: The Poetic Works*, p. 250, note 27.

71. In Riddle 30, Stork elides the masculine generic sense of audience in her translation: "To one who thirsts for knowledge and wishes to hear / We quickly and silently give our ready words" (*Through a Gloss Darkly*, p. 135). Like Lapidge and Rosier we infer a masculine audience—although the dative form "qui" is not gender-specific.

72. The metaphorical ground for this riddle is even more suggestive when we consider its possible analogue by Claudian, as identified by Orchard: both authors use the term *viscera* but "Claudian is describing the amazement of the Virgin Mary, about to give birth to Christ, the Word, whilst Aldhelm's *Enigma* deals with a book-cupboard filled with holy words" (*The Poetic Art of Aldhelm*, pp. 154–55). The rhetorical shift takes us from "real" womb—insofar as the Virgin may embody the feminine—to wooden container, and from female amazement to feminized ignorance.

73. Nunc ferri stimulus faciem proscindit amoenam
   Flexibus et sulcos obliquat adinstar aratri
   Sed semen segiti de caelo ducitur almum,
   Quod largos generat millena fruge maniplos.
   Heu! tam sancta seges diris extinguitur armis
   (Ehwald, *Aldhelmi Opera*, p. 111)

Compare again Stork's translation where feminization is less pronounced: "faciem . . . amoenam" is simply "pleasant face" (*Through a Gloss Darkly*, p. 138).

74. Semita quin potius milleno tramite tendit
   Quae non errantes ad caeli culmina vexit.
   (Ehwald, *Aldhelmi Opera*, p. 124)

75. A further analogue here is the story of the "releasing letters" in Bede's *History* discussed by Lerer (*Literacy and Power*, pp. 30–60). The captive Imma escapes from his fetters, and he is suspected of using some kind of spell or charm, "litteras solutorias," by his captors (*EH*, 4. 22). Lerer suggests some Old Norse and Old High German antecedents where women are performing the binding and loosing, evoking both a Valkyrie warrior tradition and the connection with Odin as master of runic spells (Lerer, pp. 35–37). Lerer's intention is to show how Bede rewrites this story and "replaces the supposed efficacy of these charms with the true power of the Mass and, in so doing, replaces popular stories of the marvels of words with Bede's own document of faith" (p. 39). The popular "marvellous" is replaced by the Christian "miraculous," symbolized by the Mass or the Eucharist, and these, Lerer argues "need to be understood not as popular beliefs but as learned institutionalized practices" (p. 48). The presence of the feminine at this site of oral and literate power is elided in Bede's account, as we have seen in the riddles, but also interesting is the notion of divine/ literate authority providing a passage to, and a new guarantor for the symbolic, so that we have a graphic (sic) account of the disappearance of the oral and feminine traces. See Chapter 5 for further discussion.

76. See Michael Lapidge, "The Origin of the *Collectanea*," in *Collectanea Pseudo-Bedae*, ed. Martha Bayless and Michael Lapidge, *Scriptores Latini Hiberniae* 14 (Dublin: School of Celtic Studies, Dublin Institute for Advanced Studies, 1998), p. 6.

77. "Vidi uirginem flentem et murmurantem; uiae eius sunt semitae uitae," *Collectanea Pseudo-Bedae*, pp. 144–45.

78. *Collectanea Pseudo-Bedae*, p. 245, note 198.

79. Ic wat eardfæstne   anne standan,
deafne, dumban,   se oft dæges swilgeð
þurh gropes hond   gifrum lacum.
Hwilum on þam wicum   se wonna þegn,
sweart on saloneb,   sendeð oþre
under goman him   golde dyrran,
þa æþelingas   oft wilniað,
cyningas ond cwene.   Ic þæt cyn nu gen
nemnan ne wille,   þe him to nytte swa
ond to dugþum doþ   þæt se dumba her,
eorp unwita,   ær forswilgeð

The Exeter Book, ASPR 3, ed. Krapp and Dobbie, p. 206. All references to the Exeter Book riddles are to this edition.

I know something that stands earthfast;
deaf and dumb, it often digests
useful gifts during the day handed over
by a servant. At times, in the houses of men,
some dark-skinned swarthy slave
puts more into its mouth, dearer than gold,
things such as athelings, kings and queens,
dream of. But I will not name it,
this dumb creature, this somber nitwit,
that for their use gives back to brave men
exactly what it has eaten, earlier.

Trans. Kevin Crossley-Holland, *The Exeter Book Riddles* (Harmondsworth: Penguin, 1979), p. 71. All translations of the riddles are by Crossley-Holland unless otherwise specified: we emend where we think appropriate.

80. Crossley-Holland, p. 73, *The Exeter Book*, p. 206:

81. Crossley-Holland, p. 121.

82. Crossley-Holland, p. 64, *The Exeter Book*, pp. 203–4. Crossley-Holland translates "heanmode twa" as "the feather-brained pair," which we emend to "lowly pair," emphasizing the learned runemen's condescension to these abject creatures.

83. Lerer, *Literacy and Power*, p. 119.

84. Lerer, *Literacy and Power*, p. 125.

85. Lerer, *Literacy and Power*, p. 125.

86. Tanke, " 'Wonfeax wale,' " p. 33.

87. Tanke, " 'Wonfeax wale,' " p. 39.

88. See, for example, Peter Sawyer's landmark edition *Anglo-Saxon Charters* (S), and the ongoing British Academy series begun in 1973, in which Susan Kelly's *Charters of St. Augustine's Abbey* is volume 4 (*Charters of St. Augustine's Abbey Canterbury and Minster-in-Thanet* Anglo-Saxon Charters 4 [British Academy. Oxford: Oxford University Press, 1995]), an edition which proved particularly valuable for our purposes, not

only for its detail and thoroughness, but also for its specific address of points related to monastic women. For a general overview of sources see also Susan E. Kelly, "Anglo-Saxon Lay Society and the Written Word," in *The Uses of Literacy in Early Mediaeval Europe*, ed. McKitterick, p. 39, note 12.

89. For a good general discussion of the many problems associated with charter authentication, see Whitelock (W, pp. 337–42). For an examination of the theoretical and practical aspects of the "writing of space," a current concept in the field of cultural geography, and some of its applications to the Anglo-Saxon period, see Overing and Osborn, *Landscape of Desire: Partial Stories of the Medieval Scandinavian World*.

90. Susan E. Kelly, *Charters of St. Augustine's Abbey*, p. lxiii.

91. S1258-B291-W79. References to the charters will generally be to Sawyer's edition and numbering (S), with parallel references to W. G. de Birch, ed., *Cartularium Saxonicum*, (B). Sawyer collates information and commentaries on each charter, whereas Birch includes the full text and witness lists. Translations of charter in Whitelock, *English Historical Documents* (W).

92. Kelly, "Anglo-Saxon Lay Society," p. 40.

93. See for example *Women in the Medieval English Countryside*.

94. Marc A. Meyer, "Land Charters and the Legal Position of Anglo-Saxon Women," in *The Women of England: From Anglo-Saxon Times to the Present* ed. Barbara Kanner (Hamden, Conn.: Archon Books, 1979), p. 70.

95. Meyer, "Land Charters," p. 61. Although a "provincial aristocracy" became more powerful in the tenth and eleventh centuries, and are represented in the charters as receiving bookland directly from the king, this change in social structure did not directly affect women: "Wives and daughters of these new thegns benefitted from the good fortune of their men, but did not themselves receive royal charters" (p. 61).

96. Meyer, "Land Charters," pp. 67, 69.

97. Meyer, "Land Charters," p. 79, note 104.

98. Meyer, "Land Charters," p. 79, note 104. In her argument against "golden age" theories for women in the Anglo-Saxon period Pauline Stafford contrasts this representation with some post-Conquest evidence, where the charters document a far wider range of women, and women's activities: see "Women and the Norman Conquest," p. 226.

99. Kelly, "Anglo-Saxon Lay Society," p. 42. Despite the distinction made in some charters' witness lists between the subjective form (*Ego N consensi*) and the objective form (*Signum manus N*) of subscribing to a charter, a remnant of Roman diplomatic convention which indicated the difference between the literate and the illiterate, Kelly maintains that this can be no clear indication of whether the subscriber/witness was actually literate or not (p. 42); in some cases, subscribers will declare their illiteracy (see, for example, S20-B99, and S1165-B34-W54), but the scribe who pens the names and the crosses beside them is nonetheless the only party whose literacy is demonstrable. See also Kelly, *Charters of St. Augustine's Abbey*, p. lxxxv.

100. Kelly, *Charters of St. Augustine's Abbey*, p. 42. See also pp. 37–38. For a discussion of the development of queenly status later in the period, see Pauline Stafford, "The King's Wife in Wessex, 800–1066," *Past and Present* 91 (1981): 3–27; repr. in *New Readings on Women*, ed. Damico and Olsen, pp. 56–78. See also Alistair Campbell, ed.

Encomium Emmae Reginae, with a supplementary introduction by Simon Keynes (London: Royal Historical Society, 1949; rept. Cambridge: Cambridge University Press, 1998), appendix 2. Hollis suggests that the powers of queens earlier in the period were less limited in her discussion of royal marriage, *Anglo-Saxon Women and the Church*, pp. 208–242, esp. pp. 212–3.

101. Kelly, *Charters of St. Augustine's Abbey*, pp. 37–38.

102. Hollis, *Anglo-Saxon Women and the Church*, p. 212, and note 25 for a list of royal couples appearing in witness lists.

103. S62-B238, S168-B335, S254-B158, S22-B91. It is hard to find any thread of continuity among these; S62 (777 x 781) is a grant of a monastery from Ealdred, sub-king of the Hwicce, to his kinswoman Æthelburh, witnessed by the Abbess Æthelburh herself; S168 (811) is a grant of land from Cenwulf of Mercia to Archbishop Wulfred subscribed by two abbesses, Cwenburh and Seleburg, presumably third party witnesses as they are not mentioned in the document, and apparently considered appropriate participants along with other bishops and priests in a church-related land transaction; S254 (737) is a grant of land from Æthelheard of Wessex to Winchester cathedral, again witnessed disinterestedly by abbesses Cynegils and Æscburg. The authenticity of S254 has been challenged, although the witness list could be considered genuine (Sawyer, p. 135).

104. Kelly, *Charters of St. Augustine's*, p. 42

105. S20-B99. Also printed in Kelly, *Charters of St. Augustine's*, #10, pp. 38–40.

106. See Kelly, *Charters of St. Augustine's*, p. 42, for detailed identification.

107. Ibid., p. 42.

108. S10-B42, S11-B41, S12-B73, S13-B35, S14-B40, and S18-B96; also in Kelly, *Charters of St. Augustine's*, #40–44, #46. These are substantial land grants made by three different Kentish kings, discussed in detail by Kelly, pp. 139–157, 159–162. Moreover, Minster-in-Thanet is distinguished by its entrepreneurial energy; five charters, one possibly as early as 716 x 717, grant toll remissions due on Minster ships (see Kelly, pp. xxv–xxvii). One suspects that Æbba, whose famous daughter and successor Mildrith was the beneficiary of two of these charters, might have been especially concerned even at the turn of the eighth century in the matter of tax-exemption and confirmation of church privileges outlined in S20-B99.

109. S168-B335 and S254-B158. See note 98.

110. S1436-B384.

111. S1267-B851.

112. Kelly, *Charters of St. Augustine's*, p. 72. See also p. 71 for details of the dispute, and a related charter (S1434-B378) describing the abbess's alleged intransigence. This story, and its relation to abbesses' representation in the cultural record is further complicated by the appearance of Wulfred's sister in S1434-B378, Abbess Selethryth, who Wulfred claims had given him the land that Cwenthryth refused to give up.

113. S582-B917. See also, for example, S767-B1216, where the community of nuns is the generalized charter recipient.

114. She attests the charter thus: "Ego Aelfgyth magistra prefati monasterii cum gaudio magno recepi" (S582-B917 at p. 85).

115. S799-B1304.

116. S741-B1178, S1294-B1179, S812-B1187.

117. See for example, S448-B743, S464-B763, S474-B768, S482-B778, S485-B775, S487-B787, S493-B795, S534-B868, S535-B869, S563-B903, S593-B957, S600-B953, S681-B1052, S703-B1082, S754-B1200, S762-B1218, S775-B1259. Further identifying these women as individuals and tracking down their names presents its own problems (see Meyer, "Land Charters," pp. 60–61 and esp. note 26); our intention here is to call attention to these new "titles" for women.

118. "Edgar's relations with monastic women caused more than a breath of scandal," writes Hollis (*Anglo-Saxon Women and the Church*, p. 208), and particularly his pursuit of a Wulfhild, nun at Wilton.

119. S1258-B291-W79.

120. Archbishop Æthelheard splits some differences with Abbess Cynethryth: "This also we decided in the presence of the whole synod that the abbess should receive from me the oft-mentioned monastery with its documents, and I should receive from her the lands and the deeds of the lands which she gave to me in Kent, to the end that no controversy may arise in future between us and our heirs and those of King Offa" (W79 at p. 470).

121. S1429-B156-W68 at p. 455.

122. Consider here the ways in which some mother-daughter or sister-sister relations are conditioned by the hagiographer; see for example Ridyard's discussion of Sts. Werburga and Sexburge, *Royal Saints of Anglo-Saxon England*, pp. 91–92.

123. Hollis, "The Minster-in-Thanet Foundation Story," p. 64.

124. Lerer, *Literacy and Power*, p. 91.

125. See Kelly, "Anglo-Saxon Lay Society," pp. 43–45.

126. Kelly, "Anglo-Saxon Lay Society," pp. 44–46.

127. One of most remarkable and densely layered examples of "hearing" voices within a document must be "St. Mildburg's Testament," printed and translated in H. P. R. Finberg, *The Early Charters of the West Midlands* (Leicester: Leicester University Press, 1961), pp. 201–6. See also Finberg, pp. 206–16 for a discussion of the dating and the Latin and vernacular elements of the document. Not strictly speaking a charter, it provides evidence for several lost charters (S1798-1802); neither does it contain any bequests, but in this document we not only hear the "voice" of St. Mildburg claiming and authorizing her land acquisitions for the foundation at Much Wenlock, but also repeating the testimony of previous donors, churchmen and kings, who have given land to the monastery. And she also stands as witness. She ratifies an oral history of acquisition in a document that is a veritable echo chamber of voices, where the female speaker is both subject and object, and is fully engaging, if not controlling, oral and literate modes.

128. See Florence Harmer, ed., *Anglo-Saxon Writs* (Manchester: Manchester University Press, 1952), pp. 76–77.

129. For a recent discussion of the Anglo-Saxon economy—though not one which addresses the question of women's participation—see S. R. H. Jones, "Transactional Costs, Institutional Change, and the Emergence of a Market Economy in Later Anglo-Saxon England," *Economic History Review* 46, 4 (1993): 658–78.

Chapter 3

1. S 1462, also included in Patrick Wormald, "A Handlist of Anglo-Saxon Lawsuits," *ASE* 17 (1988), as #80. We follow Wormald in using the term, "lawsuit," for this document, referred to internally as a "gewrit," but for other documents to refer interchangeably to diplomas or charters, reflecting current scholarly usage (as well as contemporary imprecision). No account of Anglo-Saxon law, however small, can now be made without Wormald's superb *The Making of English Law: King Alfred to the Twelfth Century, Legislation and Its Limits*, Vol. 1 (Oxford: Blackwell, 1999), which covers lawsuits (pp. 143–61). For the edition of the Hereford lawsuit, see A. J. Robertson, ed., *Anglo-Saxon Charters*, 2nd ed. (Cambridge: Cambridge University Press, 1956), #78; that Dorothy Whitelock intended to make this document more widely known is evident from her inclusion of it in her edition of *Sweet's Anglo-Saxon Reader in Prose and Verse*, 15th ed. (Oxford: Clarendon Press, 1975), XIIB, pp. 57–58. For ease of consultation, we refer to Whitelock's edition by line number (checked against Robertson's). For translation, see Whitelock (W, p. 556, #135). The literature on this lawsuit is scant: it is cursorily discussed by Fell, *Women in Anglo-Saxon England*, p. 78; by Blair, *An Introduction to Anglo-Saxon England*, pp. 230–31; and by H. R. Loyn, *Anglo-Saxon England and the Norman Conquest* (London: Longman, 1962), pp. 182–83. A fuller interpretation from a gendered perspective is that by van Houts, *Memory and Gender in Medieval Europe, 900–1200*, pp. 79–80. The persons mentioned in the document are identified by Robertson in the notes, pp. 399–402; see also the notes by Whitelock in *Sweet's Anglo-Saxon Reader*, pp. 246–49.

2. For the name of Edwin's father, see W, p. 556.

3. For description of the gospel book, see N. R. Ker, *Catalogue of Manuscripts Containing Anglo-Saxon* (Oxford: Clarendon Press, 1957), item 119 (a). The manuscript also records the purchase of a Hereford estate by Leofwine, brother of Leofflæd (Thurkil's wife), witnessed by Æthelstan, bishop of Hereford and Thurkil the White (two of the witnesses of our Hereford document): see Ker, item 119 (b) and Robertson, *Anglo-Saxon Charters*, #99 (with notes, p. 435), S 1469.

4. For a discussion of the practice of willing, both oral and written, see D. H. Hazeltine, "Comments on the Writings Known as Anglo-Saxon Wills, in D. Whitelock, ed. *Anglo-Saxon Wills* (Cambridge: Cambridge University Press, 1930), pp. vii–xl. See also Michael M. Sheehan, *The Will in Medieval England* (Toronto: Pontifical Institute of Mediaeval Studies, 1963), pp. 5–106.

5. Robertson, *Anglo-Saxon Charters*, p. 401.

6. Simon Keynes, *The Diplomas of King Æthelred "The Unready" (978–1016): A Study in Their Use as Historical Evidence* (Cambridge: Cambridge University Press, 1980); for the disputes about centralization, see Keynes, pp. 14–83 and the review by Pierre Chaplais of Keynes's book in the *Journal of Ecclesiastical History* 35 (1984): 262–65.

7. Keynes, *Diplomas*, pp. 51–61 (Eadred, see also S 582, 593); p. 77 (Edgar), pp. 84–97 (Æthelred).

8. For discussion of the general situation of the reformed houses and the nunneries in the late tenth century, see Pauline Stafford, *Unification and Conquest: A*

Political and Social History of England in the Tenth and Eleventh Centuries (London: Edward Arnold, 1989), pp. 192–93; and Schulenberg, "Women's Monastic Communities," pp. 261–92. The absence of female communities may be a feature of the royal diplomas as well as of the Æthelredian period. For the contrast with earlier tenth-century grants to reformed houses, where communities of both monks and nuns are identified as beneficiaries, see, e.g., S 29; and for female communities included in witness lists or by consent and cognizance in the later tenth century, see S 53 and 70.

9. See, however, S 799 (Edgar to Wulfthryth, abbess of Wilton Abbey, possibly spurious).

10. See Keynes, "Royal Government and the Written Word in Late Anglo-Saxon England," and Susan Kelly, "Anglo-Saxon Lay Society," for good surveys.

11. For examples of land charters and wills made in the husband's name, where the wife remains anonymous, see S 1420, 1509, 1470 and S 1231, 1524.

12. Whitelock, *Anglo-Saxon Wills*. For a full list of wills and bequests, see S1482-1539.

13. Stafford, *Unification and Conquest*, pp. 159–61.

14. Shire courts—apparently a tenth-century innovation—were held twice a year, above and beyond the meetings of the hundreds and wapentakes every four weeks. For general introduction, see Dorothy Whitelock, *The Beginnings of English Society*, 2nd rev. ed. (London: Penguin, 1974), pp. 137–39. See also Wormald, *The Making of English Law*, pp. 152–53.

15. In addition to the studies of literacy already cited above and in Chapter Two, see also George Hardin Brown, "The Dynamics of Literacy in Anglo-Saxon England," *Bulletin of the John Rylands Library* 77,1 (Spring 1995): 109–42.

16. For the 737 charter, see Chapter 2. Women's wills regularly feature not merely land but portable possessions such as clothing, gold, and other objects. Best known is Wynflæd's will (Whitelock, *Wills*, 3; S 1539); for discussion, see Gale R. Owen, "Wynflæd's Wardrobe," *ASE* 8 (1979): 195–222. For other examples of similar bequests, see Whitelock, *Wills*, 8, 14, 15, 21; S 1484, 1494, 1486, 1538 respectively. In the context of these longer bequests, the Hereford mother's oral will looks like a condensed formula.

17. Stafford, *Queen Emma and Queen Edith*, pp. 55–64 on "the faces of the queen" and, more generally, *Unification and Conquest*, pp. 162–79.

18. The situation is far from clear or regularized. Names, especially of women, both enter and disappear in the legal record with little apparent consistency; this feature would merit further study. For examples, see Whitelock *Wills*, 5 (S 1524; the will of Ordnoth and his wife) and contrast 11 (S 1511; the will of Birhtric and Ælfswith). Whitelock, *Wills*, 13 (S1487; Ælfhelm's will), names his sons among the beneficiaries, but identifies his wife only by her marital status. Other legal transactions appear to show a similar (lack of) pattern: for examples, see the marriage agreement between Wulfric and Archbishop Wulfstan's sister, where the sister goes unnamed (*English Historical Documents*, ed. Whitelock, 128, cf. 129; S 1459, cf. 1461) or, to pick another random example, the grant in reversion to his anonymous wife and thence to New Minster, Winchester by Alfred the thane (Robertson 27; S 1509).

19. As is best illustrated by the Anglo-Saxon royal genealogies; for general discussion, see David N. Dumville, "Kingship, Genealogies, and Regnal Lists," in *Early Medieval Kingship*, ed. P. H. Sawyer and I. N. Wood (School of History, University of

Leeds. Leeds: The editors, 1977), pp. 72–104. The royal genealogies and regnal lists offer, at best, political dimensions of the construction of royal families, and thus constitute evidence different in kind from that of the legal evidence, where kinship is usually traced to the third or fourth generation. Despite the fact that the Anglo-Saxon family is bilateral in principle; in practice male kin dominate in both legal and royal records. The most telling evidence, however, is the most obvious—there is no formal genealogy or regnal list for an Anglo-Saxon queen. Even the document that most extensively traces female descent, *On the Prowess of Earl Uhtred and the earls who succeeded him*, works to assert the legal privileges of the male, not female, relations; for brief discussion, see van Houts, *Memory and Gender in Medieval Europe, 900–1200*, pp. 77–78.

20. For a useful general introduction to the relation between genealogy, women, and family, see van Houts, *Memory and Gender in Medieval Europe, 900–1200*, pp. 65–92.

21. For discussion, see Stafford, *Unification and Conquest*, pp. 162–79, and *Queen Emma and Queen Edith*, pp. 74–75.

22. For the religious evidence, see Lees, *Tradition and Belief*, pp. 133–53, and for a general discussion of both clerical and legal evidence in the later period, see Stafford, *Unification and Conquest*, pp. 165–72.

23. As Stafford also notes in *Unification and Conquest*, pp. 164–65, p. 175.

24. The relation, overlap, and tension between the social and legal roles of widow and mother would benefit from further research, but see the suggestive comments by Stafford in *Queen Emma and Queen Edith*, pp. 66–67, 74–75, 93. For suggestive remarks about Wulfstan's particular interest in the law of widows, see Wormald, *Making of English Law*, pp. 448, 458. For a collection of essays on widows in medieval society, see Louise Mirrer, ed., *Upon My Husband's Death: Widows in the Literature and Histories of Medieval Europe* (Ann Arbor: University of Michigan Press, 1992).

25. For V Æthelred, see F. Liebermann, ed. *Die Gesetze der Angelsachsen*, vol. 1 (Halle: M. Niemayer, 1903), pp. 236–47; the relevant extracts are conveniently translated as 21, 21.1 in W, p. 408.

26. For II Cnut, see Liebermann, *Die Gesetze der Angelsachsen*, vol. 1, pp. 278–371; translated in W, 73, 73a, 73.2–73.4, 74 (p. 429). For general discussion, see Wormald, *The Making of English Law*, pp. 349–52.

27. As Stafford puts it, "The tenth- and eleventh-century kin was already strongly patrilineal and male dominated" (*Unification and Conquest*, p. 164).

28. Stafford, *Unification and Conquest*, p. 173.

29. We voice similar concerns about the terms "public" and "private" in Chapter 1.

30. As van Houts, *Memory and Gender in Medieval Europe, 900–1200*, pp. 79–80, argues.

31. S 1454. This lawsuit is not in the name of that Wynflæd whose will is discussed above, note 16. The Wynflæd dispute has occasioned more comment than the Hereford dispute, although none have conducted a detailed analysis. For edition, see Robertson, *Anglo-Saxon Charters*, #66; for discussion, see, inter alia, Stafford, *Unification and Conquest*, 173; Fell, *Women in Anglo-Saxon England*, p. 98; Wormald, *The Making*

of English Law, pp. 151–53; and Keynes, "Royal Government and the Written Word in Late Anglo-Saxon England," pp. 245–46, 249–50.

32. "The queen, or king's spouse, was alone among women in being of sufficient public moment to be listed among witnesses of royal charters: royal daughters, abbesses, noblewomen never appear. In recorded legal disputes women feature regularly only as defendants," notes Stafford, *Unification and Conquest*, p. 173. Likewise, Marc Meyer points out that, while upward social mobility is a feature of the late Anglo-Saxon landscape, women benefited primarily from the "good fortune of their men" and almost never received royal charters themselves; see "Land Charters and the Legal Position of Anglo-Saxon Women," p. 61.

33. Recent debates about the "real" Asser and whether the work is tenth century rather than ninth are neatly summarized in Carol Pasternack's review of *King Alfred the Great*, by Alfred P. Smyth (Oxford: Oxford University Press, 1995), *Medieval Feminist Newsletter* 27 (Spring 1999): 44–48.

34. The dispute between Wynflæd and Leofwine (S 1454, discussed above), is reported using indirect speech, and hence exemplary in this regard.

35. Keynes, *Diplomas*, pp. 39–83.

36. See Wormald, *The Making of English Law*, p. 152 and note 121.

37. A common term for a will is in fact "cwide" (also meaning "speech"), while many testators declare their wills using a form of "cyðan" (whose other meanings include to "utter," "tell," "relate," "make known"), as even a cursory perusal of Whitelock, *Wills*, indicates.

38. For a useful discussion of such pragmatic literacy, see Keynes, "Royal Government and the Written Word in Late Anglo-Saxon England," pp. 248–57.

39. See Whitelock's note to line 19, in *Sweet's Anglo-Saxon Reader*, p. 247.

40. For *Elene*, see Lees, "At a Crossroads," pp. 159–67; for the *Wife's Lament*, see Barrie Ruth Straus, "Women's Words as Weapons: Speech as Action in *The Wife's Lament*," *Texas Studies in Literature and Language* 23 (1981): 268–85; and for Wealhtheow, see Gillian R. Overing, *Language, Sign, and Gender in "Beowulf"* (Carbondale: Southern Illinois University Press, 1990), pp. 88–101.

41. Classic examples are, of course, Hallgerðr and Bergþóra in *Njal's Saga* and the marvelous women—Unnr, Guðrún, Auðr—in *Laxdœla Saga*; the standard translations are Magnus Magnusson and Hermann Palsson, *Njal's Saga* (Harmondsworth: Penguin, 1960) and Magnusson and Palsson, *Laxdœla Saga* (Harmondsworth: Penguin, 1969).

42. For discussion of the laws in this context, see Keynes, "Royal Government and the Written Word in Late Anglo-Saxon England."

43. Van Houts, *Memory and Gender in Medieval Europe, 900–1200*, p. 80.

44. Stafford, *Queen Emma and Queen Edith*, p. 63. Our discussion of royal female names is indebted to Stafford's work.

45. The F version of the *Chronicle* (the Bilingual Canterbury Epitome), however, adds both her names to the entry, "Ymma 'Ælfgiua.'" See Michael Swanton, ed. and trans., *The Anglo-Saxon Chronicle* (New York: Routledge, 1998), p. 134 and note 2.

46. See the entries for 1017 in the Worcester (D) and Peterborough chronicles (E). For translation, see Swanton, pp. 154–55.

47. The Peterborough *Chronicle* (E) entry for 1052 records the death of Ælfgifu Emma, as does the Bilingual Canterbury Epitome (F), while the Worcester chronicle (D) records only her Anglo-Saxon name, Ælfgifu. For translations, see Swanton, pp. 176–77.

48. Stafford, *Queen Emma and Queen Edith*, p. 89.

49. Campbell, ed., *Encomium Emmae Reginae.*

50. Stafford, *Queen Emma and Queen Edith*, p. 61.

51. For further elaboration of this crucial point, see Lees and Overing, "Misogyny and the Social Symbolic in Anglo-Saxon England," forthcoming in *Gender in Debate from the Middle Ages to the Renaissance*, ed. Thelma S. Fenster and Clare A. Lees (New York: Palgrave Press, 2002).

52. A. Campbell, ed. and trans., *The Chronicle of Æthelweard* (London: Nelson, 1962), pp. 1–2. For discussion see also van Houts, *Memory and Gender in Medieval Europe, 900–1200*, pp. 69–70, and Appendix 1 (another translation of Æthelweard's preface).

53. For discussion, see F. C. Robinson, "The Significance of Names in Old English Literature," *Anglia* 86 (1968): 14–58; and Joyce Hill, "Ælfric's Use of Etymologies," *ASE* 17 (1988): 35–44.

54. A good introduction is Michael Lapidge, "The Saintly Life in Anglo-Saxon England," in *The Cambridge Companion to Old English Literature*, ed. Godden and Lapidge (Cambridge: Cambridge University Press, 1991), pp. 243–63.

55. A useful guide to Æthelwold's importance is Barbara Yorke's introduction in *Bishop Æthelwold: His Career and Influence*, ed. Yorke (Woodbridge: Boydell, 1988), pp. 1–12.

56. Stafford, *Queen Emma and Queen Edith*, pp. 55–56. See also Mary Clayton, *The Cult of the Virgin Mary in Anglo-Saxon England* (Cambridge: Cambridge University Press, 1990).

57. *A New Critical History of Old English Literature*, ed. Stanley B. Greenfield and Daniel G. Calder, with Michael Lapidge (New York: New York University Press, 1986) remains a good introduction to the period.

58. With the exception of the copy of the *Regularis Concordia* whose altered pronouns indicate a female readership; see Joyce Hill, "The 'Regularis Concordia' and Its Latin and Old English Reflexes," *Revue Bénédictine* 101 (1991): 299–315. The extent of evidence for female readers of Latin is perhaps masked by our limited knowledge of the manuscripts. Certainly Goscelin in the post-Conquest period recalls Wilton Abbey for its community of learned women, especially Edith; see Stafford, *Queen Emma and Queen Edith*, pp. 256–57.

59. The *Encomium Emmae Reginae*, ed. Campbell; *Vita Ædwardi Regis qui apud Westmonasterium requiescit (The Life of King Edward who rests at Westminster)*, ed. and trans. Frank Barlow (London: Nelson, 1962). Our thoughts about these two works are indebted to Stafford's rich study of both queens, *Queen Emma and Queen Edith*.

60. *Encomium Emmae*, pp. 6–7.

61. See Keynes's introduction to reprinted edition of the *Encomium Emmae*, pp. lxvi–lxxi.

62. Reproduced in the *Encomium Emmae*, p. xliii.

63. Barlow, *Vita Ædwardi*, pp. 2, 14.

64. *Queen Emma and Queen Edith*, p. 51.

65. Hollis, "The Minster-in-Thanet Foundation Story"; see Chapter 2 for fuller discussion.

66. For a good introduction to these patrons and writers, see Jonathan Wilcox, ed., *Ælfric's Prefaces* (Durham: Durham Medieval Texts), pp. 2–15.

67. This argument has been made most fully by Carol Braun Pasternack for Old English poetry; see *The Textuality of Old English Poetry* (Cambridge: Cambridge University Press, 1995).

68. For a brief though related discussion of concepts of authorship, see Lees, *Tradition and Belief*, pp. 24–26. For Wulfstan Cantor, see Michael Lapidge and Michael Winterbottom, ed. *Wulfstan of Winchester: The Life of St. Æthelwold* (Oxford: Clarendon Press, 1991).

69. See his abbreviated account, "Hortatorius Sermo de Efficacia Sanctae Missae," in *Ælfric's Catholic Homilies: The Second Series Text*, ed. Malcolm Godden, *EETS* s.s. 5 (Oxford: Oxford University Press, 1979), pp. 204–5. Cited by editor, page and line number. All translations are authorial.

70. Lerer, *Literacy and Power*, pp. 30–60.

71. Ælfric acknowledges Bede's authority for the story at the beginning of the *Sermo* (p. 204), and concludes with a reference to Gregory's *Dialogues* (p. 205)—thus, the *Sermo* is framed by patristic authority. Bede's emphasis is on the salvific power of the mass, as is Ælfric's, though to a more abbreviated extent, but the real mystery—the power of the sung mass—lies at the unexpressed heart of both accounts.

72. "Sermo de Sacrificio in Die Pascae," in Godden, ed., *Ælfric's Catholic Homilies: The Second Series Text*, pp. 150–60.

73. For sources, see Theodore H. Leinbaugh, "Ælfric's *Sermo de Sacrificio in Die Pascae: Anglican Polemic in the Sixteenth and Seventeenth Centuries*," in *Anglo-Saxon Scholarship: The First Three Centuries*, ed. Carl T. Berkhout and Milton McC. Gatch (Boston: Hall, 1982), pp. 51–68; and Malcolm Godden, "The Sources for Ælfric's Homily on St Gregory," *Anglia* 86 (1968): 79–88 (at pp. 87–88).

74. *De trinitate*. ed. W. J. Mountain and Fr. Glorie. *CCSL* (50A, 1950), 15. 9. 15, p. 481.

75. Cassiodorus, *Expositio in Psalterium*. PL 70: 1271. Isidore, *Eytmologiae*, ed. W. M. Lindsay, (Oxford: Oxford University Press, 1911; repr. Oxford: Clarendon Press, 1957), 1.37.26, cited in Stork, *Through a Gloss Darkly*, p. 62.

76. For translations of both the prologue and verse prefaces, see Stork, *Through a Gloss Darkly*, pp. 90–93 (at p. 90) and pp. 98–99 (at p. 98). For the Latin, see Ehwald, *Aldhemi Opera*, pp. 35–41, 41–57.

77. Augustine, *De doctrina christiana*. ed. Joseph Martin. *CCSL* 32 (1962), pp. 63–64. For a discussion of the subsequent importance of Aldhelm's works, see Orchard, *Poetic Art of Aldhelm*, pp. 239–83.

78. Stork, *Through a Gloss Darkly*, p. 81, line 6. The manuscript is BL Royal 12.C.xxiii.

79. For a good study of Anglo-Saxon reading practices and their relation to riddles, see Nicholas Howe, "The Cultural Construction of Reading in Anglo-Saxon England," in *The Ethnography of Reading*, ed. Jonathan Boyarin (Berkeley: University of California Press, 1992), pp. 58–79 (esp. pp. 62–63).

80. For references to the editions for Aldhelm's riddles and the Exeter Book riddles, see Chapter 2, notes 65, 79.

81. Stork, *Through a Gloss Darkly*, p. 90.

82. For *The Wife's Lament* and *Wulf and Eadwacer*, see *The Exeter Book*, pp. 210–11, 179–80 respectively.

83. Anne L. Klinck has a useful summary in *The Old English Elegies: A Critical Edition and Genre Study* (Montreal and Kingston: McGill-Queen's University Press, 1992), p. 27. All quotations are from the Exeter Book, *ASPR* 3, ed. Krapp and Dobbie.

84. As suggested by the textual notes to Riddle 60 in the Exeter Book edition, and the textual notes to its translation, *The Exeter Book Riddles*, trans. Crossley-Holland, p. 126.

Chapter 4

1. For introductions to Aldhelm, see Lapidge and Herren, trans., *Aldhelm: The Prose Works*, pp. 1–19, and Orchard, *The Poetic Art of Aldhelm*, pp. 1–18. All references to Aldhelm's *De virginitate* are to the prose version, translated by Lapidge and Herren, unless otherwise indicated, cited by page. See Ehwald's edition (*Aldhelmi Opera*), where we comment on the Latin text. For Ælfric, see Wilcox, ed., *Ælfric's Prefaces*, pp. 1–15, and Clemoes, "Ælfric"; his *Lives of Saints* are edited by Skeat, *Ælfric's Lives of Saints*, cited by volume, page, and line number (where relevant). All translations from Ælfric are authorial.

2. Aldhelm mentions his intention to write a poetic version at the end of the prose *De virginitate* (Lapidge and Herren, p. 131). We have no other corroboration that the nuns of Barking saw the second poetic version, although commentators assume so.

3. Cyril Hart, *The Early Charters of Barking Abbey* (Colchester: Benham, 1953), p. 15.

4. S1246-B87. Also printed and translated in Hart, pp. 8–11.

5. Hart, *Early Charters*, p. 22.

6. Kenneth MacGowan, "Barking Abbey," *Current Archaeology* 149 (1996): 172–78.

7. MacGowan, "Barking Abbey," p. 178.

8. MacGowan, p. 178.

9. Neuman de Vegvar, "Saints and Companions to Saints: Anglo-Saxon Royal Women Monastics in Context," p. 61.

10. Christine Fell calls attention to the presence of servants in Bede's account of St. Æthelthryth where her servants help her to minister to her nuns. "Saint Æthelthryth: A Historical-Hagiographical Dichotomy Revised," *Nottingham Medieval Studies* 38 (1994): 18–32, examines Æthelthryth as queen and/or saint, and Bede as hagiographer and/or historian, and brings out a certain irony as the monastic noblewoman walks a fine line between religious function and class hierarchy: "Her humility which causes her to wait on others in particular and ritualised circumstances has not caused her to rid herself of personal servants, and the humility of Christ himself washing the feet of his disciples would seem a lesson not fully absorbed" (p. 28).

11. In his hierarchy of female chastities, Aldhelm offers the following comparisons: "Virginity is riches, chastity an average income, conjugality poverty . . . virginity is a queen, chastity a lady, conjugality a servant" (Lapidge and Herren, p. 75).

12. Neuman de Vegvar identifies Boniface's letter to Æthelbald of Mercia, written in 746–747, recalling the immorality of Osred of Northumbria (706–717) and Ceolred of Mercia (709–716) and chastizing him for his own laxity, as one turning point in the focused awareness of nuns and sexuality as problematic ("Saints and Companions," p. 60).

13. Hollis, *Anglo-Saxon Women and the Church*, p. 103.

14. "It is not permissible for men to have monastic women, nor women, men; nevertheless we shall not overthrow that which is the custom in this region, " *Die Canones Theodori Cantuariensis und ihre Uberlieferungsformen*, ed. P. W. Finsterwalder (Weimar, 1929), pp. 285–334. For translation, see John T. McNeill and Helena M. Gamer, trans., *Medieval Handbooks of Penance: A Translation of the Principal "Libri poenitentiales"* (New York: Columbia University Press, 1938), II, vi 8.

15. Hollis, *Anglo-Saxon Women and the Church*, pp. 98–108.

16. See Hollis's astute comments on the Coldingham story, a kind of "debunking" (pp. 101–2).

17. Hollis, *Anglo-Saxon Women and the Church*, p. 107.

18. Hollis, *Anglo-Saxon Women and the Church*, p. 79.

19. Ward, " 'To my dearest sister,' " p. 107.

20. For a general study of virginity, chastity, and female sanctity in the Middle Ages, see Schulenberg, "The Heroics of Virginity," pp. 29–72.

21. For Cuthberg, see Lapidge and Herren, pp. 52, 193, note 20.

22. Hollis, *Anglo-Saxon Women and the Church*, p. 80.

23. Hollis, *Anglo-Saxon Women and the Church*, p. 81.

24. Orchard, *The Poetic Art of Aldhelm*, pp. 11, 15.

25. Aldhelm studied at the school founded by Archbishop Theodore at Canterbury in the early 670s; his enthusiastic espousal of the "new" learning, namely that influx of Greek and Roman texts emphasized by Theodore (and his concomitant denigration of Celtic learning) have inevitable ideological implications in the late seventh-century battle for hegemony—doctrinal and episcopal—between Celtic and Roman ecclesiastical traditions. Once Theodore's Canterbury school had "put England on the map," Hollis avers, "Aldhelm could see no further need for Englishmen in search of learning to travel to Ireland, which for impenetrable reasons he also regarded as morally dangerous," (Hollis, *Anglo-Saxon Women and the Church*, p. 266).

26. Orchard, *The Poetic Art of Aldhelm*, p. 11.

27. *Carmen de virginitate* in *Aldhelmi Opera*, ed. Ehwald, ll. 1994–96, 435, as translated by Orchard, *The Poetic Art of Aldhelm*, p. 13, note 51.

28. Orchard, *The Poetic Art of Aldhelm*, p. 11.

29. " 'Rædan, Areccan, Smeagan': How the Anglo-Saxons Read," *ASE* 26 (1997): 1–22, at p. 15.

30. Bede's reference to the interpretive reader/listener (in this case Cædmon) as "animal ruminando" (*EH*, 4. 24) rehearses previous commentaries of Jerome and Augustine. See André Crépin, "Bede and the Vernacular," in *Famulus Christi*, ed. Gerald F. Bonner (London: SPCK, 1976), pp. 170–92 for a discussion of Bede's develop-

ment of this patristic metaphor. For a discussion of "ruminatio" and the processes of reading/interpretation, see also Lerer, *Literacy and Power*, pp. 44–48; Lerer understands Bede's reworking of this image as introducing a "new kind of 'alimentary' poetics" where the story of Cædmon provides the basis for the new "'ruminatio' of a monastic education" (p. 33). How far this applies to the female monastic reader is open to question.

31. Lerer suggests that later in the period it becomes "a trope for study and for compilation" (*Literacy and Power*, p. 73), although Aldhelm is considered to have cornered the literary market in the early middle ages with his particular rendition; his is the "locus classicus" for the image (Keynes and Lapidge, *Alfred the Great*, p. 258, note 161). Interestingly, when Asser compares King Alfred to a bee collecting "flowers" from scripture for study (ch. 88, p. 100, ch. 89, p. 100), any echoes of Aldhelm's tortuous alimentary processes have disappeared—rather like the trajectory of the disappearing body that may be identified in the literate and vernacular riddles discussed in Chapter 1. See also Lerer, p. 216, note 16, for an assortment of references to the bee image.

32. Kathryn Gravdal, *Ravishing Maidens: Writing Rape in Medieval French Literature and Law* (Philadelphia: University of Pennsylvania Press, 1991), analyzes how rape can be elided, ignored, or trivialized by medieval narrative, although its threat remains a forceful narrative presence.

33. Ehwald, *Aldhelmi Opera*, p. 294.

34. Ehwald, *Aldhelmi Opera*, p. 429, lines 1830–4.

35. Butler, *Bodies That Matter: On the Discursive Limits of "Sex"* (New York: Routledge, 1993), pp. 12–23.

36. See our discussion of women's involvement, physical and financial, in founding monasteries in Chapter 1.

37. Ehwald, *Aldhelmi Opera*, pp. 225, 349.

38. See for example Leoba's letter to Boniface asking for his comments on her composition, *The Letters of St. Boniface*, ed. Austin P. Evans (New York: Columbia University Press, 1940), 21: 59–60.

39. Orchard, *The Poetic Art of Aldhelm*, pp. 281, 239–83.

40. Gretsch, *The Intellectual Foundation of the English Benedictine Reform* (Cambridge: Cambridge University Press, 1999), p. 134. Although Gretsch does not address the question of gender in her analysis, she stresses the importance of Æthelwold's initiative in these important witnesses to the intellectual traditions of the English Benedictine reforms; see esp. chapters four and nine.

41. See Schulenberg, "Women's Monastic Communities"; Lapidge and Winterbottom, eds., *Wulfstan of Winchester: The Life of St. Æthelwold*, pp. li–xcix; and Lees, "Engendering Religious Desire," pp. 35–37.

42. See Ridyard, *Royal Saints of Anglo-Saxon England*.

43. For an analogous discussion, see Lees, *Tradition and Belief*, p. 134. The *Regularis concordia* is most conveniently edited by Dom Thomas Symons (London: Thomas Nelson, 1953), see esp. pp. 1–9.

44. Stafford, *Unification and Conquest*, p. 192. See also her discussion of Emma's sphere of influence in the reform period in *Queen Emma and Queen Edith*, pp. 140–61.

45. To the contrary, Barking is perhaps best known in the cultural history of the tenth century because of Goscelin's account of the nun at Wilton, often identified with

Wulfhild, abbess of Barking, carried off by Edgar. Only three abbesses of Barking are recorded in the period between 940 and the post-Conquest period, according to David Knowles and C. N. L. Brooke, *The Heads of Religious Houses, England and Wales, 940–1216* (Cambridge: Cambridge University Press, 1972), p. 208. The scant evidence of female religious houses both pre- and post-Conquest is discussed by Janet Burton, *Monastic and Religious Orders in Britain, 1000–1300* (Cambridge: Cambridge University Press, 1994); Barking appears to have been moderately wealthy by the time of the Doomsday Book (see Burton, pp. 2–9).

46. For Ely, see *Wulfstan of Winchester: The Life of St Æthelwold*, ed. Lapidge and Winterbottom, p. 38, and Fell, "Saint Æthelthryth: A Historical-Hagiographical Dichotomy Revisited," for the ironies of Æthelwold's move. For Nunnaminster's earlier foundation by Ealhswith, see Stafford, *Queen Emma and Queen Edith*, p. 141.

47. Following the more general proscription of the *Regularis concordia* itself. See, *An Old English Account of King Edgar's Establishment of the Monasteries* in Whitelock (W, p. 846). Æthelwold's authorship of this document is most recently assessed by Gretsch, pp. 230–33.

48. *Wulfstan of Winchester: The Life of Æthelwold*, ed. Lapidge and Winterbottom, p. 38.

49. See Stafford, *Unification and Conquest*, pp. 188–94, for a good summary of this complex evidence.

50. Stafford, *Queen Emma and Queen Edith*, pp. 107–61.

51. For discussion, see Malcolm Godden, "Money, Power, and Morality in Late Anglo-Saxon England," *ASE* 19 (1990): 41–65.

52. See, however, the evidence of the female pronouns in one manuscript of the *Regularis concordia*, discussed by Hill, in "The 'Regularis Concordia' and Its Latin and Old English Reflexes."

53. See Lees, "Engendering Religious Desire," p. 32.

54. See Wilcox, *Ælfric's Prefaces*, pp. 1–15, and Lees, "Engendering Religious Desire," p. 33.

55. See, however, Gretsch's argument for the influence of Æthelwold, Ælfric's teacher, on the reform and Æthelwold's own interest in Aldhelm in *The Intellectual Foundations of the English Benedictine Reform*, esp. pp. 425–27.

56. Greenfield and Calder, *A New Critical History of Old English Literature*, pp. 68–106, remains a useful introduction to Old English prose; important too is Lapidge's account of Anglo-Latin in the same volume (pp. 1–37). See also Wilcox, *Ælfric's Prefaces*, p. 61.

57. See Michael Lapidge, "Ælfric's *Sanctorale*," in *Holy Men and Holy Women*, ed. Szarmach, pp. 115–29; and Peter Jackson and Michael Lapidge, "The Contents of the Cotton-Corpus Legendary," also in *Holy Men and Holy Women*, pp. 131–46.

58. Wilcox, *Ælfric's Prefaces*, pp. 8–12.

59. See Joyce Hill, "The Dissemination of Ælfric's *Lives of Saints*," in *Holy Men and Holy Women*, ed. Szarmach, pp. 235–59.

60. See Lees, *Tradition and Belief*, pp. 133–53, for a related discussion.

61. See Peter Clemoes, ed., *Ælfric's Catholic Homilies: The First Series*, EETS ss. 17 (Oxford: Oxford University Press, 1997), and Godden, ed., *Ælfric's Catholic Homilies: The Second Series Text*.

62. See Paul E. Szarmach, "Ælfric's Women Saints: Eugenia," in *New Readings on Women in Old English Literature*, ed. Damico and Olsen, pp. 146–57; Frantzen, "When Women Aren't Enough"; and Gopa Roy, "A Virgin Acts Manfully: Ælfric's *Life of St Eugenia* and the Latin Versions," *Leeds Studies in English* n.s. 23 (1992): 1–27. For important studies more generally on female saints, see the anthology of essays by Jane Tibbetts Schulenburg, *Forgetful of Their Sex: Female Sanctity and Society, ca. 500–1100* (Chicago: University of Chicago Press, 1998), and Karen A. Winstead, *Virgin Martyrs: Legends of Sainthood in Late Medieval England* (Ithaca, N.Y.: Cornell University Press, 1997.

63. See Malcolm Godden, "Experiments in Genre: The Saints' Lives in Ælfric's *Catholic Homilies*," in *Holy Men and Holy Women*, ed. Szarmach, pp. 261–87.

64. A useful direction for such work is Maureen Quilligan's discussion of female voices and bodies in Christine de Pisan's *Book of the City of Ladies: The Allegory of Female Authority: Christine de Pizan's Cité des dames* (Ithaca, N.Y.: Cornell University Press, 1991). Although based on a later period than the Anglo-Saxon, Quilligan's work could be profitably considered in relation to Latin and Anglo-Saxon hagiography.

65. See Thomas D. Hill, "*Imago Dei*: Genre, Symbolism, and Anglo-Saxon Hagiography," in *Holy Men and Holy Women*, ed. Szarmach, pp. 35–50; and Lees, "At a Crossroads," pp. 159–67.

66. See Wilcox, *Ælfric's Prefaces*, pp. 62–63.

67. For a discussion of "translatio" and translation, see Lees, "Engendering Religious Desire."

68. For an edition of the three extant Anglo-Latin sources and English translation, see Jane Stevenson, ed. "Vita Sanctae Mariae Egiptiacae," *The Legend of Mary of Egypt in Medieval Insular Hagiography*, ed. Erich Poppe and Bianca Ross (Blackrock, Co., Dublin, and Portland, Oreg.: Four Courts Press, 1996), pp. 51–98. All references to the source are to this edition, by page and paragraph number. The Old English version is usually regarded as a literal translation of the Anglo-Latin but, as Andy Orchard points out in his forthcoming essay in the *Old English Newsletter*, subsidia series, such a view overlooks the stylistic alterations in the Old English. Some of these stylistic modifications are due to the translator's interest in the theme of seeing and knowing, which is already strongly present in the source. The prologue in the Old English follows the incipit in Stevenson's manuscript C (London, British Library, Cotton Claudius A. 1), where "gehwryfednysse" translates "conversio" (Stevenson, p. 51). For fuller discussion of the Latin and Anglo-Latin sources, see Stevenson, "The Holy Sinner: The Life of Mary of Egypt," in Poppe and Ross, pp. 19–50. The essays in Poppe and Ross witness the vitality of the legend in insular hagiography: for its broader medieval popularity in relation to the other prostitute saints (Mary Magdalen, Thaïs, Pelagia, Mary niece of Abraham, and Afra of Augsburg), see Ruth Mazo Karras, "Holy Harlots: Prostitute Saints in Medieval Legend," *Journal of the History of Sexuality* 1 (1990): 3–32; for a detailed study of the French reflexes of the legend, see Simon Gaunt, *Gender and Genre in Medieval French Literature* (Cambridge: Cambridge University Press, 1995), pp. 213–28. See also Karen A. Winstead, *Virgin Martyrs: Legends of Sainthood in Late Medieval England* (Ithaca, N.Y.: Cornell University Press, 1997).

69. That the power of things seen is central to medieval Christianity and its didactic strategies is to state the obvious; it is precisely this obviousness, however, that

has tended to stand in the way of its fuller analysis. For a useful study of the power of visible objects in the history of sanctity, see Cynthia Hahn, "Seeing and Believing: The Construction of Sanctity in Early-Medieval Saints' Shrines," *Speculum* 72 (1997): 1079–1106.

70. Although we do not concentrate on the penitential aspects of the text here (and Catherine Tkacz Brown examines the evidence for its Byzantine theology in her forthcoming essay in the *Old English Newsletter*, subsidia series), the Old English *Mary of Egypt* merits further study as an example of the Anglo-Saxon literature of penance studied more generally by Frantzen, *The Literature of Penance in Anglo-Saxon England*.

71. "cordis mei oculos" (Stevenson, p. 66, 16, p. 71, 19).

72. "et uidebis me iterum qualiter Deus uoluerit" (Stevenson, p. 75, 22).

73. For recent criticism of Mary's sexuality and gender, see Lees, "Engendering Religious Desire"; Karras, "Holy Harlots"; Gaunt, *Gender and Genre*. See also Hugh Magennis, "St Mary of Egypt and Ælfric: Unlikely Bedfellows in Cotton Julius E. vii?" in Poppe and Ross, pp. 99–112, and Andy Orchard, "Hot Lust in a Cold Climate: Comparison and Contrast in the Old Norse Versions of the Life of Mary of Egypt," in Poppe and Ross, pp. 175–204.

74. That Mary refuses money from her partners (cf. p. 22, lines 333–43) only emphasizes her sin of fornication; she would still be classified as a prostitute according to canon law notions of prostitution as indiscriminate sexuality; see Karras, "Holy Harlots," pp. 5–17.

75. Latin *conversio* means "a turning" (cf. Old English, "gehwryfednyss") and thus conversion is itself a metaphor; *tropus* in the Greek also means a "turn" (or in Koiné, "way" or "manner"), and is a common term for a figure in medieval Latin, thus closely related to "translatio," itself a term for metaphor. See Curtius, *European Literature and the Latin Middle Ages*, pp. 45, 128. Mary's turning away from sexual knowledge literally enacts her conversion, the figural power of which is stressed by the narrative. Similarly the literal translation of the dead body of a saint is a metaphor for that body's metaphoric transformation into spirit and sanctity. For further discussion of medieval understandings of conversion as both word and metaphor, see Karl F. Morrison, *Understanding Conversion* (Charlottesville: University Press of Virginia, 1992), pp. 1–27.

76. In some later French versions of the legend, this aged Mary is transformed into a beautiful young girl; see Gaunt, *Gender and Genre*, pp. 217–18. Mary's age thus appears to be as crucial to the dynamics of the Old English text as Zosimus's advanced years, even though it is mentioned less often. Zosimus's age signifies his apparent spiritual wisdom (cf. "þæs ealdan witan," p. 16, line 244), which is, however, hardly perfect. Mary's age appears intended to deflect attention away from her sexual attractiveness. Zosimus is fifty-three when he begins his spiritual journey (p. 4, line 47) and he is habitually referred to as an old man, "se ealda" (cf. p. 20, line 292). Mary's age is initially signified by the whiteness of her hair (p. 12, lines 176–77); that is, her age is represented as seen before being so named. She misspent seventeen years in her youth (p. 22, line 333), spent forty-seven years in the desert (p. 36, line 515), and is habitually referred to by Zosimus as a "modor" (cf. p. 46, line 711) rather than an old woman.

77. Erich Auerbach, "Figura," trans. Ralph Mannheim, in *Scenes from the Drama of European Literature* (Minneapolis: University of Minnesota Press, 1984), pp. 11–76

(at p. 61). See also James W. Earl, "Typology and Iconographic Style in Early Medieval Hagiography," *Studies in the Literary Imagination* 8 (1975): 15–46; a revised version of this essay appears in *Typology and English Medieval Literature*, ed. Hugh T. Keenan (New York: AMS Press, 1992), pp. 89–120 (with reference to Mary of Egypt at p. 90). Thomas D. Hill repeats the observation in "'Imago Dei': Genre, Symbolism, and Anglo-Saxon Hagiography," p. 44.

78. Stevenson, "Holy Sinner," p. 21.

79. In the Old Testament, Israel is often figured as a prostituted woman; for brief discussion, see Regina M. Schwartz, *The Curse of Cain: The Violent Legacy of Monotheism* (Chicago: University of Chicago Press, 1997), pp. 66–76.

80. For discussion of the holy harlot saints, see note 68.

81. As Hill reminds us in "Imago Dei."

82. Colin Chase, "Source Study as a Trick with Mirrors: Annihilation of Meaning in the Old English 'Mary of Egypt,'" in *Sources of Anglo-Saxon Culture*, ed. Paul E. Szarmach, with the assistance of Virginia Darrow Oggins (Kalamazoo, Mich.: Medieval Institute Publications, 1986), pp. 22–33. See also Andy Orchard's forthcoming essay on Mary.

83. Chase, "Source Study," p. 31.

84. Chase, "Source Study," p. 31.

85. Note also the prostitute Sibilla in the *History of the Holy Rood-Tree*, ed. Arthur S. Napier, *EETS* (os 103, 1894), pp. 26–31.

86. Magennis, "St. Mary of Egypt and Ælfric"; Lees, "Engendering Religious Desire," pp. 31–35.

87. For discussion of the text's use of liturgical time, see the forthcoming essay by Catherine Tkacz Brown.

88. The emphasis on the secretive nature of the place is slightly stronger in the Old English; contrast the Anglo-Latin, "Solitarius enim erat locus iste et plurimus uicinorum non solum inusitatus, sed incognitus" (Stevenson, p. 56, 5).

89. For "gehydde goldhord," see "absconditum thesaurum" (Stevenson p. 76, 24); the concept of Mary as a goldhoard resonates richly with Anglo-Saxon images of the gold-adorned woman, for which, see Pat Belanoff, "The Fall (?) of the Old English Poetic Image," *PMLA* 104 (1989): 822–31.

90. Later French versions of the legend take some pains to assess the relation between Mary of Egypt and the Virgin Mary; see Gaunt, *Gender and Genre*, pp. 214–16, 224–27. For evidence that the Anglo-Saxons confused this Mary with the Magdalen (an obvious enough ambiguity), see James E. Cross, "Mary Magdalen in the *Old English Martyrology*: The Earliest Extant 'Narrat Josephus' Variant of her Legend," *Speculum* 53 (1978): 16–25 (at p. 19), and Carol A. Farr, "Worthy Women on the Ruthwell Cross: Woman as Sign in Early Anglo-Saxon Monasticism," in *The Insular Tradition*, ed. Catherine E. Karkov, Michael Ryan, and Robert T. Farrell (Albany: SUNY Press, 1997), pp. 45–61 (at p. 54).

91. As the Latin prologue makes clear (Stevenson, p. 51).

92. For a useful account of Æthelweard and Æthelmær, see Jonathan Wilcox, *Ælfric's Prefaces*, pp. 9–13. Whether the translator, Paul of Naples, may be identified with Paulus Diaconus, as is sometimes assumed, is assessed by Orchard in his forthcoming essay. For the importance of Naples as an area of biblical scholarship, see

Bernhard Bischoff and Michael Lapidge, eds. *Biblical Commentaries from the Canter-bury School of Theodore and Hadrian* (Cambridge: Cambridge University Press, 1994), pp. 108–20, 155–72.

93. This point is strengthened in the Old English because the translator omits the remainder of the Latin prologue (Stevenson, pp. 51–52).

94. In addition to the spiritual labors of the translator, Mary, and Zosimus, the spiritual work of the monks in Abbot John's monastery is explicitly related to the parable of the talents (cf. p. 10, lines 141–45; Stevenson, p. 57, 6).

95. Parkes, "*Rædan, Areccan, Smeagan*: How the Anglo-Saxons Read"; see also Howe, "The Cultural Construction of Reading in Anglo-Saxon England).

96. Parkes, pp. 15–16. For discussion of the related image of the book of the heart, see Eric Jager, "The Book of the Heart: Reading and Writing the Medieval Subject," *Speculum* 71 (1996): 1–26.

97. The Old English translator uses the opportunity to stress the relation between the reference to Tobit in the prologue and this conclusion by using the same verb, "bediglian," "to conceal," in contrast to the Latin, compare Stevenson, p. 51, p. 79, 27.

98. Compare "imitabilis" (Stevenson, p. 51, incipit to ms. C).

99. The Latin lacks a similar use of repetition: "Dum autem psalleret, et in celum intentis inspiceret obtutibus, uidit a parte dextra, ubi stans sextam orabat, umbram quasi humani corporis apparentem, et prius quidem turbatus est, fantasiam alicuius spiritus existimans se uidesse" (Stevenson, p. 58, 7).

100. The alliteration, which draws the reader's attention to this passage, is the work of the Old English translator even as it preserves the meaning of the source; cf. Stevenson, p. 58, 7: "conuertens oculos, uidit aliquem in ueritate properantem ad partem occidentis. Mulier autem erat, quod uidebatur, nigerrimo corpore, pre solis ardore denigrata, et capillos capitis habens ut lana albos, modicos et ipsos, non am-plius quam usque ad ceruicem descendentes."

101. For the image of the woman burned by the sun, see Song of Songs 1: 6. The meaning of Mary's shorn hair is ambiguous; for Paul, long hair is a glory for women (cf. 1 Corinthians 11: 14–15), while the captive bride of Deuteronomy has her head shaved (Deuteronomy 21: 12).

102. The Old English translator uses the verb, "bediglian"; cf. the Latin "tegere" (cf. Stevenson, p. 60, 9), stressing through semantic choice this passage's connection to the prologue (see also the discussion above, note 97).

103. The power of the partly-clothed woman as an image for sexual or spiritual knowledge is considerable and lengthy in the Western tradition. Note, for example, that Philosophy is represented fully clothed in Cambridge, Trinity College, MS 0.3.7, f. 1 (a copy of Boethius); see *The Golden Age of Anglo-Saxon Art*, ed. Janet Backhouse, D. H. Turner, and Leslie Webster (British Museum: British Museum Publications, 1984), p. 56. For a related discussion of Philosophy as a figure, see Chapter 5. Contrast the conventional image of partly clothed (partly naked) Venus, classically rendered in Chaucer's *Parliament of Fowles*; see *The Riverside Chaucer*, ed. Larry D. Benson, 3rd ed. (Boston: Houghton Mifflin, 1987), lines 269–73. For a valuable discussion of the rela-tion between woman as figure, textuality, clothing, and interpretation in later medieval literature, see Carolyn Dinshaw, *Chaucer's Sexual Poetics* (Madison: University of Wis-consin Press, 1989).

104. Mary makes the connection explicit in the Latin: "tamen nudum meum corporem uidisti, denudabo tibi et opera meorum actuum" (Stevenson, p. 63, 12). The corresponding passage in the Old English is corrupt (cf. p. 20, lines 312–13).

105. Ironically, however, it is Mary's sexuality that has most attracted modern commentators. See note 73 above for relevant bibliography.

106. "when he looked, he saw." Repetition of the same verb in the Old English stylistically intensifies this moment of seeing; contrast the Latin, "Et respiciens, uidit" (Stevenson, p. 77, 26).

107. For the image of the lion and the *Vita Pauli*, see Stevenson, "Holy Sinner," pp. 29–30. The shining light of transformation is also associated with the monks in Abbot John's monastery, whom Zosimus sees shining in their spiritual labors (p. 6, lines 84–87).

108. The Latin is slightly more explicit: "uir qui prior me in actibus sit" (Stevenson, p. 54, 2).

109. Contrast the Latin, which does not stress the notion of temporality: "qui eum posset aliquod edificare" (Stevenson, p. 58, 7).

110. Mary is refused entry through the doors of the temple three or four times as she endeavors to fulfil her will or desire with sight of the cross (p. 28, lines 417–19). The full account of this episode (p. 28, lines 403–21) emphasizes the futility of her work, thus contrasting with the efficacy of her later spiritual labors.

111. For "heortan" see "mentem . . . intellectus" (Stevenson, p. 66, 16).

112. Contrast the Latin, "*Prospexi* in loco in quo stabam, sursum *imaginem* sancte Dei genitricis stantem" (Stevenson, p. 67, 16, emphasis added), where the Old English translator uses the common verb, "seon," thus echoing other uses of this verb in accounts of seeing (e.g., in the account of Zosimus's first sight of Mary, discussed above). Stevenson translates "imaginem" as icon (p. 90, 16). For discussion of Mary's iconic status, see Tkacz Brown's forthcoming essay, and for an important account of the role of the icon in the dynamics of medieval sight, see Janet Martin Soskice, "Sight and Vision in Medieval Christian Thought," in *Vision in Context: Historical and Contemporary Perspectives on Sight*, ed. Teresa Brennan and Martin Jay (New York: Routledge, 1996), pp. 29–43.

113. Compare the Latin, "scio enim scio quia non est condecens nec oportunum sic horridam adorare imaginem tuam uel contemplari tantis pollutis sordibus oculis" (Stevenson, p. 67, 16).

114. Compare "Dei sacramenta" (Stevenson, p. 68, 17).

115. The Old English follows the Latin closely: "Vidi gloriam quam peccatores merito non uidemus" (Stevenson, p. 68, 17).

116. Stevenson, "Holy Sinner," points out that the usual monastic behavior when seeing a woman is to run in the opposite direction (pp. 35–36).

117. The Old English stresses Zosimus's need or desire to see and to know; compare "Quid tibi uisum fuit, abba, peccatricem uidere mulierculam? Quid queris a me uidere aut discere, tantum non pigritasti laborem pertolerare?" (Stevenson, p. 60, 9).

118. The parallel syntax in the Old English makes the point more economically than the Latin; "Ille autem in terra prostratus, poscebat benedictionem secundum morem accipere. Prostrauit autem se et ipsa, et uterque iacens in terra, unus ex alio,

benedictionem deposcens, et non erat aliud ab alterutro audiri nisi tantum 'benedic' "
(Stevenson, p. 60, 9).

119. By omitting Mary's manly qualities in the prologue ("conversio virile," Stevenson, p. 51, incipit to ms. C), and the concluding explicit ("Explicit conuersio uirileque et magnum certamen venerabilis Marie Aegyptiace," Stevenson p. 79, which is also omitted from ms N—London, British Library Cotton Nero E.1—and S—Salisbury, Cathedral Library 221), the Old English translation subtly de-emphasizes Mary's status as a manly saint in some Latin reflexes of the legend.

120. Stevenson ("Holy Sinner," pp. 36–37) discusses this "quasi-erotic detail" of Zosimus's washing of Mary's feet, an incident that might be modeled on the annointing of Christ's feet in Luke 7: 38. She also notes that Hebrew "regel," "foot," is sometimes metonymic of the genitals. A simple displacement between feet and genitals might be operating in both the Latin and Old English, though in both the main emphasis of the narrative is on Zosimus's fear to touch anywhere else. In the Latin, Mary's foot touches the door of the temple and is refused entry (Stevenson, p. 66, 16; a detail omitted in the Old English).

121. Karma Lochrie, "Women's 'Pryvetees' and Fabliau Politics in the Miller's Tale," *Exemplaria* 6 (1994): 287–304.

122. In an important account of the poetics of metaphor in later medieval writing, Peter W. Travis stresses the "powerful reality of the metaphorical icon itself"; see his "Chaucer's Heliotropes and the Poetics of Metaphor," *Speculum* 72 (1997): 399–427 (at p. 407). Mary of Egypt occupies a similar space in spiritual discourse as a figure or icon of sanctity.

123. See Orchard, "Hot Lust in a Cold Climate."

124. Contrast, for example, the idealized peace in Edwin's reign, when a mother could carry her newborn child safely across with country, with the massacre of the Bangor monks a few years earlier, discussed in the Introduction.

125. This is not to deny that aristocratic women, particularly in their role as queens or royal wives, do not exert an influence in late tenth century, early eleventh century religious life (cf. Stafford, "The King's Wife in Wessex, 800–1066," in *New Readings on Women*, ed. Damico and Olsen, pp. 56–78). It is, however, to assert that the female religious themselves are less visible in the cultural record—a point sharpened when contrasted with their high visibility in the early years of Anglo-Saxon Christianity.

Chapter 5

1. *Collectanea Pseudo-Bedae*, ed. and trans. Bayless and Lapidge; *Anicii Manlii Severini Boethii Philosophiae Consolatio*, ed. Ludwig Bieler, *CCSL* 94 (1957). For translation of the *Consolatio*, see Boethius, *The Consolation of Philosophy*, trans. V. E. Watts (Harmondsworth: Penguin, 1969).

2. For the Alfredian version, see *King Alfred's Old English Version of Boethius De Consolatione Philosophiae*, ed. Walter John Sedgefield (Oxford: Clarendon Press, 1899).

3. For an overview of the various theories of the dating and composition of the *Collectanea*, see Michael Lapidge, "The Origin of the *Collectanea*" in Bayless and Lapidge, pp. 1–12; see also Martha Bayless, "The *Collectanea* and Medieval Dialogues and Riddles"; Mary Garrison, "The *Collectanea* and Medieval Florilegia" in the same volume, pp. 13–24 and 42–83 respectively.

4. Curtius, *European Literature and the Latin Middle Ages*, p. 131.

5. Quoted from Curtius, *European Literature and the Latin Middle Ages*, p. 131.

6. For examples, see Curtius, *European Literature and the Latin Middle Ages*, pp. 131–32.

7. Well known but under-analyzed. See John P. Hermann, *Allegories of War: Language and Violence in Old English Poetry* (Ann Arbor: University of Michigan Press, 1989), pp. 7–52, for useful studies of the Psychomachia material that do not, however, take gender into account.

8. Augustine, *Confessions*, trans. R. S. Pine-Coffin (Harmondsworth: Penguin, 1961), Book VIII, chapter 11, p. 176. For the Latin, together with translation and commentary, see James J. O'Donnell, ed. and trans., *Augustine: Confessions*. 3 vols. (Oxford: Clarendon Press, 1992).

9. Bede, *Allegorica expositio*, PL 91, 1027D. For an overview of similar bodily tropes, see Henri Lubac, *Exégèse médiévale: les quatre sens de l'Écriture*, 2 parts in 4 vols (Paris: Aubier, 1959–64), part 2, vol. 1, pp. 301–17.

10. "Dic mihi, quaeso, quae est illa mulier, quae innumeris filiis ubera porrigit, quae quantum sucta fuerit, tantum inundat? Mulier ista est sapientia," *Collectanea*, p. 122. The commentary on this item points only to close analogues in the Irish tradition, see p. 199.

11. For a rare exception, see Allen J. Frantzen, "When Women Aren't Enough" (at pp. 457–61).

12. The analogues to these items (which seem sufficiently related to have been copied in a single block) in Isidore's *Etymologiae*, Proverbs, and Defensor's *Liber scintillarum* are from the mainstream of patristic culture; see the textual notes to the *Collectanea*, p. 246.

13. This item is taken almost exactly from Psalm 30: 15–16. See *Collectanea*, p. 210 for discussion.

14. While item 193 does not as yet have an identified source, that for item 214 is again Scripture (Vulgate, *Sir* ix. 5); see *Collectanea*, p. 246.

15. Item 248 has close connections with the Anglo-Saxon school of Theodore (himself a major figure in this book); for elaboration, see *Collectanea*, p. 250.

16. As brilliantly articulated by Toril Moi in *What Is A Woman?* pp. 3–120.

17. For many of the texts that exemplify this tradition, see Alcuin Blamires, ed, *Woman Defamed and Woman Defended* (Oxford: Clarendon Press, 1992) and for his subsequent analysis, see *The Case for Women in Medieval Culture* (Oxford: Clarendon Press, 1997). For a more detailed analysis of the (non-) use of much of this material in Anglo-Saxon literary culture together with a further study of the *Collectanea*, see Lees and Overing, "Misogyny and the Social Symbolic in Anglo-Saxon England."

18. For discussion, see Blamires, *The Case for Women in Medieval Culture*, pp. 1–18.

19. See Lapidge, "The Origin of the *Collectanea*," for overview.

20. Lapidge, "The Origin of the *Collectanea.*"

21. In addition to the articles by Bayless ("The *Collectanea* and Medieval Dialogues and Riddles") and Garrison ("The *Collectanea* and Medieval Florilegia"), note the vernacular example of the prose *Solomon and Saturn* and *Adrian and Ritheus* dialogues; see James E. Cross and Thomas D. Hill, eds. *The Prose "Solomon and Saturn" and "Adrian and Ritheus"* (Toronto: University of Toronto Press, 1982).

22. For a preliminary study of traditionality based on Old English vernacular religious prose, see Lees, *Tradition and Belief*, esp. pp. 1–45.

23. For a good discussion of the manuscripts, see Gernot Wieland, "The Origin and Development of the Anglo-Saxon *Psychomachia* Illustrations," *ASE* 26 (1997): 169–86.

24. See O'Brien O'Keeffe, *Visible Song*, pp. 47–76, and Hermann, *Allegories of War*, pp. 32–36 for good readings of these poems. See also Patrick P. O'Neill, "On the Date, Provenance and Relationship of the 'Solomon and Saturn' Dialogues," *ASE* 26 (1997): 139–68.

25. See Hermann, *Allegories of War*, pp. 30–32 on Ælfric's Second Series Mid-Lent sermon, which does not however take into account the occasional gendering of the *conflictus* tradition; cf. "swa eac ælc ðyssera heafodleahtra hæfð micelne team. ac gif we ða modru acwellað. þonne beoð heora bearn ealle adnydde" (Godden, *Ælfric's Catholic Homilies: The Second Series Text*, p. 124, lines 490–92).

26. For a study of personification allegory in *Piers Plowman*, see Lees, "Gender and Exchange in *Piers Plowman*," in *Class and Gender in Early English Literature: Intersections*, ed. Britton J. Harwood and Gillian R. Overing (Bloomington: Indiana University Press, 1994), pp. 112–30.

27. The first clause of this sentence paraphrases Jerold C. Frakes, *The Fate of Fortune in the Early Middle Ages: The Boethian Tradition* (Leiden: E. J. Brill, 1988), p. 81, while much of our discussion is indebted to his analysis of Alfred's adaptations of Boethius, pp. 81–122.

28. In addition to Frakes, *The Fate of Fortune*, pp. 81–122, see also Malcolm Godden's useful summary in "Editing Old English and the Problem of Alfred's *Boethius*," in *The Editing of Old English*, ed. D. G. Scragg and Paul E. Szarmach (Cambridge: D. S. Brewer, 1994), pp. 163–76.

29. Lerer, *Literacy and Power*, pp. 79, 78–81.

30. As noted, but undeveloped, by Whitney F. Bolton, "How Boethian is Alfred's *Boethius?*" in *Studies in Earlier Old English Prose*, ed. Szarmach (Albany, N.Y.: SUNY Press, 1986), pp. 153–68.

31. Elaine Scarry, *Resisting Representation* (Oxford: Oxford University Press, 1994), pp. 143–80 (at p. 147).

32. Scarry, *Resisting Representation*, p. 153.

33. See Butler, *Bodies That Matter*, for a recent rereading of this classical and long-lasting trope.

34. These are critical commonplaces of Alfred's version. Good examples are Bolton, "How Boethian Is Alfred's *Boethius?*" and the account in *A New Critical History of Old English Literature*, ed. Greenfield and Calder, pp. 46–51. Clearly the time is ripe for a fresh and fuller analysis (so too Godden calls for a new edition, see his "Editing Old English and the Problem of Alfred's *Boethius*").

35. There are in fact only two manuscripts of Alfred's version to survive; see Godden, "Editing Old English and the Problem of Alfred's *Boethius*" for details.

36. See Lees's discussion of Alfred's version of Augustine's *Soliloquies* in "Engendering Religious Desire," where the desire for spiritual knowledge is developed into "an Alfredian metaphor explicitly sexual and erotic" (p. 28).

37. See for example Frantzen, *The Literature of Penance in Anglo-Saxon England*, and "Between the Lines: Queer Theory, the History of Homosexuality, and Anglo-Saxon Penitentials"; and Chapter Two of Hollis, *Anglo-Saxon Women and the Church*, pp. 46–74.

38. *The Literature of Penance in Anglo-Saxon England*, p. 204.

39. O'Brien O'Keeffe, "Body and Law in Anglo-Saxon England" *ASE* 27 (1998): 209–232, at p. 212.

40. O'Brien O'Keeffe, "Body and Law," p. 231.

41. Frantzen, *Literature of Penance in Anglo-Saxon England*, pp. 67, 201.

42. Thacker, "Monks, Preaching and Pastoral Care in Early Anglo-Saxon England," p. 160.

43. Thacker, "Monks, Preaching and Pastoral Care," p. 160.

44. *Die Canones Theodori Cantuariensis und Ihre Uberlieferungsformen*, ed. P. W. Finsterwalder, pp. 285–334, and McNeill and Gamer, trans., *Medieval Handbooks of Penance*, 1, xiv, 17; 1, viii, 7.

45. *Medieval Handbooks of Penance*, 1, ii, 21.

46. Thacker, "Monks, Preaching and Pastoral Care," p. 170.

47. *Anglo-Saxon Women and the Church*, pp. 50–51.

48. *Medieval Handbooks of Penance*, 1, vi, 4.

49. *Medieval Handbooks of Penance*, 2, ii, 6.

50. *Medieval Handbooks of Penance*, 2, ii, 14–16.

51. See Frantzen, *Literature of Penance*, p. 80, for a discussion of these and other penitential differentiations.

52. *The Literature of Penance*, pp. 66–67.

53. See Hollis, *Anglo-Saxon Women and the Church*, p. 59, note 53.

54. *Medieval Handbooks of Penance*, 2, vii, 1. See also Hollis, *Anglo-Saxon Women and the Church*, p. 163.

55. See Hollis, *Anglo-Saxon Women and the Church*, p. 111 and note 179, p. 103 and note 144. See also Theodore's penitential, *Medieval Handbooks of Penance*, 2, vi, 8, for his ruling on double houses.

56. "Monks, Preaching and Pastoral Care in Early Anglo-Saxon England," p. 148.

57. *Medieval Handbooks of Penance*, 2, i, 7.

58. *Medieval Handbooks of Penance*, 1, v, 13.

59. For this attribution of authorship see Chapter 2, n. 39.

60. *The Life of Bishop Wilfrid by Eddius Stephanus*, ed. and trans. Colgrave, chapter 34.

61. See Hollis, *Anglo-Saxon Women and the Church*, pp. 165–78.

62. Alcuin, *Epistolae*, p. 291, and Allott, *Alcuin of York*, p. 69.

63. Patrick Geary, "Sacred Commodities: The Circulation of Medieval Relics," in *The Social Life of Things: Commodities in Cultural Perspective*, ed. Arjun Appadurai (Cambridge: Cambridge University Press, 1986), pp. 169–91, envisions this dynamic in

terms of supply and demand; the relic becomes a commodity, albeit a sacred one, produced, reproduced, and even created or reinvented according to practices of circulation, such as gift, theft, and exchange.

64. *Vita Leobae Abbatissae Biscofheimensis Auctore Rudolfo Fuldensi,* ed. Waitz; Willibald, *Vita S Bonifati Archiepiscopi Auctore Willibaldo Presbytero,* ch. 6: ed. G. H. Pertz, *MGH SS* 2 (1829) pp. 331–53, ch. 11; Eigil, *Eigilis Vita S Sturmi Abbatis Fuldensi,* ed. G. H. Pertz, *MGHSS,* 2 (1829), pp. 365–77, ch. 15. All three are translated by Talbot, *Anglo-Saxon Missionaries in Germany,* pp. 205–26, 25–62, 181–202 respectively.

65. See Hollis, Chapter 9, *Anglo-Saxon Women and the Church,* pp. 271–300. See also Jane Tibbetts Schulenberg, "Female Sanctity: Public and Private Roles, ca 500–1100," for a discussion of the broader context of the erosion of Leoba's public, active role.

66. Hollis, *Anglo-Saxon Women and the Church,* p. 288.

67. Hollis, *Anglo-Saxon Women and the Church,* p. 285.

68. Hollis, *Anglo-Saxon Women and the Church,* p. 288.

69. Hollis, *Anglo-Saxon Women and the Church,* p. 288.

70. R. I. Moore, *The Formation of a Persecuting Society: Power and Deviance in Western Europe, 950–1250* (Oxford: Blackwell, 1987).

71. Indeed, David Nirenberg usefully supplements Moore's hypothesis by pointing to the importance of agency in both groups and individuals; see *Communities of Violence: Persecution of Minorities in the Middle Ages* (Princeton, N.J.: Princeton University Press, 1996), pp. 3–17.

72. For discussion, see Lees, *Tradition and Belief,* pp. 106–32.

Bibliography

Primary Sources

Ælfric. *Ælfric's Catholic Homilies: The First Series.* Ed. Peter Clemoes. *EETS* s.s. 17. Oxford: Oxford University Press, 1997.
———. *Ælfric's Catholic Homilies: The Second Series Text.* Ed. Malcolm Godden. *EETS* s.s. 5. Oxford: Oxford University Press, 1979.
———. *Ælfric's Prefaces.* Ed. Jonathan Wilcox. Durham: Durham Medieval Texts, 1994.
———. *Lives of Saints.* Ed. W. W. Skeat, *Ælfric's Lives of Saints.* Vol. 1, *EETS* 76, 82. 1881, 1885; reprinted as one volume Oxford: Oxford University Press, 1966. Vol. 2, *EETS* 94, 114. 1890, 1900; reprinted as one volume 1966.
Alcuin. *Alcuin: The Bishops, Kings, and Saints of York.* Ed. and trans. Peter Godman. Oxford: Clarendon Press, 1982.
———. *Alcuin of York, c. A.D. 732–804: His Life and Letters.* Ed. and trans. Stephen Allott. York: William Sessions Limited, 1974.
———. *Alcuini Epistolae.* Ed. E. Dümmler. *MGH, Epistolae* 4. Berlin: Weidmann, 1895.
Aldhelm. *Aldhelm: The Poetic Works.* Trans. Michael Lapidge and James L. Rosier. Cambridge: D.S. Brewer, 1985.
———. *Aldhelm: The Prose Works.* Trans. Michael Lapidge and Michael Herren. Cambridge: D.S. Brewer, 1979.
———. *Aldhelmi Opera.* Ed. R. Ehwald. *MGH AA* 15, 1912.
———. *Through a Gloss Darkly: Aldhelm's Riddles in the British Library ms. Royal 12 C.xxiii.* Ed. and trans. Nancy Porter Stork. Toronto: Pontifical Institute of Mediaeval Studies, 1990.
Alfred. *King Alfred's Old English Version of Boethius De Consolatione Philosophiae.* Ed. Walter John Sedgefield. Oxford: Clarendon Press, 1899.
Asser. *Asser's Life of Alfred.* Ed. William Henry Stevenson, 1904. Reprint Oxford: Clarendon Press, 1959.
Augustine. *Augustine: Confessions.* Ed. and trans. James J. O'Donnell. 3 vols. Oxford: Clarendon Press, 1992.
———. *Confessions.* Trans. R. S. Pine-Coffin. Harmondsworth: Penguin, 1961.
———. *De doctrina christiana.* Ed. Joseph Martin. *CCSL* 32, 1962.
———. *De trinitate.* Ed. W. J. Mountain and Fr. Glorie. *CCSL* 50A, 1950.
Barlow, Frank, ed. and trans. *Vita Ædwardi Regis qui apud Westmonasterium requiescit (The Life of King Edward Who Rests at Westminster).* London: Nelson, 1962.
Bede. *Allegorica expositio. PL* 91, 1027D.
———. *Bede's Ecclesiastical History of the English People.* Ed. and trans. Bertram Colgrave and R. A. B. Mynors. Oxford: Clarendon Press, 1969.

——. *Life of Saint Cuthbert.* In *Two Lives of Saint Cuthbert,* ed. and trans. Bertram Colgrave. Westport, Conn.: Greenwood Press, 1969.

——. *The Old English Version of Bede's Ecclesiastical History of the English People.* Ed. Thomas Miller. Part I, 2. *EETS* 96, 1891. Reprint Oxford: Oxford University Press, 1959.

Pseudo-Bede. *Collectanea Pseudo-Bedae.* Ed. Martha Bayless and Michael Lapidge. Scriptores Latini Hibernae 14. Dublin: School of Celtic Studies, Dublin Institute for Advanced Studies, 1998.

de Birch, W. G., ed. *Cartularium Saxonicum.* 3 vols. London: Whiting and Co., 1885–89.

Bischoff, Bernard, and Michael Lapidge, eds. *Biblical Commentaries from the Canterbury School of Theodore and Hadrian.* Cambridge: Cambridge University Press, 1994.

Blamires, Alcuin, ed. *Woman Defamed and Woman Defended.* Oxford: Clarendon Press, 1992.

Boethius. *Anicii Manlii Severini Boethii Philosophiae Consolatio.* Ed. Ludwig Bieler. *CCSL* 94, 1957.

——. *The Consolation of Philosophy.* Trans. V. E. Watts. Harmondsworth: Penguin, 1969.

Boniface. *Die Briefe des heiligen Bonifatius und Lullus.* Ed. Michael. Tangl. *MGH, Epistolae Selectae* 1. Berlin: Weidmannsche Buchhandlung, 1916. Trans. E. Kylie, *The English Correspondence of Saint Boniface.* London: Chatto and Windus, 1911.

——. *The Letters of St. Boniface.* Ed. Austin P. Evans. New York: Columbia University Press, 1940.

Campbell, Alistair, ed. *The Chronicle of Æthelweard.* London: Nelson, 1962.

——. ed. *Encomium Emmae Reginae,* with a supplementary introduction by Simon Keynes. London: Royal Historical Society, 1949. Reprint Cambridge: Cambridge University Press, 1998.

Cassiodorus. *Expositio in Psalterium. PL* 70: 1271.

Chaucer. *The Riverside Chaucer.* Ed. Larry D. Benson. 3rd ed. Boston: Houghton Mifflin, 1987.

Cross, James E., and Thomas D. Hill, eds. *The Prose "Solomon and Saturn" and "Adrian and Ritheus".* Toronto: University of Toronto Press, 1982.

Crossley-Holland, Kevin, trans. *The Exeter Book Riddles.* Harmondsworth: Penguin, 1979.

Dhuoda. *Handbook for William: A Carolingian Woman's Counsel for her Son by Dhuoda.* Trans. C. Neel. Lincoln: University of Nebraska Press, 1991.

Eigil. *Eigilis Vita S Sturmi Abbatis Fuldensi.* Ed. G. H. Pertz. *MGH SS* 2, 1829, 365–77.

Finberg, H. P. R., ed. *The Early Charters of the West Midlands.* Leicester: Leicester University Press, 1961.

Finsterwalder, P. W., ed. *Die Canones Theodori Cantuariensis und ihre Uberlieferungsformen.* Weimar: Böhlaus, 1929.

Haddan, Arthur West, and William Stubbs, eds. *Councils and Ecclesiastical Documents Relating to Great Britain and Ireland.* Vol. 3, 1871. Reprint Oxford: Oxford University Press, 1964.

Harmer, Florence, ed. *Anglo-Saxon Writs*. Manchester: Manchester University Press, 1952.

Horstmann, C., ed. *The Lives of Women Saints of Our Contrie of England, also some other Liues of Holie Women Written by Some of the Auncient Fathers*. EETS 86, 1886.

Isidore. *Eytmologiae*. Ed. W. M. Lindsay. Oxford: Oxford University Press, 1911. Reprint Oxford: Clarendon Press, 1957.

Kelly, Susan E., ed. *Charters of St. Augustine's Abbey Canterbury and Minster-in-Thanet*. Anglo-Saxon Charters 4, British Academy. Oxford: Oxford University Press, 1995.

Keynes, Simon, and Michael Lapidge, eds. and trans. *Alfred the Great: Asser's Life of King Arthur and Other Contemporary Sources*. Harmondsworth: Penguin, 1983.

Krapp, George Phillip, and Elliott Van Kirk Dobbie, eds. *The Anglo-Saxon Poetic Records*. 6 vols. New York: Columbia University Press, 1931–42.

Lapidge, Michael, ed. *Anglo-Saxon Litanies of the Saints*. Henry Bradshaw Society 106. London: Boydell, 1991.

Liebermann, F., ed. *Die Gesetze der Angelsachsen*. Vol. 1. Halle: Niemeyer, 1903

Magnusson, Magnus, and Hermann Palsson, trans. *Laxdæla Saga*. Harmondsworth: Penguin, 1969.

——. *Njal's Saga*. Harmondsworth: Penguin, 1960.

McNeill, John T., and Helena M. Gamer, trans. *Medieval Handbooks of Penance : A Translation of the Principal "Libri poenitentiales"*. New York: Columbia University Press, 1938.

Napier, Arthur S., ed. *History of the Holy Rood-Tree*. EETS os 103, 1894.

Robertson, A. J., ed. *Anglo-Saxon Charters*. 2nd ed. Cambridge: Cambridge University Press, 1956.

Rudolph of Fulda. *Vita Leobae Abbatissae Biscofesheimensis Auctore Rudolfo Fuldensi*. Ed. G. Waitz. MGH SS 15.1, 1887.

Sawyer, Peter, ed. *Anglo-Saxon Charters: An Annotated List and Bibliography*. London: Royal Historical Society, 1968.

Stephen of Ripon. *The Life of Bishop Wilfrid by Eddius Stephanus*. Ed and trans. Bertram Colgrave. 1927. Reprint Cambridge: Cambridge University Press, 1985.

Stevenson, Jane, ed. and trans. "Vita Sanctae Mariae Egiptiacae." In *The Legend of Mary of Egypt in Medieval Insular Hagiography*, ed. Erich Poppe and Bianca Ross, 51–98. Co. Dublin and Portland, Ore.: Four Courts Press, 1996.

Swanton, Michael, ed. and trans. *The Anglo-Saxon Chronicle*. New York: Routledge, 1998.

Symons, Dom Thomas, ed. *Regularis Concordia*. London: Thomas Nelson, 1953.

Talbot, C. H., trans. *The Anglo-Saxon Missionaries in Germany*. New York: Sheed and Ward, 1954.

Tupper, Frederick, Jr. *The Riddles of the Exeter Book*. Boston: Ginn, 1910.

Whitelock, Dorothy, ed. *Anglo-Saxon Wills*. Cambridge: Cambridge University Press, 1930.

——, ed. *English Historical Documents, c 500–1042*. Vol. 1. London: Eyre and Spottiswoode, 1955.

——, ed. *Sweet's Anglo-Saxon Reader in Prose and Verse*. 15th ed. Oxford: Clarendon Press, 1975.

Willibald. *Vita S Bonifati Archiepiscopi Auctore Willibaldo Presbytero*. Ed. G. H. Pertz. *MGH SS* 2, 1829, 331–53.

Wulfstan of Winchester. *Wulfstan of Winchester: The Life of St. Æthelwold*. Ed. Michael Lapidge and Michael Winterbottom. Oxford: Clarendon Press, 1991.

Secondary Sources

Aers, David. "Preface." *Historical Inquiries/Psychoanalytic Criticism/Gender Studies*. *JMEMS* 26, 2 (1996): 200–208.

——. "A Whisper in the Ear of Early Modernists; or, Reflections on Literary Critics Writing the 'History of the Subject.'" In *Culture and History, 1350–1600: Essays on English Community, Identities, and Writing*, ed. Aers, 177–202. Detroit: Wayne State University Press, 1992.

Aers, David, and Lynn Staley. *The Powers of the Holy: Religion, Politics, and Gender in Late Medieval English Culture*. University Park: Pennsylvania State University Press, 1996.

Auerbach, Erich. "Figura." Trans. Ralph Mannheim. Reprint in *Scenes from the Drama of European Literature*, 11–76. Minneapolis: University of Minnesota Press, 1984.

Backhouse, Janet, D. H. Turner, and Leslie Webster, eds. *The Golden Age of Anglo-Saxon Art*. London: British Museum Publications, 1984.

Bately, Janet M. "Old English Prose Before and During the Reign of Alfred." *ASE* 17 (1988): 93–138.

Bateson, Mary. "Origin and Early History of Double Monasteries." *Transactions of the Royal Historical Society* 13 (1899): 137–98.

Bayless, Martha. "The *Collectanea* and Medieval Dialogues and Riddles." In *Collectanea Pseudo-Bedae*, ed. Bayless and Michael Lapidge, 13–24. Scriptores Latini Hibernae 14. Dublin: School for Celtic Studies, Dublin Institute for Advanced Studies, 1998.

Beckwith, Sarah. *Christ's Body: Identity, Culture, and Society in Late Medieval Writings*. New York: Routledge, 1993.

Belanoff, Pat. "The Fall (?) of the Old English Poetic Image." *PMLA* 104 (1989): 822–31.

Bennett, Judith M. *Ale, Beer, and Brewsters in England: Women's Work in a Changing World, 1300–1600*. Oxford: Oxford University Press, 1996.

——. "Medieval Women, Modern Women: Across the Great Divide." In *Culture and History, 1350–1600*, ed. David Aers, 147–75. Detroit: Wayne State University Press, 1992.

——. *Women in the Medieval English Countryside*. Oxford: Oxford University Press, 1987.

——. "Women's History: A Study in Continuity and Change." *Women's History Review* 2, 2 (1993): 173–84.

Biddick, Kathleen. "Genders, Bodies, Borders: Technologies of the Visible." *Speculum* 68 (1993): 389–418.

Bischoff, Bernhard. "Die Kölner Nonnenhandschriften und das Skriptorium von Chelles." *Mittelalterlichen Studien* 1 (Stuttgart, 1966): 16–34.

Blair, Peter Hunter. *An Introduction to Anglo-Saxon England.* Cambridge: Cambridge University Press, 1959.

———. "Whitby as a Centre of Learning in the Seventh Century." In *Learning and Literature in Anglo-Saxon England: Studies Presented to Peter Clemoes on the Occasion of His Sixty-Fifth Birthday*, ed. Michael Lapidge and Helmut Gneuss, 3–32. Cambridge: Cambridge University Press, 1985.

Blamires, Alcuin. *The Case for Women in Medieval Culture.* Oxford: Clarendon Press, 1997.

Bolton, Whitney R. "How Boethian Is Alfred's *Boethius?*" In *Studies in Earlier Old English Prose*, ed. Paul E. Szarmach, 153–68. Albany: SUNY Press, 1986.

Brown, George Hardin. "The Dynamics of Literacy in Anglo-Saxon England." *Bulletin of the John Rylands Library* 77, 1 (Spring 1995): 109–42.

Burton, Janet. *Monastic and Religious Orders in Britain, 1000–1300.* Cambridge: Cambridge University Press, 1994.

Butler, Judith. *Bodies That Matter: On the Discursive Limits of "Sex".* New York: Routledge, 1993.

Bynum, Caroline Walker. *Fragmentation and Redemption: Essays on Gender and the Human Body in Medieval Religion.* New York: Zone Books, 1992.

———. *The Resurrection of the Body in Western Christianity, 200–1336.* New York: Columbia University Press, 1995.

Cameron, Deborah. *Feminism and Linguistics.* London: Macmillan, 1985.

———, ed. *Women and Their Speech Communities.* New York: Longman, 1989.

Campbell, James. "The First Century of Christianity in England." Reprint in Campbell, *Essays in Anglo-Saxon History*, 49–67. London: Hambledon Press, 1986.

Chance, Jane. *Woman as Hero in Anglo-Saxon Literature.* Syracuse, N.Y.: Syracuse University Press, 1986.

Chaplais, Pierre. Review of Simon Keynes, *The Diplomas of King Æthelred "The Unready" (978–1016): A Study in Their Use as Historical Evidence* (Cambridge: Cambridge University Press, 1980). *Journal of Ecclesiastical History* 35 (1984): 262–65.

Chase, Colin. "Source Study as a Trick with Mirrors: Annihilation of Meaning in the Old English 'Mary of Egypt.'" In *Sources of Anglo-Saxon Culture*, ed. Paul E. Szarmach, with the assistance of Virginia Darrow Oggins, 22–33. Kalamazoo, Mich.: Medieval Institute Publications, 1986.

Clayton, Mary. *The Cult of the Virgin Mary in Anglo-Saxon England.* Cambridge: Cambridge University Press, 1990.

Clemoes, Peter. "Ælfric." In *Continuations and Beginnings: Studies in Old English Literature*, ed. Eric Gerald Stanley, 176–209. London: Nelson, 1966.

Coontz, Stephanie, and Peta Henderson. "Property Forms, Political Power, and Female Labour in the Origins of Class and State Societies." In *Women's Work, Men's Property: The Origins of Gender and Class*, ed. Stephanie Coontz and Peta Henderson, 108–55. London: Verso, 1986.

Crépin, André. "Bede and the Vernacular." In *Famulus Christi*, ed. Gerald F. Bonner, 170–92. London: SPCK, 1976.

Cross, James E. "A Lost Life of Hilda of Whitby: The Evidence of the *Old English Martyrology.*" *Early Middle Ages, Acta* 6 (1979): 21–43.

——. "Mary Magdalen in the *Old English Martyrology*: The Earliest Extant 'Narrat Josephus' Variant of Her Legend." *Speculum* 53 (1978): 16–20.

Curtius, Ernst Robert. *European Literature and the Latin Middle Ages.* Trans. Willard R. Trask. London: Routledge and Kegan Paul, 1953.

Damico, Helen, and Alexandra Hennessey Olsen, eds. In *New Readings on Women in Old English Literature.* Bloomington: Indiana University Press, 1990.

Derrida, Jacques. *Of Grammatology.* Trans. Gayatri C. Spivak. Baltimore: Johns Hopkins University Press, 1976.

Desmond, Marilynn. "The Voice of Exile: Feminist Literary History and the Anonymous Anglo-Saxon Elegy." *Critical Inquiry* 16 (1990): 572–90.

Dinshaw, Carolyn. *Chaucer's Sexual Poetics.* Madison: University of Wisconsin Press, 1989.

Dockray-Miller, Mary. *Motherhood and Mothering in Anglo-Saxon England.* New York: St. Martin's Press, 2000.

Dronke, Peter. *Women Writers of the Middle Ages: A Critical Study of Texts from Perpetua to Marguerite Porete.* Cambridge: Cambridge University Press, 1984.

Dumville, David N. "Kingship, Genealogies, and Regnal Lists." In *Early Medieval Kingship,* ed. P. H. Sawyer and I. N. Wood, 72–104. Leeds: School of History, University of Leeds, 1977.

Earl, James W. "King Alfred's Talking Poems." *Pacific Coast Philology* 24 (1989): 49–61.

——. "Typology and Iconographic Style in Early Medieval Hagiography." *Studies in the Literary Imagination* 8 (1975): 15–46. Revised version in *Typology and English Medieval Literature,* ed. Hugh T. Keenan, 89–120. New York: AMS Press, 1992.

Engels, Friedrich. *The Origin of the Family, Private Property and the State.* Reprint New York: International Publishers, 1972.

Farr, Carol A. "Worthy Women on the Ruthwell Cross: Woman as Sign in Early Anglo-Saxon Monasticism." In *The Insular Tradition,* ed. Catherine E. Karkov, Michael Ryan, and Robert T. Farrell, 45–61. Albany: SUNY Press, 1997.

Fell, Christine E. "Hild, Abbess of Streonæshalch." In *Hagiography and Medieval Literature: A Symposium,* ed. Hans Bekker-Nielsen, Peter Foote, Jorgen Hojgaard Jorgensen, and Tore Nyberg, 76–99. Odense: Odense University Press, 1981.

——."Saint Æthelthryth: A Historical-Hagiographical Dichotomy Revised." *Nottingham Medieval Studies* 38 (1994): 18–32.

——. "Some Implications of the Boniface Correspondence." In *New Readings on Women in Old English Literature,* ed. Helen Damico and Alexandra Hennessey Olsen, 29–43. Bloomington: Indiana University Press, 1990.

Fell, Christine E., with Cecily Clark and Elizabeth Williams. *Women in Anglo-Saxon England.* Oxford: Blackwell, 1984.

Foley, John Miles. *Oral-Formulaic Theory and Research: An Introduction and Annotated Bibliography.* New York: Garland, 1985.

——. "Orality, Textuality, and Interpretation." In *Vox Intexta: Orality and Textuality in the Middle Ages,* ed. A. N. Doane and Carol Braun Pasternack, 34–45. Madison: University of Wisconsin Press, 1991.

——. *The Theory of Oral Composition: History and Methodology*. Bloomington: Indiana University Press, 1988.

Frakes, Jerold C. *The Fate of Fortune in the Early Middle Ages: The Boethian Tradition.* Leiden: Brill, 1988.

Frantzen, Allen J. "Between the Lines: Queer Theory, the History of Homosexuality, and Anglo-Saxon Penitentials." *JMEMS* 26, 2 (1996): 255–96.

——. *Desire for Origins: New Language, Old English, and Teaching the Tradition*. New Brunswick, N.J.: Rutgers University Press, 1990.

——. "The Fragmentation of Cultural Studies and the Fragments of Anglo-Saxon England." *Anglia* 114 (1996): 310–39.

——. *King Alfred*. Boston: Twayne, 1986.

——. *The Literature of Penance in Anglo-Saxon England*. New Brunswick, N.J.: Rutgers University Press, 1983.

——. "When Women Aren't Enough." *Speculum* 68 (1993): 445–71. Reprint in *Studying Medieval Women: Sex, Gender, Feminism*, ed. Nancy F. Partner, 143–69. Cambridge, Mass.: Medieval Academy of America, 1993.

Foucault, Michel. *The History of Sexuality*. Vol. 1, *An Introduction*. Trans. Robert Hurley. New York: Random House, 1978.

Garrison, Mary. "The *Collectanea* and Medieval Florilegia." In *Collectanea Pseudo-Bedae*, ed. Martha Bayless and Michael Lapidge, 42–83. Scriptores Latini Hibernae 14. Dublin: School for Celtic Studies, Dublin Institute for Advanced Studies, 1998.

Gaunt, Simon. *Gender and Genre in Medieval French Literature*. Cambridge: Cambridge University Press, 1995.

Geary, Patrick. "Sacred Commodities: The Circulation of Medieval Relics." In *The Social Life of Things: Commodities in Cultural Perspective*, ed. Arjun Appadurai, 169–91. Cambridge: Cambridge University Press, 1986.

Gilchrist, Roberta. *Gender and Material Culture: The Archaeology of Religious Women*. London: Routledge, 1994.

——. "The Spatial Archaeology of Gender Domains: A Case Study of Medieval English Nunneries." *Archeological Review from Cambridge* 7, 1 (1988): 21–28.

Godden, Malcolm. "Editing Old English and the Problem of Alfred's *Boethius*." In *The Editing of Old English*, ed. D. G. Scragg and Paul E. Szarmach, 163–76. Cambridge: D.S. Brewer, 1994.

——. "Experiments in Genre: The Saints' Lives in Ælfric's *Catholic Homilies*." In *Holy Men and Holy Women: Old English Prose Saints' Lives and Their Contexts*, ed. Paul E. Szarmach, 261–87. Albany: SUNY Press, 1996.

——. "Money, Power, and Morality in Late Anglo-Saxon England." *ASE* 19 (1990): 41–65.

——. "The Sources for Ælfric's Homily on St Gregory." *Anglia* 86 (1968): 79–88.

Goffart, Walter. *The Narrators of Barbarian History (A.D. 550–800)*. Princeton, N.J.: Princeton University Press, 1988.

Gravdal, Kathryn. *Ravishing Maidens: Writing Rape in Medieval French Literature and Law*. Philadelphia: University of Pennsylvania Press, 1991.

Greenfield, Stanley B., and Daniel G. Calder, with Michael Lapidge. *A New Critical History of Old English Literature*. New York: New York University Press, 1986.

Gretsch, Mecthild. *The Intellectual Foundation of the English Benedictine Reform.* Cambridge: Cambridge University Press, 1999.

Hahn, Cynthia. "Seeing and Believing: The Construction of Sanctity in Early-Medieval Saints' Shrines." *Speculum* 72 (1997): 1079–1106.

Hart, Cyril. *The Early Charters of Barking Abbey.* Colchester: Benham, 1953.

Harwood, Britton. J., "The Plot of *Piers Plowman* and the Contradictions of Feudalism." In *Speaking Two Languages: Traditional Disciplines and Contemporary Theory in Medieval Studies,* ed. Allen J. Frantzen, 91–114. Albany: SUNY Press, 1991.

Hazeltine, D. H. "Comments on the Writings Known as Anglo-Saxon Wills." In *Anglo-Saxon Wills,* ed. Dorothy Whitelock, vii–xl. Cambridge: Cambridge University Press, 1930.

Hermann, John P. *Allegories of War: Language and Violence in Old English Poetry.* Ann Arbor: University of Michigan Press, 1989.

Hill, Joyce. "Ælfric's Use of Etymologies." *ASE* 17 (1988): 35–44.

——. "The Dissemination of Ælfric's *Lives of Saints.*" In *Holy Men and Holy Women: Old English Prose Saints' Lives and Their Contexts,* ed. Paul E. Szarmach, 235–59. Albany: SUNY Press, 1996.

——. "The 'Regularis Concordia' and Its Latin and Old English Reflexes." *Revue Bénédictine* 101 (1991): 299–315.

Hill, Thomas D. "*Imago Dei*: Genre, Symbolism, and Anglo-Saxon Hagiography." In *Holy Men and Holy Women: Old English Prose Saints' Lives and Their Contexts,* ed. Paul E. Szarmach, 35–50. Albany: SUNY Press, 1996.

Hollis, Stephanie. *Anglo-Saxon Women and the Church: Sharing a Common Fate.* Woodbridge: Boydell, 1992.

——. "The Minster-in-Thanet Foundation Story." *ASE* 27 (1998): 41–64.

Houts, Elisabeth van. *Memory and Gender in Medieval Europe, 900–1200.* Toronto: Toronto University Press, 1999.

Howe, Nicholas. "Aldhelm's *Enigmata* and Isidorian Etymology." *ASE* 14 (1985): 37–59.

——. "The Cultural Construction of Reading in Anglo-Saxon England." In *The Ethnography of Reading,* ed. Jonathan Boyarin, 58–79. Berkeley: University of California Press, 1992.

Howell, Martha C. *Women, Production and Patriarchy in Late Medieval Cities.* Chicago: University of Chicago Press, 1986.

Irvine, Martin. "Medieval Textuality and the Archaeology of Textual Culture." In *Speaking Two Languages: Traditional Disciplines and Contemporary Theory in Medieval Studies,* ed. Allen J. Frantzen, 181–210. Albany: SUNY Press, 1991.

Jackson, Peter, and Michael Lapidge. "The Contents of the Cotton-Corpus Legendary." In *Holy Men and Holy Women: Old English Prose Saints' Lives and Their Contexts,* ed. Paul E. Szarmach, 131–46. Albany: SUNY Press, 1996.

Jager, Eric. "The Book of the Heart: Reading and Writing the Medieval Subject." *Speculum* 71 (1996): 1–26.

Jolly, Karen Louise. *Popular Religion in Late Anglo-Saxon England.* Chapel Hill: University of North Carolina Press, 1996.

Jones, S. R. H. "Transactional Costs, Institutional Change, and the Emergence of a Market Economy in Later Anglo-Saxon England." *Economic History Review* 46, 4 (1993): 658–78.

Justice, Steven. *Writing and Rebellion: England in 1381.* Berkeley: University of California Press, 1994.

Kadel, Andrew. *Matrology: A Bibliography of Writings by Christian Women from the First to the Fifteenth Centuries.* New York: Continuum Press, 1995.

Karras, Ruth Mazo. "Holy Harlots: Prostitute Saints in Medieval Legend." *Journal of the History of Sexuality* 1 (1990): 3–32.

Kay, Sarah, and Miri Rubin, eds. *Framing Medieval Bodies.* Manchester: Manchester University Press, 1994.

Kelly, Susan E. "Anglo-Saxon Lay Society and the Written Word." In *The Uses of Literacy in Early Mediaeval Europe,* ed. Rosamond McKitterick, 36–62. Cambridge: Cambridge University Press, 1990.

Ker, N. R. *Catalogue of Manuscripts Containing Anglo-Saxon.* Oxford: Clarendon Press, 1957.

Keynes, Simon. *The Diplomas of King Æthelred "The Unready" (978–1016): A Study in Their Use as Historical Evidence.* Cambridge: Cambridge University Press, 1980.

——. "Royal Government and Written Word in Late Anglo-Saxon England." In *The Uses of Literacy in Early Mediaeval Europe,* ed. Rosamond McKitterick, 226–57. Cambridge: Cambridge University Press, 1990.

Kiernan, Kevin S. "Reading Cædmon's 'Hymn' with Someone Else's Glosses." *Representations* 32 (1990): 157–74.

Klinck, Anne L. *The Old English Elegies: A Critical Edition and Genre Study.* Montreal and Kingston: McGill-Queen's University Press, 1992.

Knowles, David, and C. N. L. Brooke. *The Heads of Religious Houses, England and Wales, 940–1216.* Cambridge: Cambridge University Press, 1972

Kristeva, Julia. *Tales of Love.* Trans. Leon S. Roudiez. New York: Columbia University Press, 1987.

Laistner, M. L. W. *Thought and Letters in Western Europe, A.D. 500–900.* 1931. Reprint Ithaca, N.Y.: Cornell University Press, 1957.

Lapidge, Michael. "Ælfric's *Sanctorale.*" In *Holy Men and Holy Women: Old English Prose Saints' Lives and Their Contexts,* ed. Paul E. Szarmach, 115–29. Albany: SUNY Press, 1996.

——. "Aldhelm's Latin Poetry and Old English Verse." *Comparative Literature* 31 (1979): 209–31.

——. "The Origin of the *Collectanea.*" In *Collectanea Pseudo-Bedae,* ed. Martha Bayless and Michael Lapidge, 1–12. Scriptores Latini Hibernae 14. Dublin: School for Celtic Studies, Dublin Institute for Advanced Studies, 1998.

——. "The Saintly Life in Anglo-Saxon England." In *The Cambridge Companion to Old English Literature,* ed. Malcolm Godden and Michael Lapidge, 243–63. Cambridge: Cambridge University Press, 1991.

Lees, Clare A. "At a Crossroads: Old English and Feminist Criticism." In *Reading Old English Texts,* ed. Katherine O'Brien O'Keeffe, 146–69. Cambridge: Cambridge University Press, 1997.

——. "Engendering Religious Desire: Sex, Knowledge, and Christian Identity in Anglo-Saxon England." *JMEMS* 27, 1 (1997): 17–45.

——. "Gender and Exchange in *Piers Plowman.*" In *Class and Gender in Early English*

Literature: Intersections, ed. Britton J. Harwood and Gillian R. Overing, 112–30. Bloomington: Indiana University Press, 1994.

———. *Tradition and Belief: Religious Writing in Late Anglo-Saxon England.* Minneapolis: University of Minnesota Press, 1999.

Lees, Clare A., and Gillian R. Overing. "Before History, Before Difference: Bodies, Metaphor and the Church in Anglo-Saxon England." *Yale Journal of Criticism* 11 (1998): 315–34.

———. "Birthing Bishops and Fathering Poets: Bede, Hild, and the Relations of Cultural Production." *Exemplaria* 6 (1994): 35–65.

———. "Misogyny and the Social Symbolic in Anglo-Saxon England." In *Gender in Debate from the Middle Ages to the Renaissance*, ed. Thelma S. Fenster and Clare A. Lees. New York: Palgrave Press, 2002.

Leinbaugh, Theodore H. "Ælfric's *Sermo de Sacrificio in Die Pascae*: Anglican Polemic in the Sixteenth and Seventeenth Centuries." In *Anglo-Saxon Scholarship: The First Three Centuries*, ed. Carl T. Berkhout and Milton McC. Gatch, 51–68. Boston: Hall, 1982.

Lendinara, Patrizia. "The World of Anglo-Saxon Learning." In *The Cambridge Companion to Old English Literature*, ed. Malcolm Godden and Michael Lapidge, 264–81. Cambridge: Cambridge University Press, 1991.

Lerer, Seth. *Literacy and Power in Anglo-Saxon Literature.* Lincoln: University of Nebraska Press, 1991.

Leucke, Jane Marie. "The Unique Experience of Anglo-Saxon Nuns." *Medieval Religious Women*, vol. 2. *Peaceweavers*, ed. Lillian Thomas Shank and John A. Nichols, 55–65. Kalamazoo, Mich.: Cistercian Publications, 1987.

Levison, Wilhelm. *England and the Continent in the Eighth Century.* 1946. Reprint Oxford: Clarendon Press, 1966.

Leyser, Henrietta. *Medieval Women: A Social History of Women in England, 450–1500.* London: Orion Books, 1995.

Lochrie, Karma. "Desiring Foucault." *JMEMS* 27, 1 (1997): 3–16.

———. "The Language of Transgression: Body, Flesh, and Word in Mystical Discourse." In *Speaking Two Languages: Traditional Disciplines and Contemporary Theory in Medieval Studies*, ed. Allen J. Frantzen, 115–40. Albany: SUNY Press, 1991.

———. "Women's 'Pryvetees' and Fabliau Politics in the Miller's Tale." *Exemplaria* 6 (1994): 287–304.

Lomperis, Linda, and Sarah Stanbury, eds. *Feminist Approaches to the Body in Medieval Literature.* Philadelphia: University of Pennsylvania Press, 1993.

Loyn, H. R. *Anglo-Saxon England and the Norman Conquest.* London: Longman, 1962.

Lubac, Henri. *Exégèse médiévale: les quatre sens de l'Écriture.* 2 parts in 4 vols. Paris: Aubier, 1959–64.

Lynch, Joseph H. *Christianizing Kinship: Ritual Sponsorship in Anglo-Saxon England.* Ithaca, N.Y.: Cornell University Press, 1998.

MacGowan, Kenneth. "Barking Abbey." *Current Archaeology* 149 (1996): 172–78.

Magennis, Hugh. " 'No Sex Please, We're Anglo-Saxons'? Attitudes to Sexuality in Old English Prose and Poetry." *Leeds Studies in English* n.s. 26 (1995): 1–27.

———. "St. Mary of Egypt and Ælfric: Unlikely Bedfellows in Cotton Julius E. vii?" In *The Legend of Mary of Egypt in Medieval Insular Hagiography*, ed. Erich Poppe and Bianca Ross, 99–112. Blackrock, Co., Dublin and Portland, Ore.: Four Courts Press, 1996.

McKitterick, Rosamond. *The Carolingians and the Written Word*. Cambridge: Cambridge University Press, 1989.

———. "Nuns' Scriptoria in England and Francia in the Eighth Century." *Francia: Forschungen zur westeuropäischen Geschichte* 19 (1992): 1–35.

———, ed. *The Uses of Literacy in Early Medieval Europe*. Cambridge: Cambridge University Press, 1990.

McLaughlin, T. P. "Abelard's Rule for Religious Women." *MS* 18 (1956): 241–92.

McNamara, Jo Ann, and Suzanne Wemple, "The Power of Women Through the Family in Medieval Europe, 500–1100." *Feminist Studies* 1 (1973): 126–41.

Meyer, Marc A. "Land Charters and the Legal Position of Anglo-Saxon Women." In *The Women of England from Anglo-Saxon Times to the Present*, ed. Barbara Kanner, 57–82. Hamden, Conn.: Archon Books, 1979.

Mirrer, Louise, ed. *Upon My Husband's Death: Widows in the Literature and Histories of Medieval Europe*. Ann Arbor: University of Michigan Press, 1992.

Moi, Toril. *What Is a Woman? and Other Essays*. Oxford: Oxford University Press, 1999.

Moore, R. I. *The Formation of a Persecuting Society: Power and Deviance in Western Europe, 950–1250*. Oxford: Blackwell, 1987.

Morrison, Karl F. *Understanding Conversion*. Charlottesville: University Press of Virginia, 1992.

Muckle, J. T. "The Letter of Heloise on Religious Life and Abelard's First Reply." *MS* 17 (1955): 240–81.

———. "The Personal Letters Between Abelard and Heloise." *MS* 15 (1953): 47–94.

Nelson, Janet. "Reconstructing a Royal Family: Reflections on Alfred, from Asser, Chapter 2." In *People and Places in Northern Europe, 500–1100: Essays in Honour of Peter Hayes Sawyer*, ed. Ian Wood and Neils Lund, 47–66. Woodbridge: Boydell.

———. "Wealth and Wisdom: The Politics of Alfred the Great." In *Kings and Kingship Acta* 11 (1986 for 1984) (ed. Joel Rosenthal): 31–52.

———. "Women and the Word in the Early Middle Ages." In *Women in the Church*, ed. W. J. Sheils and Diana Wood, 53–78. Studies in Church History 27. Oxford: Blackwell for Ecclesiastical History Society, 1990.

Neuman de Vegvar, Carol. "Saints and Companions to Saints: Anglo-Saxon Royal Women Monastics in Context." In *Holy Men and Holy Women: Old English Prose Saints' Lives and Their Contexts*, ed. Paul E. Szarmach, 50–93. Albany: SUNY Press, 1996.

Nicholson, Joan. "*Feminae gloriosae*: Women in the Age of Bede." In *Medieval Women*, ed. Derek Baker. Studies in Church History Subsidia 1, 15–29. Oxford: Blackwell, 1978.

Nirenberg, David. *Communities of Violence: Persecution of Minorities in the Middle Ages*. Princeton, N.J.: Princeton University Press, 1996.

O'Brien O'Keeffe, Katherine. "Body and Law in Anglo-Saxon England." *ASE* 27 (1998): 209–32.

———. "Orality and the Developing Text of Cædmon's *Hymn*." *Speculum* 62 (1987): 1–20.

———. *Visible Song: Transitional Literacy in Old English Verse*. Cambridge: Cambridge University Press, 1990.

O'Neill, Patrick P. "On the Date, Provenance and Relationship of the 'Solomon and Saturn' Dialogues." *ASE* 26 (1997): 139–68.

Ong, Walter. *Orality and Literacy: The Technologizing of the Written Word.* London: Methuen, 1982.

Orchard, Andy. "Hot Lust in a Cold Climate: Comparison and Contrast in the Old Norse Versions of the Life of Mary of Egypt." In *The Legend of Mary of Egypt in Medieval Insular Hagiography*, ed. Erich Poppe and Bianca Ross, 175–204. Blackrock, Co., Dublin and Portland, Oregon: Four Courts Press, 1996.

———. *The Poetic Art of Aldhelm.* Cambridge: Cambridge University Press, 1994.

Ortner, Sherry B., and Harriet Whitehead, eds. *Sexual Meanings: The Cultural Construction of Gender and Sexuality.* Cambridge: Cambridge University Press, 1981.

Overing, Gillian R. *Language, Sign, and Gender in Beowulf.* Carbondale: Southern Illinois University Press, 1990.

Overing, Gillian R., and Marijane Osborn. *Landscape of Desire: Partial Stories of the Medieval Scandinavian World.* Minneapolis: University of Minnesota Press, 1994.

Owen, Gale, R. "Wynflæd's Wardrobe." *ASE* 8 (1979): 195–222.

Parkes, M. B. " 'Rædan, Areccan, Smeagan': How the Anglo-Saxons Read." *ASE* 26 (1997): 1–22.

Parks, Ward. "The Textualization of Orality in Literary Criticism." In *Vox Intexta: Orality and Textuality in the Middle Ages*, ed. A. N. Doane and Carol Braun Pasternack, 46–61. Madison: University of Wisconsin Press, 1991.

Pasternack, Carol Braun. "Post-Structuralist Theories: The Subject and the Text." In *Reading Old English Texts*, ed. Katherine O'Brien O'Keeffe, 170–91. Cambridge: Cambridge University Press, 1997.

———. Review of Alfred P. Smyth, *King Alfred the Great* (Oxford: Oxford University Press, 1995). *Medieval Feminist Newsletter* 27 (Spring 1999): 44–48.

———. *The Textuality of Old English Poetry.* Cambridge: Cambridge University Press, 1995.

Patterson, Lee. *Chaucer and the Subject of History.* Madison: University of Wisconsin Press, 1991.

———. "On the Margin: Postmodernism, Ironic History, and Medieval Studies." In *The New Philology*, ed. Stephen G. Nichols. *Speculum* 65 (1990): 87–108.

———. "The Return to Philology." In *The Past and Future of Medieval Studies*, ed. John Van Engen, 231–44. Notre Dame, Ind.: University of Notre Dame Press, 1994.

Quilligan, Maureen. *Book of the City of Ladies: The Allegory of Female Authority: Christine de Pizan's Cité des dames.* Ithaca, N.Y.: Cornell University Press, 1991.

Rasmussen, Ann Marie. *Mothers and Daughters in Medieval German Literature.* Syracuse, N.Y.: Syracuse University Press, 1997.

Reiter, Rayna R., ed. *Toward an Anthropology of Women.* New York: Monthly Review Press, 1975.

Ridyard, Susan. *The Royal Saints of Anglo-Saxon England: A Study of West Saxon and East Anglian Cults.* Cambridge: Cambridge University Press, 1988.

Roberts, Jane, Janet L. Nelson, and Malcolm Godden, eds. *Alfred the Wise: Studies in Honor of Janet Bately on the Occasion of Her 65th Birthday.* Cambridge: D.S. Brewer, 1997.

Robinson, F. C. "The Significance of Names in Old English Literature." *Anglia* 86 (1968): 14–58.

Rollason, D. W. "Hagiography and Politics in Early Northumbria." In *Holy Men and Holy Women: Old English Prose Saints' Lives and Their Contexts,* ed. Paul E. Szarmach, 95–96. Albany: SUNY Press, 1996.

———. *The Mildrith Legend: A Study in Early Medieval Hagiography in England.* Leicester: Leicester University Press, 1982.

———. *Saints and Relics in Anglo-Saxon England.* Oxford: Blackwell, 1989.

Roy, Gopa. "A Virgin Acts Manfully: Ælfric's *Life of St. Eugenia* and the Latin Versions." *Leeds Studies in English* n.s. 23 (1992): 1–27.

Rubin, Miri. "The Eucharist and the Construction of Medieval Identities." In *Culture and History, 1350–1600: Essays on English Community, Identities, and Writing,* ed. David Aers, 43–63. Detroit: Wayne State University Press, 1992.

Scarry, Elaine. *Resisting Representation.* Oxford: Oxford University Press, 1994.

Schaefer, Ursula. "Hearing from Books: The Rise of Fictionality in Old English Poetry." In *Vox Intexta: Orality and Textuality in the Middle Ages,* ed. A. N. Doane and Carol Braun Pasternack, 117–36. Madison: University of Wisconsin Press, 1991.

Schulenburg, Jane Tibbetts. "Female Sanctity: Public and Private Roles, ca. 500–1100." In *Women and Power in the Middle Ages,* ed. Mary Erler and Maryanne Kowaleski, 102–25. Athens: University of Georgia Press, 1988.

———. *Forgetful of Their Sex: Female Sanctity and Society, ca. 500–1100.* Chicago: University of Chicago Press, 1998.

———. "The Heroics of Virginity." In *Women in the Middle Ages and the Renaissance: Literary and Historical Perspectives,* ed. Mary Beth Rose, 29–72. Syracuse, N.Y.: Syracuse University Press, 1986.

———. "Saints' Lives as a Source for the History of Women, 500–1100." In *Medieval Women and the Sources of Medieval History,* ed. Joel T. Rosenthal, 285–320. Athens: University of Georgia Press, 1990.

———. "Strict Active Enclosure and Its Effects on the Female Monastic Experience." In *Medieval Religious Women,* vol. 1, *Distant Echoes,* ed. John A. Nichols and Lillian Thomas Shank, 51–86. Kalamazoo, Mich.: Cistercian Publications, 1984.

———. "Women's Monastic Communities, 500–1100: Patterns of Expansion and Decline." *Signs* 14 (1988–89): 261–92.

Schüssler Fiorenza, Elisabeth. *But She Said: Feminist Practices of Biblical Interpretation.* Boston: New Beacon Press, 1992.

Schwartz, Regina M. *The Curse of Cain: The Violent Legacy of Monotheism.* Chicago: University of Chicago Press, 1997.

Sheehan, Michael M. *The Will in Medieval England.* Toronto: Pontifical Institute of Mediaeval Studies, 1963.

Sims-Williams, Patrick. *Religion and Literature in Western England, 600–800.* Cambridge Studies in Anglo-Saxon England 3. Cambridge: Cambridge University Press, 1990.

———. "An Unpublished Seventh- or Eighth-Century Anglo-Latin Letter in Boulogne-sur-Mer MS 74." *Medium Ævum* 48 (1979): 1–22.

Smith, Lesley, and Jane H. M. Taylor, eds. *Women, the Book, and the Worldly: Selected*

Proceedings of the St. Hilda's Conference, 1993, vol. 2. Cambridge: D.S. Brewer, 1995.

Soskice, Janet Martin. "Sight and Vision in Medieval Christian Thought." In *Vision in Context: Historical and Contemporary Perspectives on Sight*, ed. Teresa Brennan and Martin Jay, 29–43. New York: Routledge, 1996.

Stafford, Pauline. "The King's Wife in Wessex, 800–1066." *Past and Present* 91 (1981): 3–27. Reprint in *New Readings on Women in Old English Literature*, ed. Helen Damico and Alexandra Hennessey Olsen, 56–78. Bloomington: Indiana University Press, 1990.

———. *Queen Emma and Queen Edith: Queenship and Women's Power in Eleventh-Century England*. Oxford: Blackwell, 1997.

———. *Unification and Conquest: A Political and Social History of England in the Tenth and Eleventh Centuries*. London: Edward Arnold, 1989.

———. "Women and the Norman Conquest." *Transactions of the Royal Historical Society* 6th ser. 4 (1994): 221–49.

Stenton, Frank M. "The Historical Bearing of Place-Name Studies: The Place of Women in Anglo-Saxon Society." Reprint in *New Readings on Women in Old English Literature*, ed. Helen Damico and Alexandra Hennessey Olsen, 79–88. Bloomington: Indiana University Press, 1990.

Stevenson, Jane. "The Holy Sinner: The Life of Mary of Egypt." In *The Legend of Mary of Egypt in Medieval Insular Hagiography*, ed. Erich Poppe and Bianca Ross, 19–50. Blackrock, Co., Dublin and Portland, Ore.: Four Courts Press, 1996.

Stock, Brian. *The Implications of Literacy: Written Language and Models of Interpretation in the Eleventh and Twelfth Centuries*. Princeton, N.J.: Princeton University Press, 1983.

Straus, Barrie Ruth. "Women's Words as Weapons: Speech as Action in *The Wife's Lament*." *Texas Studies in Literature and Language* 23 (1981): 268–85.

Szarmach, Paul E. "Ælfric's Women Saints: Eugenia." In *New Readings on Women in Old English Literature*, ed. Helen Damico and Alexandra Hennessey Olsen, 146–57. Bloomington: Indiana University Press, 1990.

———, ed. *Holy Men and Holy Women: Old English Prose Saints' Lives and Their Contexts*. Albany: SUNY Press, 1996.

Tanke, John W. " 'Wonfeax wale': Ideology and Figuration in the Sexual Riddles of the Exeter Book." In *Class and Gender in Early English Literature: Intersections*, ed. Britton J. Harwood and Gillian R. Overing, 21–42. Bloomington: Indiana University Press, 1994.

Thacker, Alan. "Monks, Preaching and Pastoral Care in Early Anglo-Saxon England." In *Pastoral Care Before the Parish*, ed. John Blair and Richard Sharpe, 137–70. Leicester: Leicester University Press, 1992.

Travis, Peter W. "Chaucer's Heliotropes and the Poetics of Metaphor." *Speculum* 72 (1997): 399–427.

Ward, Benedicta. " 'To My Dearest Sister': Bede and the Educated Woman." In *Women, the Book, and the Godly: Selected Proceedings of the St. Hilda's Conference, 1993*, vol. 1, ed. Lesley Smith and Jane H. M. Taylor, 105–11. Cambridge: D.S. Brewer, 1995.

Wemple, Suzanne F. "Sanctity and Power: The Dual Pursuit of Early Medieval Women." In *Becoming Visible: Women in European History*, ed. Renate Bridenthal and Claudia Koonz, 90–118. Boston: Houghton Mifflin, 1977.

Whitelock, Dorothy. *The Beginnings of English Society*. 2nd. rev. ed. London: Penguin, 1974.

———. "The Old English Bede." *Proceedings of the British Academy* 48 (1962): 57–90.

Wieland, Gernot. "The Origin and Development of the Anglo-Saxon *Psychomachia* Illustrations." *ASE* 26 (1997): 169–86.

Williams, Raymond. *Culture*. London: Fontana, 1981.

Winstead, Karen A. *Virgin Martyrs: Legends of Sainthood in Late Medieval England*. Ithaca, N.Y.: Cornell University Press, 1997.

Wormald, Patrick."A Handlist of Anglo-Saxon Lawsuits." *ASE* 17 (1988): 247–81.

———. *The Making of English Law: King Alfred to the Twelfth Century*. Vol. 1. Oxford: Blackwell, 1999.

———. "The Uses of Literacy in Anglo-Saxon England and Its Neighbours." *Transactions of the Royal Historical Society* 5th ser. 27 (1977): 95–114.

Yorke, Barbara, ed. *Bishop Æthelwold: His Career and Influence*, ed. Yorke, 1–12. Woodbridge: Boydell, 1988.

Index

abbesses: at Barking, 185n64, 206n45; and Benedictine Reform, 67, 126, 180n34; role of, 30, 32, 180n34; in written records, 65–68, 75, 196nn103, 112. *See also* Hild; monasticism, female

Abelard, Peter, 180n34

absence, female: of Æfflæd, 27, 54; of bodies, 123, 149–50; of Breguswith, 26; and communication, 106, 107; in *De virginitate*, 122, 123; in ecclesiastic record, 191n51; feminist scholarship and, 6, 40–41; in Hereford lawsuit, 78, 81, 89; of Hild, 11, 21, 22, 26, 27–29, 30, 77, 155; in *The Husband's Message*, 107; and literacy, 44, 48, 93; metaphors of, 153, 160, 163; of monastic women, 26, 124; and naming, 45, 53–54, 81, 86–87, 191n51; and orality, 38–39, 41, 44, 48, 57, 58; of Osburh, 37, 47–49, 77; in penitentials, 166–67; reading and, 107–9; in riddles, 58, 102–4, 107, 122; of "unexceptional" women, 75; and violence, 150; women participating in own, 26, 29, 124; in written documents, 54, 75, 78–79, 81, 82–83, 93–94, 191n51. *See also* agency, female

Æbba, 65–66, 68, 166, 196n108

Æbbe (mother of Leoba), 23, 51

Aediluulf, 125

Ælfflæd, 27, 51–54, 182n40

Ælfgifu. *See* Emma/Ælfgifu

Ælfgyth, 67

Ælfric: and Aldhelm, 127–28, 129, 130, 131–32; Easter Sunday sermon, 43, 96, 101, 102, 103; on Eucharist, 43, 96–100; female saints of, 135, 149–50; on Imma, 95, 96, 100; and vernacular literacy, 127–28; writings of, 39, 94–95, 127, 128, 186n69. *See also Lives of Saints* (Ælfric)

Ælfric (father of Leofwine), 82

Ælfthryth, 46, 75, 82

Æscburg, Abbess, 196n103

Æthelberht I, 34, 183n55

Æthelburg, 34–35, 37, 169, 185nn61, 64

Æthelburh, Abbess, 196n103

Æthelheard, Archbishop, 196n103, 197n120

Æthelhild, 75

Æthelmær, 128, 137

Æthelred, 75, 91

Æthelred II (the Unready), 75, 82, 90

V Æthelred, 80

Æthelstan, Bishop, 72, 76

Æthelthryth, 52, 126; in Bede, 37, 131, 185n64, 204n10; hagiography of, 37–38, 92, 183n55, 204n10; in *Lives of Saints*, 128–29, 130, 131; as monastic noblewoman, 204n10; name of, 54, 191n51; necklace of, 25, 131, 150

Æthelweard, 46, 91, 94–95, 128, 137

Æthelwold, 92, 95, 126, 206n40

Æthelwulf, 49, 189nn30, 31

Æthilred of Mercia, 53

Ætla, 27

Agape (*De virginitate*), 119, 121

Agatha (*Lives of Saints*), 128, 131

agency, double, 1–2, 11, 50, 166. *See also* agency, female

agency, female: and Christian subjectivity, 171; and Christian symbolic, 171; and cultural production, 30–31; in *De virginitate*, 117–18; double agency, 1–2, 11, 50, 166; and dreams, 25; in Hereford lawsuit, 83–89, 171; of Hild, 21, 26, 34, 171; literacy and, 44, 48, 93; in monasticism, 30, 180n34; naming and, 78–79, 87, 89–92; and orality, 27, 44, 83–89; status and, 89–92; structural view of, 171–72. *See also* absence, female

Agnes: in *De virginitate*, 118, 121; in *Lives of Saints*, 128, 129, 131

Alcuin, 54, 168, 169, 191nn51, 53

Aldfrith, 51

Aldhelm: and Ælfric, 127–28, 129, 130, 131–32; and Bede, 113, 125; category of virginity,